HOPE'S KIDS
A VOTING RIGHTS SUMMER

Alan Venable

One Monkey Books
San Francisco

One Monkey Books
156 Diamond Street
San Francisco, CA 94114
OneMonkeyBooks.com

Publisher@OneMonkeyBooks.com

ISBN 978-1-940722-02-3

Cover photo by Mary Ann Efroymson

CONTENTS

THINKING OF

Harold McKenzie
Everett Jackson
John Lee Anderson
Furman Hart, Jr.
J. Alfred Curry
Donnessa Coblyn
Mrs. Bruce

"I don't remember anything," she said. And then the tiny glimpses—snapshots of our time in the south. The carefully swept dirt floor, spotless table, the commemorative plates on the walls of JFK... and Jackie.... Lesley remembered a bed with a swayed mattress with the coverlet pulled tight across the top...the pride and care in these simple homes with no running water. And the day that we arrived just as a family was sitting down to lunch—the father and the children and the mother eating grits and greens. How much they didn't want us there: maybe to protect their privacy, maybe out of shame for the meagerness of the meal, maybe because we meant danger.

—Phyllis Greenfield Ross

Oh, he was a wise man and patient. And a true diplomat.

—Genevieve Chandler Peterkin

GONE TO CAROLINA

1. TOWN SQUARE STREET

Genevieve Chandler Peterkin wrote that her husband Bill Peterkin's home—Fort Motte, Calhoun County, South Carolina—was a place that came with "a great deal of historical baggage." Not far from the swampy Congaree River, it's one of those by-passed rural spots where street names advertise long-faded dreams. The hamlet's name commemorates an 18th-century siege in which South Carolina patriots defeated the Redcoats. These days, its rectangular, mile-round, Town Square Street fronts a handful of houses and mobile homes.

The nearby historic plantation with the greatest poetic claim is Lang Syne, where the Peterkins once farmed 1,500 acres, mostly cotton. They also ran a small bank. Around 1900, a 17-year-old Carolinian, Julia Mood, moved to Fort Motte to staff a one-room school for whites. A few years later she married into the Peterkin line and became the mistress of Lang Syne, one of three or four white folk there. Nearly three decades later she garnered the South's first Pulitzer Prize with her sensational novel *Scarlet Sister Mary*. Like just about all she ever wrote, the book was based on knowledge and insight she'd built up over the years about the lives of the several hundred blacks on Lang Syne, including many still housed in its old slave quarters. Julia's soul was not a restful one, and she poured it into her works. Nearly everything she wrote was about the blacks, and her close observation and sensibility earned praise from black historian and leader W.E.B. DuBois.

Of course, it isn't unusual for American whites to express their own yearnings through projections on American blacks. I know I was doing the same, coming of age in Pittsburgh in the late 1950s. By then for me, the attractions of Shane and John Wayne had faded in favor of Negro heroes.

Today Calhoun County's famous name is actress Viola Davis, born just outside the town of St. Matthews the summer that I and other young civil rights workers were canvassing there house to house. Who knows but on her birthday we might have knocked at her parents' door. I relish the possibility, as I do her winning an Oscar in August Wilson's "Fences," a drama set in Pittsburgh, my home town, around when I was growing up.

My own nominee for outstanding Calhoun County native is a self-effacing farmer I was privileged to work with that summer of 1965. His name was Hope Williams Jr., born in Fort Motte in 1910, the youngest of twelve grandchildren of slaves. Skeptical as I've grown about idealizing others, I still hold onto Hope. That's why his photo fronts this book.

For various good reasons, I've changed or omitted some names in this book. While at it, I've changed mine, too, in part because there are two other Alans in this account, in part to lessen confusion in a narrative that draws on other first-person accounts, and perhaps in part because, though I hadn't yet discovered Melville, I was part of a hunt for a great white whale. So call me "Ish."

2. WALTHAM

Like Melville's innocent, Ish also made decisions more often on urges than rigorous thought when, at the end of his junior year college, he looked around for a summer calling bigger than himself. The summer before, a friend had gone south with COFO's Mississippi Summer. He knew Gail Falk from church and a network of left-leaning high school students who'd met at Quaker weekend workshops on topics like capitalism and race. Her going to Radcliffe College had been part of how he'd ended up at Harvard.

At the end of spring '64, Ish and a mutual friend had talked with Gail about her pending plan to go south and had come away unnerved at the risks and doubtful about how much it might accomplish. Ish's own '64 summer commitment was counseling at a camp in sleepy Vermont. Camp Killooleet was run by the left-leaning, musically inclined Seeger family, serving kids mainly from New York. Good-natured, baseball-crazy Michael Goodman was the most winning 8-year-old in the cabin. Shortly after arrival, the camp learned that Michael's 20-year-old cousin Andrew Goodman had just gone down to Mississippi. June 21, as camp began, Andrew and two other young men went missing in Neshoba County. When their broken bodies were dug up in August, Ish felt like a coward for not having gone.

Ish and Michael

That November Johnson cruised back to the White House on misplaced hopes he might not push us deeper into Vietnam. Then winter confrontations in Selma bled into the spring. By that time LBJ was bombing North Vietnam. Dismayed by emerging events, Ish dropped in on a Student Nonviolent Coordinating Committee office to volunteer for the upcoming summer. A harried white staffer informed him that SNCC was no longer sending young liberals south, but mentioned that students at Brandeis were forming a chapter of a ten-week project called "SCOPE" to register voters down there. SCOPE was a multi-state effort being assembled by SCLC (Southern Christian Leadership Conference), Dr. King's Atlanta-based organization.

"No More Selmas," said the leaflet Ish got from Brandeis, a phrase attuned to the special meaning the Selma marches had gained in Boton when a Boston man was killed. James Reeb, a Unitarian minister, had been staffing a Boston desegregation program for the American Friends (Quaker) Service Committee. Tuesday March 9, the evening he arrived in Selma, he was beaten into a coma by whites. The suspenseful two days he lingered fueled a picket line around the massive Federal Building in Boston, urging the feds to send down marshals. Friday night after he passed, demonstrators occupied the twelve-story building. Among the dozens dragged out early Sunday were eleven students from Brandeis.

That's a lot from a suburban campus of 1,600, but Brandeis wasn't your typical college. From its founding in 1948 as a Jewish secular institution, it had promoted involvement in social justice. In 1960, for example, faculty and students had picketed Boston Woolworth stores in support of lunch-counter sit-ins down south.

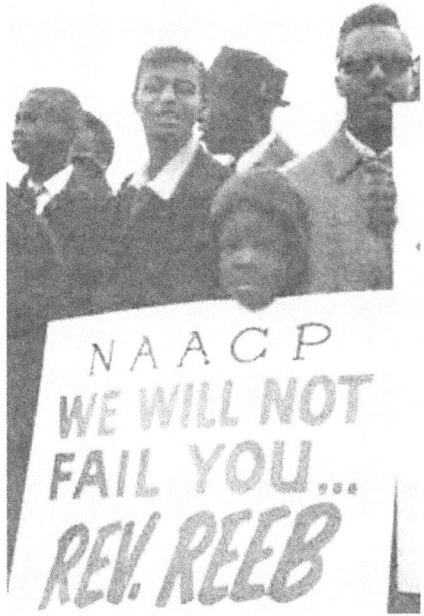

Wellesley College News photo by Robin Reisig.

Brandeis people were also involved in picketing Hayes-Bickford, a popular cafeteria chain, for discriminatory employment. In March 1964, SCLC praised Brandeis for sponsoring a nationwide student fast to raise cash for relief of hunger in Mississippi. Brandeis' most notable faculty link to rising student radical thought was New Left political theorist Herbert Marcuse, and students from his courses would be part of Brandeis SCOPE. More pragmatically, an important link was activist and popular lecturer Jacob "Jerry" Cohen. In the summer of 1965, he would be on leave co-writing *Freedom When?*

From the Brandeis paper, *The Justice.*

with James Farmer, the early-1940s founder of the non-violent, direct-action Congress of Racial Equality (CORE).

SCOPE (short for Summer Community Organizing and Political Education) was the brainchild of SCLC's pugnacious Hosea Williams (1926-2000), who'd started life poor and orphaned in Georgia.

Around age twenty, Hosea was a staff sergeant in Germany when a bomb hit his foxhole, killing everyone around him. After a year in veterans' hospitals, he returned one hot summer day to Georgia where the police in a bus station roughed him up for drinking from a "white" water fountain (the only one working that day). The returning warrior would not forget that.

After finishing college he taught high school and worked about ten years as a US Department of Agriculture chemist in Georgia. Along with that, in the 1950s he rose as an NAACP leader known for provocative but effective strategies. In 1963 he went on leave from the USDA, resigned from his NAACP leadership and moved over to SCLC.

According to *The New York Times*, Martin Luther King, Jr., loved this "rambunctious, fearless and blunt" leader. Hosea was Martin's heavy (nonviolent) artillery, "my wild man, my Castro" whom King dispatched in '64 to the segregated beaches of St. Augustine. As the *Times* would summarize his role, "Mr. Williams would recruit volunteers, teach them the elements of nonviolence

Martin Luther King Jr. at Brandeis, 1957.

and exhort them with prayers and shouts of 'Freedom now!' Then he would take them on the march in defiance of court orders, armed assault and the prospect of jail." The strategy was "a strong dose of Hosea Williams and his foghorn voice" to soften white officials into negotiating with SCLC's more diplomatic Rev. Andrew Young.

The basic early idea of SCLC-SCOPE was that colleges would form chapters of SCOPE with faculty as administrators and students as rank-and-file workers; each chapter would take on a southern county for ten weeks of voter registration. In late 1964 Hosea visited Brandeis and enlisted Leonard Zion, a rabbi and assistant dean of student affairs. Dean Zion envisioned Brandeis SCOPE as a complement to an ongoing Brandeis project run by the Northern Student Movement in Boston's Roxbury district. Also connected to that, it happened, was Baptist Rev. Virgil Wood, SCLC's man in Massachusetts. In line with Hosea's early idea of faculty involvement, Dean Zion envisioned SCOPE also as a way to launch relations between Brandeis and some black southern college that would continue beyond the summer. To get things rolling, he called on Mississippi Summer returnee David Gelfand and graduate scholar Carol Estes, though neither planned to go south with the group. By mid-winter, more students were getting involved. Two early members were juniors Elias Dickerman from Honduras and David Jacobson from Chicago. David's father, J.Z. Jacobson, was a visionary teacher, writer and well-known art critic who, back in 1941, had published a short book attempting to fathom Nazi ideology and to express some hope for humanity in that apocalyptic time.

David remembers Al Engelman as a professor who got involved early, ad-

David J.   Elias   Bill G.

vising the group about how to prepare. Bill Greenhill, a senior from Scarsdale, took on most of the planning, research and communications co-signed by Dean Zion. Planning information from SCLC was scant because Hosea Williams, who had intended to focus himself on SCOPE as of January 1, was largely tied up until April with other commitments. As Andrew Young would remember SCLC in the spring of 1965, it was still just 150 staff nationwide, "expected by the nation to overturn segregation everywhere. We were too few, but we poured our lives into this challenge."

As the spring advanced, more faculty gave background workshops to about sixty interested students, and students took on assignments for publicity, fund-raising and so forth.

Where in the South would we go? SCLC was targeting scores of rural counties across the south and, experimentally, some cities as well. The latter option appealed to Dean Zion, who envisioned the summer as the starting point for longer ties between Brandeis and some southern black college, most likely found in a sizable town. Out of half a dozen urban locales, the group settled on Richland County in the hilly Midlands of South Carolina. Of that county's 200,000 population, about four-fifths lived in Columbia, capital of the state. The city had a sizable black middle and professional class, clustered around two private black institutions, Allen University and Benedict College. Downtown was USC, the public state university, which had begun an orderly to-ken integration in 1963. On the north side of town was private, white Columbia College. These white schools and white city commercial establishments gave menial employment to numerous blacks. More were employed at Fort Jackson, a large Army base just east of the city. Other employers were city, county, and state level governments, though none employed blacks at any pay grade higher than janitor. Federal jobs (mainly postal) were open to blacks. Columbia's percolating economy included a black commercial district along Washington Street. As a result, though good jobs were limited, county black unemployment was relatively low. Median county white income was $5,800. For blacks it was $2,200, $800 less than the federal poverty line for families. (How did those last two statistics compare with stats for Allegheny County PA? Ish wasn't eager to know.)

Still, all this and the presence of a relatively strong NAACP suggest that

Richland wasn't really a county where SCLC's SCOPE was urgently needed, and it isn't clear how much SCLC really wanted Brandeis to go there. As part of its planning, SCLC starred Columbia and seven other cities on an undated five-state map, but the map may have drawn after Brandeis had made its choice. Richland County was part of the 6th Congressional District, which SCLC (in its wildest dreams) considered key to unseating US Senator Strom Thurmond in 1966, but this hadn't led SCLC to include Richland among its top-twenty priority South Carolina counties.

One or two Brandeis faculty were stimulating parental consents by promising that Brandeis SCOPE would play things safer with their kids than other SCOPE chapters might do. At the same time, here and there in the volunteer pool ran discontent at the choice of urban Richland County. Deep down, canvassing safely inside black urban neighborhoods wasn't what some had in mind. Like Ish, many were awed by accounts of gutsy SNCC workers sneaking into the Mississippi Delta, dodging sheriffs and KKK by crawling ditches at night to talk up change among black sharecroppers. Not that we had that kind of courage, but some were already wondering how far the group might venture outside the city. SCLC wasn't SNCC, and Brandeis SCOPE would be too large to slip into a rural county.

By late May, Bill Greenhill had compiled an eight-page report about the county. One surprise was that in 1951 Columbia had been named one of about ten "All-America Cities," on account of a new city-manager structure and "citizen" participation; and again in 1964 for progress including "urban renewal" and "improving race relations."

NAACP leader James Felder paints a drowsy view of still basically segregated Columbia in the early 1960s: "Unlike Charleston, blacks in Columbia were not known for staging a lot of protests. In many ways, they felt insulated from the prejudices of the white community because of educational institutions [and] powerful black economic engines in the community." Glossing over limitations, Felder mentions black banking, insurance and mortgage businesses that provided services denied to blacks by white-owned firms; I.S. Leevy's "department store" (more like a dry goods and clothing store than a Gimbels); a struggling, fifty-bed private black hospital; black-owned small stores and restaurants; and black Blue Ribbon taxi.

Moore's history of Columbia sums up how city desegregation was proceeding mostly quietly but steadily in the early 1960s through back-room deals. In April 1962, for example, a handful of prominent local black men secretly approached the mayor, pragmatic Lester Bates. They suggested negotiating in private with him about quietly integrating places like parks, lunch counters and theaters. Bates saw the sense in that alternative to Alabama, where city reputations were shredding as white firemen trained hoses and police used cattle prods and dogs unrestrained against demonstrating blacks. So gradually, with backroom, face-saving maneuvers, places were being opened up and signs of segregation removed from public fountains and restrooms. Up in Waltham, Brandeis SCOPE had little inkling of these parlays. Few Columbians knew about them, either.

Bates' polity was in step with broader economic strategy. Despite having re-raised the Confederate battle flag atop the statehouse in 1961, state-level officials were dialing back the racial rhetoric. Since the end of World War II they'd been luring northern industrial money down to their poor, union-proof state. The point was that none should confuse the Palmetto State with the lawless, deeper Deep South.

Relevant to its voting rights mission, Brandeis SCOPE had learned that Richland County whites outnumbered blacks. It also knew that over half of eligible whites were registered to vote, compared with a quarter of eligible blacks.

Hope's Kids

It had learned that over 24,000 potential black voters were still off the rolls. In Columbia, the white proportion of registered voters was 80%, versus 30% for blacks.

Brandeis freshman Margot Thornton had signed up for publicity. In late April she and politics professor Norton Long flew to Columbia briefly to meet a few local black leaders. From that came some encouraging contacts recorded in Greenhill's report, and the promise of a local black sponsors' committee to officially welcome SCOPE. Its chair was 28-year-old, white, Arkansas native Dick Miles (a future US ambassador), who was staffing the South Carolina component of a multi-state Voter Education Project. VEP was a joint creation of CORE, SNCC, SCLC, and NAACP. Dick's role with SCOPE fit well with SC-VEP's mission of tracking and coordinating statewide registration efforts.

Margot

How many would be in the group? A month before it headed south, the group boiled down to 23 students or graduating seniors (listed at the end of this book). There was said to be screening, though in the end only one was rejected, or possibly none. Of the 23, eighteen attended Brandeis; five came from other Boston colleges. Ages ranged from 17 to 23. Ten were finishing freshman year. Having formed at Brandeis, most were Jewish; at least six were not. Four had grown up in the South or had a southern parent. Margot Thornton was the only black. Her dad was from Haiti, where Margot understood he'd grown up free of white racist exposure. She recalls, "He believed anything you wanted to do, you could do." .

Ish joined the group in May. At the one or two free-wheeling meetings he attended, he wondered who if anyone was looked to as a leader. At that point the group had three "program directors": COFO veteran Dave Gelfand who wasn't going with the group; Arthur "Terry" Parsons, a first-year grad student about to be drafted; and quiet-mannered Bill Greenhill, who'd already decided not to head up the group in the South.

Ish was also confused by overlapping names: two Bills (Greenhill and Kornrich); two Davids (Jacobson and Kricker); two Rickys (Richard Gurbst and Frederick Schaffer); two Elizabeths (Betty Milgram and Liz Hafkin); a Kathleen ("Thais" Courts) a Kathy (Davis), a Catherine ("Citti"—pronounced Kitty—Allsup); plus three Alans (Venable, Segal, and Kern).

Phyllis

Then there was Phyllis Greenfield, a long-boned, long-faced, guitar-playing freshman curled awkwardly at the base of a bookcase, her chestnut hair high in an unkempt bun. Whoa. A conscientious monogamist, Ish had already chosen the girl of his dreams—a peppery, Hungarian-American-Unitarian lass. Judy would have gone south, too, if she'd been able to persuade her mother to sign the release for a daughter whose paprika level could get her in dutch. In the end, Judy would devote her summer to counseling black kids in Kansas City. Wise mother, Judy thinks today.

Now the question was money. SCLC was paying for things like the training, advising field-staff living expenses and stipends ($10 a week) for up to four local volunteers in each county, but each chapter would cover its own transportation, member costs, phone bills, and most everything else. For Brandeis that would also include helping out a number of Brandeis scholarship students with money to make up for summer earnings they'd need to forgo in order to take part in SCOPE.

Dr. King was coming to Boston April 23 to lead a march of 40,000 to a rally on Boston Common. The day before, Dean Zion wrote to him special delivery hinting King might swing by Waltham to help them raise $40,000 Zion thought it would take to send forty students and fifteen faculty down. Unfortunately, King was tied up in the march, rally, and back-to-back meetings with state politicians.

When the chapter winnowed down to 23, the budget shrank to roughly $21,000. By late May, the group had raised only $2,000, and its treasurer, David Kricker—a nervous, friendly junior from a working-class progressive family in Woodstock NY—was wracking his brains. So was Elias Dickerman who'd been trying to fill the gap since April. Raised in a small Central American Jewish community in the Honduran capital, Tegulcipa, Elias had more moxie and savvy than anyone else in the group and was using his twice-weekly campus radio slots to drum up money and other support. At some point he'd also pressed his pliant roommate David Jacobson into a sleep-sapping effort.

David K.

More money must have come from a late appeal to parents; whatever that amounted to, the shortfall must still have been huge. Four basic expenses made up about three-fourths of the $21,000. The additional fourth was intended for items that disappeared from the plan, such as flying sixteen Brandeis faculty down for visits; in the end, just a handful would come. There were four essential items.

- Stipends for Brandeis scholarship students, in lieu of summer earnings they would need for college in the fall.

- Long-distance bus fares down in June and back at the end of August.

- $10 weekly living expenses per Brandeis student (assuming they might get more or less free summer-long housing and a fair number of meals). Non-Brandeis members would pay for themselves.

- Gas and office supplies, though nothing for an office or cars. In theory the group could borrow cars or get rides from local folk. Being mainly in a city, they could also hoof it or ride the bus.

In the final weeks of school, with everyone hunkered down over term papers and finals, campus donations had petered out. David Kricker's last resort as treasurer was getting SCOPE members to return other departing students' dorm keys to the college office in exchange for keeping the two-buck deposit. Then Brandeis President Sachar found $5,000 to cover the scholarship student stipends. But the gap was still great.

David J. still misses the sleep he lost as Elias elbowed him on, but finally something paid off: a personal appeal that Elias mailed to Drew Pearson, the nationally syndicated *Washington Post* columnist of "Washington Merry-Go-Round." Maybe Elias had learned of a small donation Pearson had made to SCLC in 1964, or maybe he knew only of Pearson's broad support for civil rights. Elias pleaded for any amount and Pearson mailed him a check for $10,000. It was really Elias and Pearson who enabled Brandeis SCOPE.

Looking back, Ish wonders how informed we 20-year-olds were about the cause we were joining and what we were likely to find. What did we know beyond what filtered down through Walter Cronkite on CBS, *The Times*, *The Boston Globe*, *Newsweek*, *I.F. Stone's Weekly*, flyers, rumors, and topical song? And what sort of inter-racial experience did we already have?

Many of us (probably most) had already been involved in peace, civil rights, or similar causes through family progressive or labor ties, some going back several decades. As for Ish, since childhood he'd been intrigued by stories and themes from Civil War times when an Ohio branch of the family had been part of the Underground Railroad. He'd read his great-grandfather's pamphlet *Down South Before the War* about an 1850s excursion down the Mississippi to witness slavery firsthand.

Of course, Pittsburgh schools were integrated, though the numbers of blacks in Ish's weren't large. In his grade school and high school the single most admired student was future novelist John Edgar Wideman. Through chess and sports Ish got to know and like a number of blacks. He knew a few others from Scouting. As Scoutmaster, his father had welcomed them and their fathers into the troop. The family's Unitarian church attracted refugees from Jewish, Christian and other backgrounds, and included a few blacks as well. The pastor, Ed Cahill, had led Atlanta's Unitarians through "integration, not just desegregation" beginning in 1957. While Ish was signing up with SCOPE, his law-student brother Gil was planning to join a summer legal team in Jackson.

Ish's parents employed a black housekeeper, Mattie Belle Herring, to help clean a large house and launder for a family of four boys. In the black migration of the early war years, after finishing high school, Mattie Belle migrated north and began five decades of work in their home. The family did more than most about looking out for a housekeeper's welfare. In addition to Social Security, the parents enrolled Mattie Belle in the retirement plan that grew out of the father's consulting business.

Mattie rode the bus back to Alabama many summers for family and class reunions, but about her earlier life down there the four boys never learned much. It wasn't the kind of family that asked a lot of personal questions. But Ish's attachment to and awkward feelings about her—married, childless, helping to raise him—imbued his thoughts about race.

Two doors away lived a fierce, hysterical Scotch-Irish housewife from central Pennsylvania, mother of a favorite playmate, who openly hated blacks of all ages, but as a loyal neighbor treated Mattie with respect. (Years after leaving Pennsylvania Ish learned that what he'd always thought was a liberal state, proud of its Quaker roots, was described by some as "Pittsburgh and Philadelphia with Alabama in between.")

At Harvard he'd met wise old Gordon Allport and read his *The Nature of Prejudice*. He'd researched a term paper about the backgrounds of the handful of black males who'd been part of his high school graduation class, whose lives outside school he'd known nothing about.

About South Carolina specifically, Ish had gathered some history beyond Fort Sumter from Tom Pettigrew's seminal course on race relations in the South. Perhaps from that he'd learned how the state's proportion of blacks had shrunk. Around 1880, three-fifths of the state's population was black. In the next four decades, 142 documented lynchings coupled with anti-black riots and other oppression had forced enough black families out so that by 1920 they were down to roughly half. (South Carolina history scholar Elizabeth Robeson says that on one hand the state actually had the lowest number of lynchings among all the former Confederate states; on the other, 99% of South Carolinian victims were black, whereas other states lynched sizable numbers of whites as well.)

Through the 1920s the black population shrank another 8% while the white population grew by 15%. Kaleidoscopic oppression continued. By 1960, only 35% of South Carolina's people were black. Still, opportunistic, manly-man US Senator Strom Thurmond won landslide re-elections in substantial part by his codes of "states' rights" and "federal tyranny" for blacks taking over the South. He hadn't always been anti-federal. In the '30s, like most South Carolinians he'd been all in favor of Roosevelt's Depression-fighting programs, which benefited both races. Nor in his private life was Strom ever an authentic model of purity and separation. In 1925 he'd fathered a daughter, Essie Mae, with a 16-year-old black maid employed by his family who apparently remained his mistress for another twenty years until he married at age 46. In 1965 the publicly unacknowledged daughter was forty years old, still under the senator's financial protection, and still no more than a rumor to whites.

Around 1940 began the state's long, slow dismantling of legalized segregation, when local NAACP chapters finally succeeded in creating a state-level organization. White resistance was so intense that for many years the SC-NAACP could not publicize its telephone number or address. On the legal level, things began to happen, thanks to courageous rulings from 1944 to 1951 by federal judge J. Waties Waring, a white Charleston aristocrat whose marriage to a New York woman pried him loose from the status quo. Waring shocked his homies with judgments that black teachers could not be paid less than white ones and that the state Democratic Party (the only party that mattered) could not bar blacks from joining it and voting in its primaries. (To his credit, then Governor Thurmond did not resist.) But generally progress was halting and slow and mainly relied on federal courts.

After *Brown v. Board of Education* (1954), black voices quickened, the Klan revived, and white Citizens Councils formed to resist the decision's vast implications. Shortly after *Brown v. Board*, a young black Columbia woman, Sarah Mae Flemming, boarded a bus and, finding all the black seats taken, sat down at the back of the section for whites. The white bus driver (all drivers were white and held police powers inside their buses) demanded she stand, then punched her in the stomach and forced her off. Her response was a federal lawsuit that awarded her constitutional rights to sit wherever she wanted. A South Carolina state judge thwarted its effect in the state, but the ruling became the basis for Rosa Parks' victory two years later in Montgomery. (Another ten years would pass before Columbia transit hired its first black driver.) Meanwhile, two years later in South Carolina, the fight was over new "anti-communist" legislation that for about a year prohibited local, county, and state employees (including teachers) from being members of the NAACP. Through the second half of the 1950s, things straggled along in Columbia and Richland County, though by 1955, nearby Orangeburg blacks had launched a solid, sustainable campaign of suits and demonstrations that, in 1965, would intersect with SCOPE.

In 1960-61, attacks on students at sit-ins and Freedom Riders across the South evoked a sickness and shame throughout much of our "land of the free." The sit-ins began in 1960 when four NAACP college students from North Carolina A&T took seats at a white-only lunch counter in Greensboro. CORE quickly jumped in to help spread their example. Later that year, sit-ins began in Orangeburg, and two years later in Columbia as strident groups like CORE prodded NAACP leadership into those kinds of actions. (When arrests in cities like Orangeburg grew larger—into the thousands—most often it was the NAACP that came up with lawyers and bail.)

In mid-1964, the federal *Civil Rights Act* set off a new surge of change. For example, the law forbade discrimination in businesses like restaurants or hotels considered part of interstate commerce. In cities like Columbia, the act also prompted new voter registration campaigns. All this a full decade after *Brown v. Board*.

On the eve of SCOPE's arrival, voting rights progress was stalled in Congress, pending the *Voting Rights Act* that would eliminate state literacy tests designed to keep blacks off the rolls. SCLC had hoped the bill would be signed by July of SCOPE summer, but June was running out, and still it hadn't passed. This meant we'd need to begin our door-to-door work with literacy testing still in place to varying degrees throughout the state. Our VEP (Voter Education Project) handout (see next page) embodied the law that was still in effect. The form required applicants to declare their race and to either own property or demonstrate "that I can both read and write a section of the Constitution of South Carolina." Our impression back in Waltham had been that literacy testing was no great obstacle to registering. We hadn't yet witnessed how a registrar could arbitrarily let any illiterate white adult breeze through registration, while making it torture for literate blacks. We didn't guess that "read and write" could be construed to mean "interpret."

In theory, fifty years of compulsory school attendance should have brought full literacy to the state, but child farm labor and other dynamics still cut off the schooling of many more blacks than whites. So we hoped to run literacy classes for blacks of all ages, along with workshops on practical problems like requesting the paving of streets or enrolling in existing services. We'd heard that some members of the South Carolina Student Council on Human Relations, an interracial student group centered in Columbia, had tutored and canvassed for voter registration, and we hoped to work with them.

So that's where we were heading. Besides a towel, sleeping bag, and travelers' checks for ten weeks' subsistence, what was Ish supposed to bring? SCLC's short list included books; his choices were Gandhi's essays *Non-Violent Resistance (Satyagraha)* and a pocket New Testament in which he'd underlined relevant verses. Throughout his public schooling, daily patriotic morning pledges had been supplemented with the Lord's Prayer (Protestant version) and ten verses from the King James Bible. Since then he'd largely avoided religion, but he did want to be able to talk the talk if called upon to speak in church.

SCLC also recommended a flashlight, writing supplies, and possibly a camera. A fan of the New Lost City Ramblers, Ish was bringing his autoharp. For the summer heat, afternoon downpours and sink-washability, he'd wear icky nylon shirts; for Sundays a $30, washable seersucker suit. As 19-year-old freshman Lynn Goldsmith observed, washing wouldn't really get rid of the stickiness but would be "nice to try." David Kricker remembers that whatever one wore, the day-long heat "fried everyone's brains" and at night we would flounder in sweat.

SAMPLE
State of South Carolina
APPLICATION FOR REGISTRATION

Dated at _____, S. C., _____ day of _____, 19____

I _____

hereby apply for registration as an elector and certify under
oath that:

1. I am a female, a member of the _____ race, born at
   male

_____, on ____

I reside at _____ Street in the town or city of
_____ or

on _____ Road in _____

Township or Parish in _____ County. My nearest

voting place is _____. My weight is ____ lbs.,

my height is ____ ft. ____ in., the color of my eyes ____

the color of my hair ____

( ) 2. I (a) will have resided in South Carolina for at least one year, in this
County for at least six months and in my voting precinct for at least three
months prior to any election at which I will be entitled to vote if a registration certificate is issued to me upon this application, or

( ) (b) am a minister or spouse of a minister in charge of an organized
church in this State, or

( ) (c) am a teacher of public school or spouse of a teacher and will have
resided in South Carolina for a period of six months prior to any such
election.

( ) 3. I am not an idiot, or insane, a pauper supported at public expense or
confined in any public prison.

4. I will demonstrate to the Registration Board that

( ) (a) I can both read and write a section of the Constitution of South
Carolina; or

( ) (b) I own and have paid all taxes due last year on property in this State
assessed at $300.00 or more.

( ) 5. I (a) have never been convicted of any of the following crimes: burglary,
arson, obtaining goods or money under false pretenses, prejury, forgery,
robbery, bribery, adultery, bigamy, wifebeating, housebreaking, receiving
stolen goods, breach of trust with fraudulent intent, fornication, sodomy,
incest, assault with intent to ravish, miscegenation, larceny, or crimes
against the election laws; or

( ) (b) Have been legally pardoned for such conviction.

Sworn to and subscribed before me ⎫ _____

this _____ day of ⎬   Applicant

_____, 19____ ⎭ Examined and found (not) qualified

_____   _____
Member of Registration Board   Member of Registration Board

VOTELESS People Are Hopeless People

(Courtesy of S. C. Voter Education Project)

L ate afternoon June 12, most of Brandeis SCOPE boarded a Greyhound in New York for a 23-hour ride to Atlanta. Lynn, Phyllis, Margot, Citti ("Kitty") Allsup, and Frederick "Ricky" Schaffer overflowed onto a second, otherwise empty bus. In a photo probably taken in a common room in Atlanta, you can pick out four of these five.

In Atlanta, clockwise from lamp: Alan Kern, David J.'s forehead, Margot, Lesley Straley, Betty Milgram, Phyllis, Citti, Bill G., Ish's forehead, Lynn, Mary Ann Efroymson, Liz Hafkin.

Phyllis' hometown was Teaneck, New Jersey. Her mother, Sophie Greenfield, was a social worker who'd once worked in August Wilson's Hill District in Pittsburgh. The Greenfields marched in progressive causes. Because of earlier associations with communists, Phyllis' lawyer-dad Mike had been barred from employment by the progressive organizations he'd wanted to represent. In lieu he was running a racially integrated children's play cosmetics factory in New Jersey where Phyllis worked the assembly line one summer, befriending everyone around her. A pianist, she'd planned to major in music but, discovering what felt to her like destructive pressures in the Branideis music department, she'd shifted to preparing herself to follow her mother's profession. On the bus, she took out her guitar and soon sang into friendship with harmonica-toting Ricky Schaffer.

Lynn Goldsmith was another 18-year-old from progressive roots. When not teaching physics at Princeton, her father coordinated a nearby Freedom Center. Both parents—George and Sonya Goldsmith—would be helping us all summer. Familiar with radical groups in Princeton, confident, energetic, with strong social mojo, Lynn could be strident and feisty. "Felt good," she'd write, late summer, after a "friendly fistfight" with Mickey Shur, a young leader of the New York Columbia University chapter of SCOPE in Orangeburg County, forty miles south of Columbia.

Citti ("Kitty") Allsup, another freshman with Brandeis SCOPE, was a wilder card: daughter of conservative Protestant missionaries who'd fled Cuba as Castro took over. In 1968 she would describe herself as having grown up "in a minister's house where women met to eat cookies, sew rag dolls and talk about how to save poor Africans." Rebellious, deeply idealistic, sweet, iron-willed, and searching for community, she'd fought the bleakness of her first year at Wheaton, a women's college southeast of Boston, by joining Boston CORE.

At the Richmond stop for a meal, they noticed segregated bathrooms and eating: a large modern cafeteria—recently officially integrated by hard struggle but still filled entirely with whites—next door to a tiny, ill-lit "restaurant" for blacks and civil rights types passing through.

Ricky Schaffer had spent time his first year at Harvard hanging out in SDS discussions on empowering the working class, and his ruminations home that summer to a college roommate ran along those lines. South of Richmond, he and Margot had a good, long talk, during which he thought about how the group had yet to work out a leadership structure for the next eleven weeks. Other, smaller SCOPE chapters with faculty members or older grad students may have had an easier time with this, but for us the leadership question was playing out in unflattering ways. It's tempting to let some old dogs lie, but Ish still thinks there's something to learn here, as did Bill Greenhill years ago when he wrote about Brandeis SCOPE leadership issues in a social work graduate school paper. In it, did Bill share Ish's sense that Bill himself might have been the group's best social leader? Unfortunately, Bill chucked the paper years ago.

On the bus, Ricky Schaffer mentally noted Margot's level-headedness and civil rights experience. She mentioned how even her 12-year-old brother was already into the struggle. This fit with Rick's thinking then that, as the only black in the group, she was "in a sense" already the leader. Freshman Lesley Straley, another level head, remembers Margot also as a likely leader, "poised, extremely confident, clear." But Margot was rightly wary of being chosen on account of her color and of trying to steer an unwieldy group of older students who hashed and re-hashed every move.

To Margot Ricky described his dissatisfaction with differences between somewhat older, pulpit-led SCLC—with its focus on high-profile, TV-friendly events—and younger, elusive, hardscrabble SNCC. Margot agreed with Ricky about the difference but didn't think it would have much bearing on what our group would be doing. Despite his doubts about the value of enfolding more blacks in a lazy American bourgeoisie, Ricky hoped for the best in Richland County. As he wrote to his roommate, "The most active civil rights group there is the clergy, and although they are middle-class, they have shown much willingness to work for the aims and for the organization of the lower classes."

At the stop in Charlotte NC, Ricky studied a sullen, skinny little black girl seated in the waiting room. A plump white girl stood nearby, and as their glances met, the black child stuck out a long, pink tongue. "And with it," he wrote, "she points back at the white girl all the insults and humiliation that she has suffered and shall suffer because her tongue does not match her skin."

Lynn found it easy at first to converse with other, non-SCOPE riders, but after entering South Carolina "the Negroes tended to be quiet and keep to themselves." At one stop the bus was entirely full, save one seat next to an elderly black woman. A white man got on and stood the duration of his forty-minute ride.

Long past midnight at the back of the bus, Phyllis penned her feelings as the Deep South seemed to close in. They'd been driving down Route 1 for hours—"dark and quiet except for the sounds of breathing. I was struck by the loneliness of the landscape—darkness, miles of fields bordered by woods, endless distance between small, dimly lit houses, then a single bulb burning in a little shack set back against the woods." She wondered how others on the bus could sleep as she and they headed "where no one can find us, or hear us if we call. What have I done?" Terrified, she didn't want to be here. She never shared these feelings with anyone or knew that anyone else was afraid.

3. ATLANTA

For more about the six-day SCOPE training in Atlanta, explore other sources at the back of this book. About 400 volunteers attended the sessions in Morris Brown College's Joe Louis gym. (SCLC -SCOPE would eventually involve 650 from 120 colleges.) Between speeches, workshops, films, and meals that over the week became more and more Spartan, we slept in the college dorms and mingled outside on the lawn.

Phyllis' first letter home confronted the gulf between Teaneck and the "middle-class" black homes surrounding the campus. What she saw was a shanty-town of rickety houses, interspersed with Depression-era housing constructed by the WPA: "colorless dismal duplicates—grey-brown mirrored

Terry hits a funny bone on the Morris Brown College lawn. Photo Carol Sable.

images. Like a prison. If it were the north I'd be sorry they were so sturdy, or they might have been torn down." But the people seemed warm and friendly.

She couldn't remember feeling so secure within a community, "and for the first time the people who stick out are the whites—they seem so pale."

She caught herself generalizing too quickly about people we'd started to meet. "Perhaps it sounds bad, but I think of the Negro people as such—as well as individuals. 'Negro people shout'—we heard that from Andy Young today. Why?" In the face of repression and frustration, shouting struck her as psychologically sound "and a lot cheaper than a psychiatrist." Later in training she'd grapple with other stereotypes she possessed, like an underlying bias against "blond and blue-eyed American whites."

Sessions ranged through history, economics, poverty, farm labor, federal law, literacy. In between speeches Phyllis met a heady mix of "elderly Negroes who have gone from house to house teaching reading and writing—kids who left school, men and women who left jobs to run freedom houses, demonstrate—the Selma marchers, lively, anxious to get going." She spoke to some who'd worked in one Alabama community for several years.

Ish was less able to mix. He listened to speakers and intellectualized about the religious roots of movement culture. Most of the blacks at the training were southern. He glanced at a cluster of young black men in faded overalls or jeans—battle-scarred veterans of SNCC standing apart, guarded and cynical in this SCLC scene. Among themselves they sang in shades and phrases he could not begin to reproduce. One played a mournful wooden flute. How different they were from most of the SCLC leaders. Among the latter, intensely inspiring, 29-year-old Mississippian Rev. James Bevel stood out in overalls, yarmulke, and message, at least to Liz Hafkin and Ish. Jim and his wife Diane were dynamic recruiters of youth. As SCLC's head of direct action he introduced Gandhian non-violence and methods of self-defense, reminding us to cover our heads and, if we were on the ground, try to ward off kicks to the kidneys.

Dr. King spoke Monday night, building for Phyllis "to a climax of black and white, all religions, hand in hand crying, 'Free at last! Free at last!' And I was filled with unity and gladness—tears an insufficient release." But Hosea's

James Bevel leads one of numerous SCOPE workshops on non-violence.
Photo *Atlanta Inquirer.*

orchestration made her uneasy. After the speech he stood, repeatedly shouting, "Who's our leader?" to which we chorused, "Martin Luther King!" "Sometimes, when we rise *en masse*," wrote Phyllis, "I think of Hitler, and sometimes I can't just yell 'Freedom' to 'What do you want?' It sticks in my throat even if I believe it."

Though King was essential, for many of us our moderator, Bayard Rustin (1912-1987), was key. To Ricky Schaffer he was a large disheveled man, with long, hard gray hair, and a crooked smile. "With the first words he speaks, it is hard to keep from feeling, here is a man I would trust completely." A pacifist and war resister imprisoned in World War II, Bayard had also mentored James Farmer in the creation of CORE, was director of the labor-oriented A. Philip Randolph Institute, and had organized the 1963 March on Washington where King had delivered "I have a dream."

In talking to us, King had included "non-believers" as part of the movement, but Thais Courts felt a wider cultural divide in Atlanta between Christian and non than between races. In this aspect, she, too, found Bayard Rustin the most exciting and persuasive—"his reasoned, intellectual manner," his language of "philosophical scholarship that we northern students knew so well."

Phyllis wrote of him as "the one who spoke not only of love, but also of fear. He didn't say, 'I am not afraid because I will go home to my God if I die.' He said, 'I go on if I am afraid—and I am always afraid—because I must live with myself—because I love humanity and life.'"

During the singing of "We Shall Overcome" at the end of a session, Ricky Schaffer joined his right hand with that of a little girl who lived at the Freedom House

Bayard Rustin.
Photo Frederick (Ricky) Schaffer.

in Atlanta, thinking he had "never seen before the same joy and innocence and sorrow that were in her eyes as she sang and swayed." His left hand held that of tall, young Leroy Mouton who had been in the car Viola Liuzzo had been driving when she'd been murdered three months earlier outside Selma. People like Leroy reminded him we were taking on a gentler challenge than SCOPErs bound for Alabama where Governor Wallace still promised "segregation now, segregation tomorrow, segregation forever."

We met Pat Gandy, our SCLC field advisor. Tall, thin, red-headed, white, Pat was 28, a native of Georgia, ex-Navy, and five-year movement veteran. He was one of the few daring southern whites who'd thrown their lives into the struggle. Arrested many times and beaten more than once, he had a wild streak and liked to rile things up.

Hope's Kids

Early morning on Tuesday, Lynn and some others held an "emergency meeting" to talk about whether all of us should go to Richland County. Some felt we weren't all bound to Richland and could go instead to surrounding rural counties. Others argued against dispersing because Brandeis controlled the stipend money for scholarship kids at the end of the summer, and a split might jeopardize those payments. Another reason not to split was we'd already committed ourselves to leaders in Richland, though to whom exactly was vague. Besides, some of us and our parents had been promised a "safe" assignment. In Elias' recollection, some of these kids were now protesting playing it safe.

On Tuesday night, Hosea Williams attended a larger meeting of our group. By this time Lynn was hoping to slip away to some more rural county adjacent to Richland, but she wrote that Hosea had come to tell us why *he* had suggested a split. For one thing, our chapter really was too big. VEP's Dick Miles had never been keen on tying up so many in Richland, and Hosea agreed. He proposed we send three Brandeis-student members and three non-Brandeis members to a different county. Most likely he'd been talking with some of us on the side. Most likely the non-Brandeis trio was meant to include Citti, Ricky Schaffer and Mary Ann Efroymson, Wellesley '65. Most likely the Brandeis three were meant to be Lynn and her friends Bill Kornrich and Thais. After the meeting Lynn argued long with David Kricker who remained against any split, as did Elias, Bill Greenhill, and Phyllis. Then someone telephoned Waltham and was told the group should stay in one county.

Hosea Williams

Behind all this lay interpersonal tensions, some deriving from encounters before the group had formed. Political? Personal? Brandeis is a pretty small place. Ish still doesn't know what, but some friction stood between Bill Greenhill and Elias; some other perhaps between Elias and Thais, and possibly others.

To a meeting on Wednesday, Hosea brought Ben Mack, a Columbia man, now field secretary for SC-SCOPE. Oddly, this may have been the first we knew about Ben, and maybe he had just been given the role. Before, he'd been a trainer in SCLC's Citizenship Education Program, a leadership workshop based on John's Island on the Carolina coast. David Jacobson thinks Ben was around age forty, with several young children. From Ben's comments in workshop about communicating with adults, Ish got the impression of a modest, quiet-spoken, practical and sometimes wry individual, perhaps a former teacher. Hosea and Ben told us that inside Richland County some of us could spread out to its rural fringe. Perhaps they proposed this as a way of postponing the issue, thinking once we arrived in-county, other splits could be wangled. From SCLC's point of view, it must have been awkward dealing with an overlarge group that resisted being spread out in smaller units. Separately, Pat Gandy was also urging us to divide and fan out, but the group ignored his suggestion as well.

Whoever approached encountered a leaderless group in which no decisions at all could be made. At last, on Thursday afternoon in Atlanta we convened to put someone in charge. It must have been understood the leader would be someone from Brandeis. With Bill Greenhill and Terry out of the running, Elias became the obvious choice. Several people believed his inclination, at that stage in his life, was more to command than facilitate, but what to do when no one else seemed inclined? Freshman Margot was wary. Some other woman? The prejudice of the time ran against that. An older Phyllis might have unified and taken us surprising places. But she must have felt herself too fragile, and other personal reasons made her hesitate to lead among men. All summer Ish sensed her wish that a male would march out front. In any case, cool, calculated decisions would not have come easy to one as compassionate as she.

The Thursday meeting devolved into struggle. "Many tactless things were said," as Lynn wrote shortly after. "The group refuses to accept any leadership or organization—they are afraid of putting one person in the position of coordinator." Bill Greenhill gave his support to Elias despite any personal quarrel, but not without feeling that Elias' great self-confidence inclined him to "do what he wanted, when he wanted." Bill's support of Elias matched their shared opinion that the chapter should stay intact in Richland.

Lynn backed Elias, thinking him "the only capable person," though "often hard to get along with." She found herself telling "these stubborn kids [that] an organization, especially in civil rights, must have *organization* to make decisions." It was "not always going to have time to sit around and discuss each and every issue." What she thought she helped achieve was a temporary willingness to designate Elias as spokesman. Still, she foresaw "a difficult summer," and her support for Elias as leader in Richland relied in some part on her sureness that she herself would not be there.

Thais was among the ones unlikely to work well with Elias. Today, her summary of the meeting was that the group had insisted his powers be "clearly, clearly limited. We talked for a long, long time, each person bringing up a new limitation. Everything had to be brought to the group. We even said things like, 'Every communication with Atlanta has to be shown to the group.' Limitation after limitation was brought up, discussed and agreed upon."

How workable was that going to be? The meeting must have wounded Elias but also inflamed his fighting spirit and pride at having saved the group's financial butt. Still, the question was more or less settled, and when training ended June 18, we'd head en *masse* to Richland County and see what happened next.

Hope's Kids

In Atlanta, SCLC had on its hands 400 life-hungry late-adolescents. On Friday, the last day of training, it convened separate meetings for boys and girls to urge a celibate summer. Phyllis for one was grateful. Naturally given to hugging and walking arm-in-arm with friends, she'd already written home about a troubling incident in a car the previous night with a black youth we'll call Ted. Ted insisted she sit next to him in a front seat, which, she wrote, "I'm not supposed to do—integrated couples are not supposed to drive at night—he'd been drinking and went through a red light—he wasn't drunk—only a little beer on his breath—I took the wheel because a policeman was behind us...but didn't stop us."

Ricky Schaffer was also aboard. Ted stopped and Ricky replaced him as driver. Phyllis "got in back and Ted insisted on joining me, and to my surprise he became very friendly with me physically—to the extent that he decided that he alone was going to escort me home and I had to rather force company on us—it shook me up—I felt tested and it bothered me—perhaps this is unique but I doubt it. There is an affectionate atmosphere here that I know I wouldn't like with an all-white group—I get constantly pinched on the cheek, patted and winked at, and I feel comfortable and liked—but if it came from white men, I know it would be different—because this is like a family and I feel like these are my brothers and sisters—a new feeling for me."

In the girls' Friday session on sex, Andrew Young laid out dress codes and rules against drinking or dating. According to Phyllis the session was mainly about black male attraction to white girls, which had "such complex motivation and now that we've discussed it I feel much better. Our session began with the progressive emasculation of the Negro male and the placing of the white woman on a pedestal—the effects are a more-than-usually aggressive approach—but nevertheless not frightening. I've already realized I must restrain any physical demonstration of affection as it is interpreted so freely and promptly returned twofold—but the atmosphere is warm and reassuring." Couples were urged to split up into different counties and generally not work as a team. In Phyl's mind this relieved tension "because it leaves room for close relationships with girls and boys."

Andrew Young in Atlanta.
Photo *Atlanta Inquirer.*

At the time Lynn, too, was glad that SCLC was laying out rules, "glad these things were said because everyone should understand them—our conduct and relationships with Negroes and our fellow workers." In coming weeks, her view would change; and already she—a hipper teen than Phyllis—had joined the partying that went on off campus each night that week. She noted the attractiveness of the veterans of SNCC and men like Rev. Young. "All the girls are so turned on by him. He is a really beautiful person. I am amazed at his openness and sincerity. He is able to speak about anything, no matter how personal to us or himself."

Our SCLC leaders must have felt we needed to "just say no" more firmly than they did. Lynn was a fetching young woman, and big Atlanta had night spots where movement people gathered. After our inconclusive Wednesday-night squabble, she'd gone to a party celebrating the election that day of Julian Bond and seven other black men to the Georgia state legislature—a first since Reconstruction. At the party Pat Gandy cornered her and took her to another party at Bill's Play Lounge. Pat was "more polite than northern men, very nice" to Lynn and treated her "like a lady." She wasn't entirely charmed, but she did let him buy her a beer and told him she was too tired to dance. They listened to the music. She got back to the dorm at 3:00 a.m.

Generally, she found that the girls were "swamped by offers from the boys, and it is often hard to handle the situation." Relationships could be "very touchy." Friday afternoon and eve she got invitations to various events that night but was again tired and didn't take them seriously. However, a staff party caught her interest, and when Pat told her she "had to" go with him ("a nice way to put it!") she returned to her dorm to prepare. On the way back she ran into a boy who'd already invited her out that night. She explained what had happened and escaped from him and a few other insistent lads. As she rejoined Pat, a tall and extremely handsome young black named Bob "physically" escorted her away, and she let Bob hang onto her after Pat drove them to the party. She felt Pat deserved it for thinking she was his by virtue of rank.

Back in the car later that evening with ten other kids, the driver (white) was being careless. According to Lynn, a flashing blue light pulled them over. A black cop stepped up to the car and pointed out that one of the doors was open. Then they ran a red light and a white cop pulled them over, but also let them off to drive to another, post-midnight party. When Lynn left that one with four other kids, she didn't know they were making a booze run. But liquor was hard to find after midnight. They searched for an hour before she finally got back to the dorm at 2:00.

Ish could be wrong but doesn't recall himself or any other guy in Brandeis SCOPE being terribly suave, though mustachioed sophomore Alan Kern smoked a pipe. The girls varied. Liz Hafkin played down the feminine side. Seventeen-year-old freshman Betty Milgram seemed proper and cautious. Carol Sable, a 20-year-old junior from Upstate New York was an earnest questioner and listener with a playful streak. Lesley Straley, the thick-braided freshman with roots in Unitarian Ohio, could have been Ish's tomboy sister. Her father taught physics at UNC Chapel Hill (a.k.a. "Communist Hill" according to Senator Jesse Helms), where the family was part of the movement. Sex wasn't yet on her radar.

Hope's Kids

Thais was something else. A few years later, Jimi Hendrix would capture her well with "Foxey," thinks Ish. Only after the project did he learn much about her. In an interview for his senior thesis she told him she'd become "Thais"

Hosea with Carol.
Photo Lynn Goldberg.

Alan K.

Betty

Lesley

in part because it brought more responses than "Kathleen" or "Peggy" on the ride-share board she used to reach New York on weekends. Did she know then that "Thais" was also the sensuous eponymous beauty in the novel by Anatole France? Thais' father was northern and Jewish, but her mother had grown up Presbyterian in South Carolina, which, says Kathleen today, "meant you didn't talk about sex, religion or politics." With that in mind, she may not have told her parents how, one restless spring on a lark, with minimal clothing under her coat, she'd auditioned for the Playboy Club in Boston. Still under age to bunny for Brahmins, instead she was offered long ears and cottontail suit for a similar job

Mingling in Atlanta, The Brandeis SCOPErs are Carol Sable (l.), Ricky Schaffer (c.), David Jacobson (r.).

in New Orleans. It sounded slouchy; Thais declined. (Years later she practiced law instead.)

To Ish, Thais seemed admirably out in the vanguard of sexual liberation, but his Puritan soul was challenged to square that with her intellect and other ideals. Living in an all-white Massachusetts town, her mother had rejected segregation and discrimination and was proud but "a little worried" about her taking part in SCOPE. To allay this concern, Thais had downplayed danger, pointing out *The New Yorker* ads in which South Carolina was recruiting industry from the north and explaining how that kept a lid on.

Thais

RICHLAND

4. Modjeska's Watch

Training ended mid-Saturday. Late that afternoon we set off for Columbia 200 miles away by bus and overloaded cars. On its six-hour milk run, the Greyhound stopping in little towns or by the road. The Georgia sunset was pretty but Lynn missed the companionship of Atlanta. Across the state line, South Carolina looked poor and ugly in the diminishing light. Bare red soil "eroded into mountains and valleys of waste." Unfamiliar billboards flowed by as did old cars in broken states along the roadside.

At midnight among those picking us up was Rev. William McKinley Bowman (1914-2000). His white '65 white Caddie bemused us at first as only a status symbol, but there was more to the man than chrome. He'd been active in civil rights since at least 1940 when he'd been among those breathing new life into the NAACP. In 1954 Bowman began a popular DJ Gospel show on white-owned local radio WOIC. He'd worked extensively on voter registration and, in the early '60s, organized lunch-counter sit-ins. As for vanity

Rev. Bowman. Photo courtesy Audrey B. Felkel.

behind the wheel, we'd yet to learn what it was to drive out on rain-slicked clay-mud roads to pastorless rural churches, as Bowman did—like other city-based preachers—or through sudden torrential downpours to some summer revival. For a sometime-itinerant preacher, a solid car made sense.

Bowman took us back to Second Nazareth Baptist Church on Elmwood Avenue in a northeastern corner of town. By 2:00 a.m. Lynn was bedding down in the parsonage with the Bowmans' teen-aged kids. In twos and threes the rest of us were parceled out to other homes. A mix of economic levels near richer Waverly district (where Columbia's black professional and business class lived), Bowman's neighborhood looked working class and not especially bad off.

Second Nazareth Baptist. Postcard.

Phyllis, Margot, Betty, and Lesley were installed in a ramshackle boarding house shared with four young black women, including students and in-service teachers. The fee was $10 per person per week—out of a weekly SCOPE al-

Col. College

Ward 19

Farrow Rd.

Main

Monticello

Black Bottom

Elmwood
Cemetery

Simkins
cottage

Elmwood

Elmwood Ave.

Gov.
mansion

2nd Naz. Bapt.

Howard
School

Arsenal Hill

YWCA

Wheatley

SC Pen.

Taylor St.

YWCA

YMCA

Twp.
Aud.

Benedict Col.

Allen U.

Washington St.

919

Col.
Hosp.

Waverly

Zion
Bapt.

Court-
house

Gervais St.

West
Columbia

Capitol

Ward 9

Congaree River

Assembly St.

Harden St.

USC

Columbia

(Grid based on an undated
map published after 1965)

Lexington county

Richland County

Fairground

Airport

1 mile

Zion Pilgrim
Bapt.

Sugar Hill Lane

Arthurtown

From the State House
looking up Main, 1965.
Photo Vernon Merritt III, *Black Star.*

lowance that may have been boosted to $15. It was run by Mrs. Bradley, wife of an elderly mortician thirty year older than she. Phyllis watched her in her sewing room where she took in local work. "She's rather lonely. It isn't the family situation we wanted, but it's fun in its own way, and temporary."

Phyllis recalls connecting deeply with few others in SCOPE, though at the time she did feel non-romantically "rather close to David Kricker, Ricky Schaffer, even to Elias. It's those kind of relaxed relationships that make this experience so cope-able, so livable, so pleasant!" Her most rewarding friendship, however, with Lesley, took off in the boarding house setting. Lesley was "a panic. She's one of the sweetest and most clever people I know. She lives upstairs with a girl named Rina or Rena, a secretary about our age whom I've come to like very much." Lesley was a fellow serious musician, violist. In 2005, they reminisced fondly about living together, sharing a mirror as each of them bronzed, "and feeling as though we were black," followed by Phyllis' feeling of shock to realize, "Oh, I'm not," though her hair did curl in the heat.

Liz Hafkin and another SCOPEr were housed elsewhere by an elderly woman who had retired from work as a maid. She gave them her air-conditioned bedroom and fed them enormous Sunday meals. Ish and one or two others were welcomed into the modest, Evergreen Circle home of an eighteen-gear trucker named Williams, his wife Bernice, their 8-year-old daughter, and another relative. Thais was taken in by a couple with teenaged children. The husband had a federal job, probably postal. With the warmth of parents they helped her through migraines.

Hope's Kids

Kathy Davis was a Wellesley classmate of Mary Ann. Both from Indianapolis, they'd known each other as children. *The Wellesley College News* had publicized Brandeis SCOPE and had listed Kathy as a contact. Kathy recruited Mary Ann. Awareness was high on their campus: a hundred Wellesley women had joined the April march in Boston. In Columbia Kathy first shared the apartment of a woman whose teenage son was away. She remembers her host—"very nice, matter-of-fact, a good cook"— and herself both leaving early in the morning, meeting again at night.

Kathy

Elias and David Jacobson moved in with the elderly Caldwells on Ridgeway Street, close to Ben Mack in Columbia's northwest Ridgewood district (out Monticello, just beyond city limits). Kathy moved there also, when her first host's son came home. She liked the Caldwells, too, and having more people around. Quiet Mr. Caldwell worked as a laborer, Mrs. Caldwell as maid. "Good people." The house was modest, some nearby streets paved, some not.

Formerly the Caldwells', 2016.

Staying with the Caldwells embedded David all summer in the neighborhood, but for most of us initial housing didn't put us in touch with a community. In lieu of advance work by SCLC, most of the initial housing must have been arranged by Bowman and his congregation. David thinks our offer to pay $10 weekly attracted some hosts, though others refused to accept it. He also thinks we were easily perceived as "dangling money in front of the eyes of the African American community"—a poor start for collaboration.

Being so spread out brought transportation problems and weakened our general coordination. We would have an office, but in other counties, smaller SCOPE groups were better able to unify around some version of "freedom house" where interested local people could drop by freely and possibly join the work. Could we transition to the sort of "SCOPE house" (three side-by-side structures!) that the chapter from New York's Columbia University had been lent by nuns in Orangeburg County? Phyllis hoped we could.

Second Nazareth Baptists weren't the only group marking our midnight arrival. A few hours before, two dozen KKK had posed for photos on the State House steps, departing out to a rally in Irmo, a white supremacist stronghold on the Richland-Lexington county line. On an inside page, the daily *Columbia Record* would show a smiling young mother and infant daughter in angelic matching Klan robes. But the editor's comment was not approving: "If Columbia is 'the South at its best,' the Klan is the South, and the nation, at its worst."

34

Sunday morning we re-assembled for services with the small, summer congregation and—amazing to us—*two* choirs. Along with the warmth of the welcome, some were struck by how well off the congregation appeared,

Formerly the Mack home, 2016.

and Lynn was happily amazed a collection taken on our behalf took in over $60. Phyllis thought it "not the usual church…too many men for it to be typical. The organ, the microphone, the fine building and clothing were all too luxurious." In retrospect, Margot questions assumptions we were making about what was typical of black churches and the significance of being well-dressed. As the summer advanced, we hedged our usage of "rich" and "poor" in reference to blacks *or* whites. Economically, South Carolina was a very poor state. As Thais put it, "By rich, I mean not poor."

Sunday evening, we returned for another religious-style service of official welcome from our dozen sponsor organizations. Rev. Bowman had noticed Phyllis' guitar and—telling her that the meeting would be broadcast live—asked her to bring it and lead some songs. She rounded up Ish to join her. How strange it felt to be on the radio "leading" freedom songs our hosts knew better than we. But the place began to rock. People clapped and called out verses and, in Phyllis' words, "in the warmth, beads of sweat made smiling faces shine with happiness—and kids like you've never seen—a closeness—even just the way people sit together in the pews—and instead of 'Good Shabbas' it's 'Peace to you, brother.' Well, we were a success. First we sang 'This Land is Your Land,' 'Down by the Riverside,' and 'Good News, Chariot's Coming.' I was shaking, but as the crowd got the rhythm and began swaying I relaxed and Ish was fine." Truth is, his legs were shaking, too.

Phyllis coaxed several reluctant older ladies to join the circle for "We Shall Overcome," holding their hands to get them to sing. Toward the end, one squeezed back with feeling. Then children swamped the musicians. One boy even allowed, "You white folks is getting what we blacks has had all along."

At the back of this book is a list of leaders and groups on the program that night. Oddly, though Ben Mack's name appears for SCLC, the program assigns him no speaking role. Instead, a 65-year-old woman got up to describe our purpose and oversee a second collection on our behalf, severely advising the gathering to fill the plates with "quiet money," not the kind that clinks. At the time and throughout the summer, few of us besides Elias knew much about this amazing woman and how much she was doing for SCOPE.

Hope's Kids

It was she, Modjeska Monteith (Mrs. A.W.) Simkins (1899-1992), who helped Ben plant us in the county. There's still no full biography, but a brief one—*Modjeska Monteith Simkins: A South Carolina Revolutionary*—says she was the daughter of a highly successful master brick mason, Henry Monteith. Her given name acknowledges Turkish-American roots. Her mother Rachel was active in the 1905-1909 Niagara Movement, founded by W.E.B. Dubois and others to press for integration. Though Modjeska's parents were successful Columbians, they raised her in rural surroundings, commuting in to schools attached to Benedict College. From childhood she was aware of a secular human rights movement that extended far beyond her state. As a teen she attended meetings of the nascent Richland NAACP.

After graduating from Benedict College, she spent most of the 1920s teaching math at Booker T. Washington High. In the 1930s she was hired to lead the Negro Work Program of a state-financed effort to reduce endemic tuberculosis. This took her throughout the state, encountering backwater blacks, absorbing rare, deep knowledge of and empathy with many thousands rarely glimpsed by Columbia's black elite.

Her modjesty, some years later. Photo SCPN.

At the end of the 1930s she joined young Rev. Bowman and others in building a state-level NAACP. Around 1943, probably by mutual agreement, she left state employment to devote herself to deeper change. Sometime in the '40s she also created a Richland County Citizens Committee to mobilize projects that the middle-class-based NAACP was reluctant to sponsor. In later years, she said, it was mainly this group that brought about the integration the buses and parks. Personally drawn to stronger politics than the NAACP would dare, in 1946 she organized a major progressive event in Columbia called the Southern Negro Youth Congress, drawing nearly a thousand energized, postwar, young southern blacks. For that she welcomed strong support from the American Communist Party. (There was nothing illegal about that, and the major parties couldn't care less.) The week-long conference featured Dubois, communist historian Herbert Aptheker and Paul Robeson, the legendary performer whose career would be destroyed for his open Soviet-friendly views.

In spite of bias against women as NAACP leaders, from 1941 to 1957 Modjeska served as its state secretary and dynamo behind the scenes. In the 1940s she teamed with NAACP lawyer Thurgood Marshall, paving his way for lawsuits including a Clarendon County case that became the centerpiece of *Brown v. Board*

of Education of Topeka. (Backroom deals among others led to its being named by its Kansas component, sheltering South Carolina's image.) It was she who, in 1954, urged Sarah Mae Flemming to file suit against the bus company and personally funded the early stages. From early on, she and Thurgood worked closely together. When he first stayed in town, she put him up at her cottage on Marion Street where she focused on her movement work. Later he stayed at the Simbeth Motel, which she'd founded to accommodate black travelers in a region where hotels uniformly refused them. The Simbeth was in Dentsville, a black community northeast of the city. Still, whites drove by to shoot it up. Tradi-tion has it that when the night rid-ers came after Thurgood, he'd be whisked away to a funeral parlor to sleep in a well-padded coffin. (By the early 1960s there would be one or two other black motels.)

Modjeska's cottage at 2025 Marion, now office of the South Carolina Progressive Network.

In 1957, pressured by the great red scare, SC-NAACP removed Modjeska from among its leaders, dumping her in the wake of the 1956 state law that declared the NAACP a "communist" organization and banned membership by government employees. Modjeska was unapologetic about her connections with communists and unashamed of being "named." As she said, "I'm up on that list, along with hundreds of organizations. Why? Because we didn't follow like sheep in the path of the people in power." But other state and national NAACP leaders were hugely intimidated by McCarthy and his followers. Among other vulnerabilities, they feared being stripped of IRS exemption.

In hindsight, Gov. Robert McNair's biographer Philip Grose calls Modjeska implacable and approves of SC-NAACP's ouster of her and replacement by Rev. I.D. Newman—the NAACP man who'd assisted the FBI in gathering dirt on Modjeska. Not that Newman wasn't also a brave NAACP leader. Historian Millicent Brown says his "commitment to youths, and support for their willing-ness to be put on the front line of attacks from police, school administrators, merchants, and peers made him a welcomed person on the scene and in the jails." But Modjeska, not he, was the one fully capable of debating white guys into the floor. What white male politico's ego (for which she had little public patience) could take that from a female black!? As Grose puts it more sweetly, dudes like McNair would find in Newman "a kinder, gentler" foe than Simkins.

On her death in 1992, another NAACP stalwart of the time, James Felder, described how, not only had she "cranked out more press releases and letters to the editor than all of the civil rights groups in South Carolina combined," and not only was she a "crowd pleaser" and "a fierce warrior for preserving freedom for all of us...just as at ease registering winos to vote on Read Street as she was entertaining Thurgood Marshall...a legend in her own time...who woke up every morning with freedom on her mind."

South Carolina Progressive Network activist Brett Bursey stresses how, although Modjeska could be a righteous force, she was never arrogant or self-righteous. She simply, modestly took on the role of everyperson. But in that role she did speak straight. At one point of frustration, she quipped, there wasn't "too much wrong with South Carolina that a few deaths couldn't resolve...a few white folks that once they die, this state would be a much better place." But she also stuck it to prominent black men she regarded as complacent, and she did not spare the well-off Waverly crowd. She had a tongue. Even today, one older middle-class black Columbian tells Ish she just wasn't proper.

"Some people are like contented cows," Modjeska would opine. "Their eyes and mouths are wide open, but their minds are sound asleep." And "If you've got enough sense in your noggin, you're going to know the fight is there—not just for black people, but for all mankind." In 1964, she was calling the black men invited onto city committees "cherry-picked...a buffer state. They jump when the mayor says 'frog.'" But later on, according to Moore, she acknowledged Mayor Bates' rich contributions, saying, "He did more for progress in Columbia than any other mayor before or since." Moore also credits direct actions or threats of same by her Richland County Citizens Committee with driving the mayor and prominent blacks to bargain productively in private.

(Simkins' treatment by self-consciously middle-class NAACP runs along similar lines with a turning point in Hosea Williams' career. Until his shift to SCLC in 1963, he had been a valuable if sometimes shocking asset of the NAACP. However, on the verge of being inducted onto its national board he was rejected amid concern with the fact that his parents had never been married.)

Perhaps the station that broadcast our welcome at Second Nazareth was Bowman's WOIC; or it may have been a short-lived, black-owned station on which in 1964 Modjeska had begun a weekly show about freedom and justice.

Did Elias and Modjeska ever find time to discuss the power of radio? Ish learned about her only by writing this book, though he does recall—among very few memories—speaking with her briefly in Columbia in August when she greeted him and Citti at a weekend conference. At the time he didn't even recall her having welcomed us in June. Suddenly here was this physically and mentally remarkable elder sharing an all-too-short moment. He remembers feeling that, behind the gentle gaze, there was more she wanted to say. Was she noticing how his unusual surname was also that of the Imperial Wizard of the Georgia KKK (no relation)? Or was she more focused on Citti?

Only looking back does he see the oddness of Modjeska—by then no more than a rank-and-file NAACP member—co-leading our welcome at Bowman's church. There's something odd as well about the passage in that eight-page plan compiled in May that listed possible local partners. It had mentioned an Interdenominational Ministerial Alliance and a Northern Richland County Civic Group. It *hadn't* mentioned the NAACP, the dominant state and local civil rights group. Nor had it mentioned Professor Long and Margot having contacted Ben Mack or anyone else from SCLC in the county; perhaps there was none at the time of their visit.

So what if any understanding was there between Brandeis SCLC-SCOPE and the locally dominant NAACP? In a spring planning memo, Hosea Williams had specified that SCOPE was "not to be used to promote expansion of SCLC. Whatever organization in the local community accepts SCOPE, it will be given full authority, without interference, to supervise its activities." Had that hand-off been made? Not really.

The summer of SCOPE, a crew from Stanford University student radio station KZSU traveled the South recording interviews with various civil rights projects and spokespeople, including lawyer Earl W. Coblyn. Earl was a northerner based in Orangeburg, chairman of an SC-NAACP committee for economic opportunity and local advisor to the Columbia University SCOPE chapter in Orangeburg. To the KZSU reporters, in line with Modjeska, he said that the NAACP was too attached to its middle-class urban base and doing too little about still largely voteless and powerless rural blacks.

At the same time, SCLC had never been strong in the state. Sometime before 1960, said Earl, King had visited the state on an invitation from two people "interested in his coming." Earl didn't mention names, but one was Modjeska, who faulted the NAACP for not embracing King as the movement's overall leader. The other was long-time civil rights advocate I.S. Leevy (1876-1968), a Columbia entrepreneur who'd founded numerous businesses over the years, including the state's first black-owned service station (1930) and a Columbia "department store." We'd see his cameo in churches all over on much-used stick-and-cardboard fans. On one side they showe off his funeral home. On the other they urged people to vote and told them how to register. Like Modjeska, he'd also played a major role in the '40s blooming of the NAACP and since 1961 he had sat on SCLC's board.

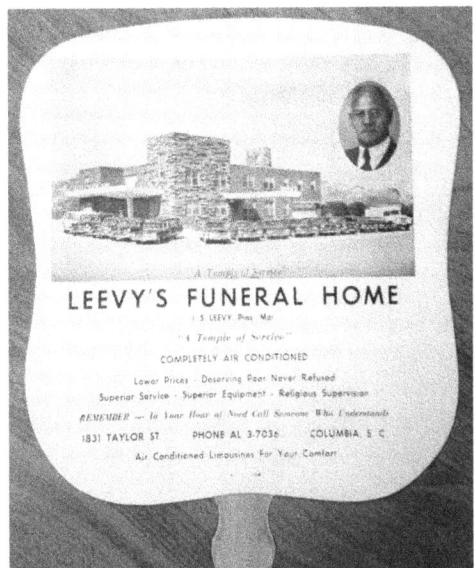

LEEVY'S FUNERAL HOME

Most likely Leevy was not at our welcome, being blind, 90, and close to the end. But the list of sponsors included his name as chairman of the Richland VEP. Also listed (but not a presenter) was SC-NAACP secretary I.D. Newman.

Of Dr. King's earlier visit, NAACP lawyer Earl Coblyn said he'd not been "too warmly received." Minutes from a late-August SCLC Atlanta executive meeting would add that in South Carolina many SCOPE efforts were "thwarted by NAACP." What with our welcome by Rev. Bowman and some later contact that summer, it seems off base to say SCOPE was "thwarted" in Richland County (maybe Newman worked with Elias in ways that Ish knows nothing about), but neither were we much embraced except by several individual ministers and gadfly Modjeska. She made it her business to settle us in, alongside other fish she was frying those ten weeks, like challenging employment discrimination at Fort Jackson and sorting out problems at Simbeth Motel.

David Jacobson admires how Elias shepherded us through this early phase. In the end, he thinks, advice came mainly from busy but patient Ben Mack. Whatever our connections were now, our May plan had concluded that the county's registration drives had not been well coordinated, and we hoped to improve on that. As for reaching beyond the middle class, the plan had mentioned a man named William Blakely, who spoke for a small "lower class" group in Lower Richland, the poorest rural part of the county. We hoped to get down his way.

That first Sunday evening must have been when we first heard about Black Bottom, a Congaree River bottomland on the north side of town, laid out as Camp Fornance in the Spanish-American War. By the 1930s it was shanty and Depression housing. Formerly poor white, most of it was now bottom-poor black, with poor whites hanging on at one end. Phyllis was given to understand that city boundaries had been redrawn some years before to place it outside city limits and therefore outside city expense. She asked Second Nazareth people about it, but no one had ever been there and most were afraid to go: "Some expressed disgust. They suggested we work elsewhere. They had reached a plateau of success and did not want to 'look back.'"

Their reaction made Black Bottom the place we wanted to take on first. Right away Phyllis imagined living there or elsewhere outside Columbia proper: "NAACP people will be in Columbia itself, and the city is fairly well under way." Outlying places had much greater need "for exploration and organization.... contact, care—perhaps we'll switch off." Anyway, she assured her parents, we'd be placed in groups with a "field worker...and always less than twenty miles from Columbia, and we'll be meeting in Columbia as a group several times a week." For their further peace of mind she added that Dean Zion and several professors would join us soon and, more creatively on her part, that "a committee of top SCLC staff will 'pass thru' twice a week to see if we have any problems." But could she sell the Brooklyn Bridge?

One evering a week Elias would drive to an evening meeting with local advisors, often being tailed homeward by police or unidentified whites. Other than that, we were told not to be out past dark, nor to stray into white parts of town. Cautious Ish complied, but from the get-go others were bolder. Our night of arrival, a youth preparing to drive a car back to Atlanta by dawn asked Lynn to step out with him for coffee. "I shouldn't have," she wrote for her parents, "because mixed couples are not allowed, but we were only going up the street, and it was after 2:00."

The first Sunday morning, Phyllis, Lesley, Margot, and Betty joined housemates Teshine, Rina and Geneva, for breakfast. Then instead of attending at Second Nazareth, "Donning our loveliest frocks we set off to church—white gloves and hats—I had neither but it didn't matter—Second Calvary Baptist. As Hosea Williams said, one main problem with the Negro community is that it has too many churches—there are at least eight within easy walking distance— all in the midst of the middle-income Negro district—almost all Baptist." The Father's Day's service turned out pretty tame, the minister quoting Dr. Spock.

A funeral that followed was less subdued. In Atlanta Phyllis had learned from Arthur Days, an Alabama preacher, that funerals were great for meeting the living. She had never seen a corpse, "and the wailing and weeping and crying out would have been devastating if I had not felt so estranged by the newness of the experience. Then we got a hellfire sermon about every word, deed, thought, being written in our 'books' and about 'the Lamb's book of life' wherein is written the names of those who've joined the church—and of the great Judgment Day—Amen!"

From church the young ladies strolled beside the Allen and Benedict campuses. Phyllis noticed how soldiers from Fort Jackson were accepted around there in mixed-race groups, though it was "an oddity to see us girls integrated, and all eyes are on us." She'd heard that the city was opening up, though one downtown restaurant was still in court resisting integration. That was Little Joe's Sandwich Shop on Main Street, a fifty-seat restaurant version of six "Piggie Park" drive-in barbecues owned by restaurateur Maurice Bessinger.

Bessinger was president of his own National Association for the Preservation of White People and head of South Carolina's Wallace-for-President group. According to Bill Kornrich, in addition to a picture of smiling piglet "Little Joe," the sandwich shop had a white line painted out front and a sign declaring where Bessinger's "white property" began. When Little Joe's opened in 1963 and was promptly picketed, Bessinger had arranged for picketers to be jailed for trespass. He had testified in court that this was not about race but "the right of a small businessman to select his customer.... You can't be a racist and a Christian, and I am a Christian." His Baptist Bible compelled him "to oppose any integration of the races whatever" along with the federal income tax, though he did render his 1040s unto Caesar. In 2001 he still asserted that state law had forbidden him to integrate and that all sensible blacks were perfectly happy with segregation.

However, Bill was under the impression that Bessinger had already made concessions at least regarding back-door-only rules at Piggie Parks in other counties.

In his own explorations, Kornrich was wandering past barrooms and pool halls out at the west end of Washington Street. He called it, not unfondly, "the Harlem of Columbia, it's really the worst people. I just went to a bar, and everybody at the bar knew me by the end of the week. Saturday I met some guy who is drunk, and he took a couple of punches at me, and all his friends were worried that, you know, 'you hit a white guy, are you crazy?' It took me about a half an hour to explain that I understood that he was tired and had just tied one on. They just stared. 'How can a white person talk to us as people?'" (By summer's end Bill would conclude that the main thing we were able to do was provide experiences in which South Carolina blacks could talk with whites on an equal footing. In Hosea Williams' post-summer assessment, this ranked as some achievement.)

Bill's roommate and buddy Ricky Gurbst took note of another drive-in restaurant, Doug Broom's: "He won't serve Negroes. Well, he does; but he makes it tough on them. You have to get out of the car, and if you're alone he may not serve you. If you go as four or five, he'll serve you. On the other side of town, there's another place he owns, called the V.I.P. Room, a restaurant and night club for Negroes. At one place he's not going to take their money, but at the other, he's going to take it."

5. STREETS

Our first Monday morning we reconvened to learn how and where we would start. Dick Miles had lent us boxes of index-card records of previously canvassed areas including lower- and middle-class neighborhoods and places like the semi-rural stockyard area out by Farrow Road where a thousand people lived without plumbing. We would comb these areas for hold-outs. But grimmer Black Bottom was fresh on our minds, and probably on Pat Gandy's, too, when he drove a gang out there. On the ride Lynn saw "some very poor houses...many unpaved streets and shacks, even within the city." Back at the church they picked up more SCOPErs, making eleven in the car. "The back end dragged as we toured from the governor's mansion to the other side of the railroad tracks," exploring an area between the mansion and the century -old penitentiary by Arsenal Hill (erected 1867, demolished 1994, and commonly known as "Arsenal Hell").

Held later that day was our first church picnic, most likely hosted by Bowman's flock. Lynn admired the scene: "These people know what a picnic is! We played kickball to work up an appetite for the most abundant array of food I have ever seen. Tables and tables. Chicken, spare ribs, salads, cakes, punch. After stuffing ourselves we sang and talked to people. They all want to help us and take us under their wings."

That night some of us met with Modjeska's Richland County Citizens Committee (RCCC). In after years, Modjeska would call it a shell group. Its president was Adam Stewart, a middle-aged mechanic employed as a "lot boy" by a Columbia Ford dealer. Adam lived some miles north of town.

Two Baptist ministers showed up at the meeting from Camden in neighboring Kershaw County. One was Rev. James Solomon Gadsden. The other was Rev. J. Alfred Curry, chairman of the Kershaw County NAACP voter registration drive. Since passage of the 1964 *Civil Rights Act*, they and another clergy had attempted to integrate two Camden restaurants—Tony's and Pines Drive-In. From one they'd were forced to scram when the female owner pointed a shotgun.

They'd come to the RCCC meeting to recruit some SCOPErs to Camden. Unaware that Kershaw County was not at all where SCLC would have preferred its resources—even less so than in Richland—understanding only that Kershaw was more rural than Richland, some of us thrilled at the chance.

After the meeting, Pat Gandy and the ministers drove Lynn, Bill Kornrich, Ricky Gurbst, Thais, Terry, and Mary Ann out into black Columbia night life, and Lynn's opinion of Pat improved. He'd invited them out "for coffee" in the private room of a tavern where they could dance to a Piccolo juke box. There the ministers and kids got drunk and danced and talked up the move.

Lynn was excited at the prospect of getting past picnics: "They want us and need us, and we want to go. Our voices got louder and louder, and we acted wilder and wilder, happy to have found a place. Most of all, we will each have our 'own' family, and will live as part of it." Though "hard to manage when they were drunk," the ministers sincerely "wanted to come our way as much as we wanted to go theirs." In fact the picnic mindset still ruled in Camden as well, and the group move would stall for three weeks while Curry and Gadsden persuaded their flocks and lined up housing. In the meantime, the would-be Kershaw crew would continue to canvass in Richland.

Tuesday June 22, in boy-girl pairs, we set out in and around Black Bottom. One local driver had dropped an engagement to ferry us around all day. Lynn felt sick glancing back and forth between the grounds of the governor's mansion and the shacks on the other side of the street. The soil was eroded clay and sand that quickly coated her with dust. Here and there people told her they'd heard about us on the radio. In a house with many adults and children, she played jacks with the kids and explained about voting. "I encouraged school,

Black Bottom had numerous "shotgun shacks": wooden houses laid out with front and back doors aligned such that a shotgun blast could pass right through if both doors were open. The South Carolina State Museum dates this photo 1924, but the automobile suggests later.

and helped them write their names. I was surprised that many of the children will be attending summer school. Even the youngest kids go to playschool."

To Bill Kornrich also Black Bottom was "eye-opening...terrible. Men, women, and diseased children sit on the porches passing time somehow. But these people were warm and willing to listen. They knew about education and voting and, literate or not, wanted to talk and were happy to see us. Many had a little education and were glad to have someone help them with the difficult application. We helped them fill out sample forms to take to the courthouse to copy." Others were totally illiterate, and only the pending *Voting Rights Act* afforded them any hope of voting, but even the children wanted to look at the form.

Lynn's crew stopped at a grocery owned by a white woman who had been there thirty years and had seen the population shift from white to black: "She told us about the people, their jobs (most get welfare), their education, what they do. She knew the people and their ways. They came to her and bought penny candy and cookies from big tins, and grape and orange sodas. Little children came in rags, and put out their bumpy hands for 'nic' wo' [nickel's worth] of cookies.'" Lynn could barely understand what they said but saw happiness in their rotted-tooth smiles.

"We came to an ancient lady standing barefoot in her okra patch, pounding stakes with a large flat stone. She said she was sick but looked quite strong. She was most proud that her daughter was already registered and would help her with the application. With our transportation, she would get to the courthouse. A small child hoeing nearby was sent inside to put the sample form in the Bible with the important papers.

"We had few problems, and everyone was hospitable. Some were reluctant to trust us and would not give their names until after much coaxing. The only white people these people know are insurance agents, rent collectors, house condemners, and so on. We had to gain their confidence by talking with them a long time.

"More than once we met a registered person—or one who was not—who wanted to tell all the neighbors about registration and urge them to go. This was really thrilling. It takes such courage to go down and face the registrar when they can barely read or write, sometimes even after they have failed before. They bear a shame and degradation no one should suffer." People seemed excited to hear about a first "mass meeting" we were setting up.

Working together, Phyllis and Ish blundered into and scooted back out of a white patch the map had shown as black. Right away Ish discovered how poorly he understood what people were saying. What the heck did they mean by "reddish to wote"? Ah. *Register. Vote.*

Phyllis soon concluded the two did best when they split up the task. At a given door, she would "talk about the family and the calluses on Mrs. Harris' feet, and the shame of the past election, and Ish plugs SCOPE and gets the necessary information across." While Ish talked to the elderly man on a porch, she took aside a young woman, 29, "who couldn't read and hardly knew the alphabet, and we went over a sample registration form. We did a little syllable reading. She was obviously bright, picking it up quickly. Good luck, Mrs. Gordon."

What stirred Phyllis most that morning was a plea from a Mrs. Bruce to seek out a nearby teen-aged mother with a starving 7-month-old—a story thread we'll pick up again later. Lunch was peanut-butter-and-jelly sandwiches back at Bowman's church, then rest until the heat receded. After that we would canvass Arsenal Hill, around Howard School and Arsenal Playground, a less poor area, until 6:00.

We wanted local teens to canvass with us door to door. Phyllis simply went up to them, introduced herself and explained our needs. While Ish was at a house, she met 16-year-old Anthony and 17-year-old Ronnie, who walked the neighborhood with them a while, talking about the jazz they sang and eventually offering to help at our first mass meeting.

At Arsenal Hill Playground they found a city club for seniors—all white except for Ronnie's grandmother who was there as a maid. The ladies peered "almost rudely" at Phyllis' SCOPE button as she asked if she could post a notice about the meeting. Twenty minutes later, six blocks away, a Parks and Playgrounds car pulled up and the driver asked what they had wanted in the office, saying they could advertise in the playground, not on the building, adding that his was a liberal state; Columbia didn't need help. No one was stopping anyone from doing anything.

The day was exhausting, but that evening Ricky Schaffer returned alone to the Howard School playground, looking for other high school students willing to go around with us: "A group of really tough students was playing tackle football on a small field. I was standing next to one fellow when another approached him and tapped him on the pocket (I later realized that he did this to see if the first kid was carrying a knife—which he was). The boy next to me said, 'Don't mess with me, man; I'll cut you.' The other nodded in the direction of the street and said, 'Come on.' To my great relief the first replied, 'Not to-night, man.'"

Ricky watched the game for a while, talking with individual sideliners as he summoned the courage to speak to them as a group. His first fear was he wouldn't get through to them at all. His second was being unable to interest them in "something so dreary as voter registration." In that case he felt he'd need to switch to something more like direct action, which he couldn't honestly say our group was ready to pursue. He knew it sounded affected, but to his roommate he described his speech like this:

> "'Hey, listen up a sec. My name is Rick Schaffer; I'm working for Dr. Martin Luther King's Southern Christian Leadership Conference in Columbia on a voter registration project, and we need your help in our work. Now, I've spent some time in Harlem, and those guys there ain't any tougher than you. But there isn't a drive-in restaurant in New York City that they can't go in. I said I thought you were tough, but I don't think it's tough when you can't eat in Doug Broom's drive-in if you want to. And it ain't tough if the city can ship all of Booker T. Washington High School five miles out (the high school was bought by the University of South Carolina, and a new one is being built way the hell out of town) so that a thousand Negro students have to be bussed three miles extra, but not a single white student has to. And I don't think it's tough when you can't swim in any municipal swimming pool that you want to.

> "The vote may be able to change this nonsense. We have been going from house to house, and often we get the response, 'But if I register, my white boss may fire me,' or, 'well I've never registered before and I don't know if I should now.' These people are scared, and perhaps with good reason. But one thing's for sure; if they don't vote, things aren't going to be any different for you.'"

Ricky told them we'd be accepted more readily if guys like them would join the work and how it should continue after we left. Afterward, he was feeling low until one of them gave him a ride and said he'd come with friends to help on Wednesday.

That evening or the next day, Phyllis talked with basketball players in between games and came away optimistic: "They're working with us now—it takes very little—these kids want to help us."

Wednesday's canvass fanned out at the west end of Washington Street, not far from the bars and a branch of Victory

Formerly the Victory Savings branch at 919 Washington.

Savings Bank at 919. This first and only black-owned South Carolina bank had been founded in 1921 by a group including (naturally) I.S. Leevy and Modjeska's family. Victory's purpose was to avail small loans to blacks routinely (sometimes in reprisal) turned down by white-owned banks. Modjeska had been involved with it for years. She worked as a teller at times and owned the building at 919.

Zion Baptist, 2016.

At the end of the street sat big Zion Baptist Church. In 1961 it had been the gathering point for a march of nearly 200 students that had led to a US Supreme Court confirmation of constitutional protections for marchers. Its pastor, Jesse M. Walker, had offered it for our meeting on Thursday.

To Lynn, Tuesday's canvass had seemed chaotic but Wednesday's better prepared by Elias and a committee: "Our morning was handed to us in a package—people to do research, people to do office work, people to recruit young workers. I went out in the field again, with little luck in finding help. One lady suggested the Boy Scouts. There are apparently no church youth groups." Lunch was peaches, a penny each at a tiny grocery. Later back at Zion, they picked up a thousand leaflets to pass out in the neighborhood.

Thursday Phyllis saw the work resume "in its drop-in-the-bucket fashion." She helped a few women write the sample, "brought Mrs. Harris pads for her shoes, promised Mrs. Paterson a magnifying glass—made lunch for the whole bunch—talked to the owners of several grocery stores, a man in a poolroom and one in a barber shop. The most active women are the beauticians."

She drew weird looks when she rode with Frank, a Negro boy. "I was in the back seat—the usual precaution—but the stares are amazingly offensive, even the funny noises coming out of these warped mouths—and yet, these fellows are probably good to their wives and kids." She asked Frank about the laws on intermarriage. Frank said that if the couple came married from out of state, no one bothered them, but four years ago a Negro had been lynched for marrying a white woman, and eight years ago a white man was, too; they never touched either woman. She wrote, "Frank lives in a 'good part of town' and his mother has a gun which she used once to prove to three white men that they really might not come in—all in one beautiful, old southern city. They don't take us seriously because there have been registration drives before and Watson won by a 70% margin."

She meant Congressman Albert Watson, a KKK ally and self-proclaimed champion of "hard-core rednecks." In 1964 he'd opposed the *Civil Rights Act*, saying it "threatens the very foundations of our republic and is a fraud on the American people, particularly the Negroes." Two months before we arrived he'd won re-election saying the NAACP was duping other blacks. By odd double-standard, The *Columbia Record* faulted the city's mostly black Ward 9 for voting against him "in a bloc."

By then we were no longer being driven all over town. Lynn set out that morning on an hour's walk in melting heat, probably back to Black Bottom. Wherever it was, conditions looked even worse than before. One house had "no doors or windows, the porch had holes, there was no paint—but—there was a huge TV, a phonograph, a radio, a telephone, and the lady we spoke to had been registered. This is very common. The values are very strange. Often a mother will complain she hasn't enough food for her children, but she sits home all day and watches TV.

Alan S.

"Many people we can't help for one reason or another. Their only hope is passage of the voting bill. We tell them we will keep them informed. We worked in groups of six to a block, and I was partners with Alan Segal. Alan let me do a house next door to him by myself. I prefer to be by myself, because boys think girls can't do it and they keep doing all the talking." But Gurbst and Kornrich yelled at Alan for letting her do it alone.

The canvassing ran late that day. It was chaos getting home to suppers, then back to Zion Baptist in time for the 8:00 p.m. meeting. Only in our northern imaginations would gatherings start "on time." Phyllis and Ish caught a first ride over to start the evening with song.

We were getting ahead of ourselves in expecting to turn out people so soon in communities we barely knew. Ben Mack was probably out of town and letting us learn the hard way about not getting ahead of our base. Lynn wrote that the gathering didn't draw "the masses we had planned" and that we would have been wiser to get a smaller church, rather than rattle around. Also, it must not have helped that our leaflet gave no address and had called the Zion Baptist "*Second* Zion Baptist." Had Ish done that, confounding the name of Rev. Walker's church with that of Rev. Bowman's *Second* Nazareth? Church names would confuse him all summer.

But Phyllis' basketball buddies did come.

That night Lynn talked again with Rev. Curry, now representing three ministers who wanted SCOPE in Kershaw County. Looming larger in her mind was Pat Gandy, our SCLC advisor. She was desperate to talk about him with someone. Pat came across well at the Zion Baptist meeting, had "really got to the people," but he seemed to be taking over the group. On Tuesday, *The Columbia Record* had run a straightforward, front-page piece about Richland and seven other counties where SCOPE would be working. In an interview with the paper, Pat had mentioned our focus on voting, adding, "wherever there is a need, we expect to lend a hand." He mentioned segregation fences still in place at a state park beach, despite federal orders two years before that required state park desegregation. (The parks would not be fully outwardly desegregated until a year after we left.)

More disturbingly, mid-week while Ben was away, Pat made some amazing announcements. Thursday's edition of *The State*—Columbia's other main paper—ran the headline "Gandy Opposes U.S. In Viet Nam, World War II" and quoted Pat as saying that, after Pearl Harbor, the United States had been wrong in declaring war on Japan and Germany; instead, we should have arranged a non-violent peace march on both.

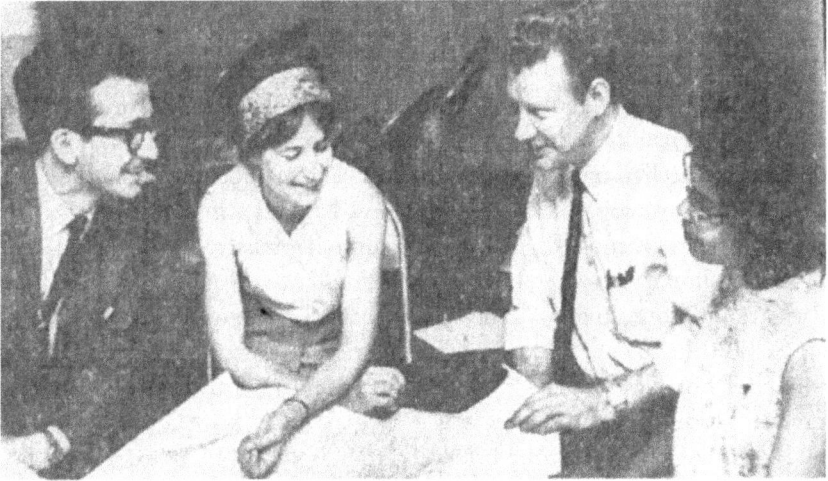

Elias, Kathy, Pat, Margot. *The State*, June 24, 1965.

Pat was putting some english on Dr. King's recent denunciation of the escalation in Vietnam. Pat's words could only offend most Columbia whites *and* blacks, especially considering their jobs at Fort Jackson—not to mention astonishing Brandeis. Lynn heard better sense from Pat when he and Margot appeared on Thursday evening TV. Still, she shuddered, "He can't be trusted, and also drinks—in the church, too! We are helpless, and can turn to no one."

Meanwhile, per the same edition of *The State*, the County Board of Registration was showing good will by increasing the number of voter registration days that summer. In off-election years like this one, county law required registration be open only one day a month. *The State* said officials were stretching the budget to forestall accusations that anyone stood in the way of black registration. They would open the rolls for two solid weeks, the first at the outset of July, the second in August. This seemed like an accomplishment for us, inasmuch as the article connected that move to our presence—but only if we could turn people out.

For the first week Bowman's parsonage had been our temporary office. Friday we moved into upper-floor space at 919½ Washington Street, next door to Victory Savings. The 919½ building also belonged to Modjeska. Since the '40s she'd used it to house progressive groups and events, including a short-lived but courageous black newspaper, the *Lighthouse Informer*. When other housing ran short, SCOPErs would sleep on the office floor.

Hope's Kids

By Friday we were entering areas for which we had VEP records. Initially in this we were joined by what Phyllis described as "a large number of Negro youths from the NAACP task force." But after the first week, she doesn't mention such collaboration in Columbia. Liz Hafkin remembers canvassing somewhere outside the city with Benedict College students: "The Benedict students had been doing it quite a while and were really skilled at it."

Looking back, even apart from the looseness of our connection to local groups, Ish sees reasons not to have expected many to join us going door to door. Young women and men like Rev. Bowman's eldest son Joe—who drove us around early on—had already been canvassing in recent efforts and turning out for demonstrations. Just two months before our arrival, hundreds of students had marched on the capitol grounds. Now students were on vacation or working summer jobs. Ricky Schaffer and Ish had a mutual student friend at Harvard, Tom Gordon, the son of a Columbia minister. Ish had met Tom just before freshman year when both worked on a dorm-cleaning crew. Now he and Ricky found Tom driving a Blue Ribbon cab to continue to pay for college. In all, SCOPE hadn't shown up at quite the right moment to mesh with local efforts, and hot summer days were not so convenient, attractive or even efficient times for locals to join us.

According to Phyllis our Friday partnering with NAACP kids did not include working in mixed-race couples, both for safety reasons vis-à-vis local whites, and black community discomfort. The group worked Ward 19 on the southeast skirts of town, which seemed "a happier neighborhood but less of a challenge. I felt—I think we all did—that we didn't belong there as much as Black Bottom."

Rain Saturday cooled down the heat. At the office that morning, still worrying about Pat and other internal issues, Lynn noticed apprehensively, "It doesn't seem to make any difference if we are late now. We are losing our organization." She was disappointed also to find that *The State* had quoted Governor McNair as saying we'd found nothing wrong in Columbia and were wondering why we were there. "Nothing wrong" was a stretch, but bore its grain of truth.

"Wow!" she thought and together with others dashed off a letter to the paper calling attention to the dirt-road slums surrounding the governor's mansion and infants like the starving baby Phyllis and Citti were now beginning to help in Black Bottom. The letter never ran.

Later that day a discussion was held about renting a shack in Black Bottom for $21 a month—"really fixing it up," as Phyllis reassured her parents. "It wouldn't take much time with 23 of us—plus an exterminator—and living there. The idea of 'family living' isn't realistic in the city as much as in the rural areas. If a family can afford to keep us—even receiving $10 a week which most don't like to accept—they either are financially high above the people we work with, or else the parents both work. In these cases their children are already married. Typically the woman works from or leaves the house at 6:00 a.m. to return home about 9:00. Family life just isn't. Besides, if we had the house, we could live where it's really bad, we would have a center for literacy classes, we could have informal get-togethers with our neighbors. We wouldn't be 'wards' of the community, so to speak, and we would 'experience' rather than watch as guests. What do you think? It was my idea so you can rip it apart."

Lynn endorsed the concept not for herself but for others who would remain in the county. That evening Phyllis and others fattened at another picnic with the extended family of "Grandma Williams" in a pleasant, black northeastern suburb called Hollywood Hills. Then the Williams took them to the Savoy, a dance and drinking club where Phyllis was glad to see kids our age, "nothing formal or ritzy—a lot of fun and something new—everybody dances with everybody's partner and we joined in and really enjoyed." This may also have been the same roadhouse where, according to Thais, "They don't sell liquor but you bring your own and they put a setup on your table—a Coke and a paper cup. I went with the kids of the family I was staying with. The music was excellent—James Brown. I danced."

6. URBAN BLUES

A dreadful Sunday night chapter meeting began our second week. Later, Lynn struggled to sum it up: "I am very disturbed. Elias left. I think he was pushed up against the wall and could no longer function as coordinator."

The meeting began with objections to sudden instructions, passed on by Elias, for some of us to enter Newberry County. Like Kershaw, Newberry borders Richland to the north. The order must have come from Hosea and seemed to imply backing out of Kershaw with which we were already building ties. But Kershaw had a substantial middle-class black community in Camden, its prosperous county seat. Newberry was bleaker, needier; scarier, too. Calhoun County, bordering Richland to the south, was another scary but strategically compelling target. There we could help a tiny group on the cusp of forming a new branch of the NAACP. More than either Richland or Kershaw, Calhoun made sense in terms of SCLC's overall state electoral goals.

Next day, Hosea Williams would rescind the Newberry order, dispatching there instead some volunteers who'd arrived in Atlanta too late for the training. But this didn't repair the damage we'd done to ourselves on Sunday night. The sudden order wasn't Elias' decision, and Lynn felt the way we had raised the matter had made him feel we were all against him. Then, she wrote, we'd insisted on re-organizing to delegate more responsibility. To that, Elias responded that if there was nothing further concerning him, he would like to be excused. "When we protested, he flew into a rage and stomped out."

No one says who started putting the screws on Elias, but Lynn was not alone in thinking he'd been overstepping his bounds and showing little tact in how he dealt with others inside the group. "However, we are at fault, because we did not help him any. We only antagonized him further by jumping on things when we didn't know the facts." We all had a lot to learn about teamwork.

To KZSU in August, Betty and Thais both acknowledged that the group had acted badly. "After all, he's a person," said Thais, "and we should have made a bigger effort to not completely leave him with everyone against him." Phyllis felt that some had acted selfishly towards Elias. "They wanted more of a share in the planning but demanded it in such a way as to make it personally offensive and painful to him—he's had trouble with these same people before and he's tried so hard to please them."

Phyllis followed Elias out, hoping to turn him around or at least to stall him until he was "calm enough to drive safely—sanely—poor kid, he was really unhappy." Outside, Elias told Phyllis things about his past that few if any of us had heard. Ish doesn't know how much of his statements she reported back to the group, nor which were accurate in her account, or true in point of fact; but here are details she passed on to her folks: "Like everyone else, Elias has personal problems. His family disowned him several years ago when he took part in rebel activities in his country—he's about 26 or 27, I think, and in his country that's considered fairly old. He was engaged once—to Miss Peru 1958—that was in 1960." Some weeks later, Phyllis wrote of his telling her that he was 29 and had been married, but his wife had died in childbirth. It's all very odd. In fact, Elias was just turning twenty.

Outside by the car, by Phyllis' account, Elias said he was leaving town. She tried to dissuade him. When he drove away she returned in tears to share some of what he'd told her, to chastise the group, and to launch a discussion of frankness and love: "If we can 't learn from this we're really in sad shape—and the various people who had caused the rift decided to visit him and express their desire that he remain with us." Lynn was proud of her performance.

Afterward, Phyllis wondered how Elias could proceed: "Once he left the room, unable to listen to criticism and surmount the personal element, he relinquished his position of leadership. I wonder if he can return as a regular member. He was never just one of us, even before he was elected, he always took more responsibility, initiative than anyone else. That's why he's leader now. We'll see."

The girls were more swayed than the boys by Phyllis, supporting her criticism of the group. In Lynn's view, "The boys attacked Elias' lack of strength to stay in his place."

After the painful meeting, Thais was among those asking Elias to return, but not as leader, she explained to KZSU. She said the group felt pressured to accept him back as leader out of fear that "Brandeis University was going to intervene at any minute and come flurrying down with a cutoff of funds, because they had made it very clear that we had some sort of emotional commitment, or whatever, to Richland County. Some very confusing and confused issues." In the same interview, Betty speculated that Elias—our primary contact with Brandeis—himself had generated fear of intervention from Waltham. Another voice chimed in that, from what he'd heard, Elias "could do whatever he likes with the administration." Interestingly, in a separate talk with KZSU, Elias confided, "Actually, the administration—it's not exactly the administration—will determine the policy; but the administration as it stands now, will do whatever I tell them. Now don't ask me how I got into the position where I could tell the administration of the university what they're supposed to do. But that's the story."

Elias still keenly remembers how hard it was to lead his peers. Brandeis students, he says, "ran an interesting gamut, with individuals who were very significantly independently minded, rebellious in nature, disdainful of the administration, and opposed to a number of administrative goals and positions." By 1965, he says, there had been a number of anti-administration protests regarding Brandeis' stance on issues such as university investments, governance of student life and the Vietnam war. Elias faced personality challenges also from non-Brandeis members of our group. Ricky Schaffer, Citti and Mary Ann were all strong-willed—Kathy and Ish not so much.

By the end of the Sunday night saga, Lynn understood that the group would try to bring Elias back, but "most likely" not as a leader. She saw that "our group is much too large, and how unwieldy it is. I am anxious for it to get reorganized, and to see myself in another county."

Monday June 28, Ben Mack stepped in and, as Lynn described it, "put things right." Speaking for SCLC, he "plowed through each problem like it didn't even exist. He is so amazing. Everything seems to work out perfectly." Again Elias would be in charge. After all, as someone told KZSU in August, "His ability to arrange housing, transportation, speak to leaders in the community—tasks like that he assumed well." Someone had to give orders, especially at the outset because everyone was so inexperienced. "We did not know what to do at first," one SCOPEr confessed. "I didn't have the spirit of initiative at first. I didn't try and look around and find things to do. I thought we would be told how to organize." Cautious Betty agreed that the group had been unhappy in the first days, "wasting mornings when we were all bored and sitting around the office." But really not everyone sat around. It wasn't Lynn's style, for one; and from that summer day to this, to Ish's knowledge, his lifelong friend Phyllis has yet to "sit around."

At a later meeting on Monday, most of us were relieved to be told that Brandeis SCOPE would split. On a date still pending, five would go to Kershaw County. Tomorrow at 10:00 a.m., Pat Gandy would ferry five others down to

Calhoun County. Those eager to go drew lots. The five who drew Calhoun were Lynn, Mary Ann, Terry, Thais, and freshman John Babin. Later that day, Thais fell sick; thinking she would still be unwell next morning, she yielded her place to Carol Sable. Hmm. Does old Ish suspect that Thais' temporary illness had something to do with the fact that Bill Kornrich was headed to *Kershaw*? By dropping out of line for Calhoun, she joined the Kershaw line instead.

For those who remained in Richland, the decision to calve worked short-term wonders. Two days later Phyllis noticed the office settling down. "Elias is staying on and that's real relief. Ish has really taken charge, though. He is much more tactful than Elias, and everyone feels good about his being leader."

Ish doesn't remember "taking charge." For years he'd been backing away from gavels. In high school he'd declined to run for class president but happily accepted running for VP, sure that a more gregarious classmate would be the right top choice. He finds now that, true to form, he wrote home mid-July describing himself as "second in command." That was just before Elias shifted him down to Calhoun.

As of the Fourth of July, Phyllis noticed Ben Mack and Pat Gandy working together on our behalf. "They introduce us to local leaders, suggest methods—we discuss our needs and problems. Then the local leaders tell us what they need—we all get together with the Columbia Citizens Committee [Dick Miles' committee? Modjeska's? Both?]. Then Elias and Ish organize or one of us helps them—that's more usual—everyone pretty much administrates—and we split up to attack specific wards." Wistfully perhaps she added, "We do nothing on our own."

In the long run the crisis didn't much improve transparency and must have made Elias' less eager to share. In August someone remarked that when he first re-took the helm "he was allowing people to do what they wanted, and things were going along pretty smoothly. Then after ten or so days, everything returned to its normal state, and we were right back where we were."

Bill Greenhill says he loyally continued to do what he could to serve the mission and the group's commitment to Richland County and exercised what leadership he could. By early August others who remained in Richland had adapted also in various ways. As Phyllis remembers, "Though our SCOPE group gathered frequently for updates and assignments, we never discussed our feelings."

The Calhoun five split off in late June, the Kershaw five in mid-July. Meanwhile, Elias would continue administering in and from Columbia, controlling expenditures, vehicles, and connections with Waltham, and attempting to carry out orders from Atlanta.

7. COLUMBIA VENTURES

S o: back to Monday, June 28, when Ben ironed everything out. That same day Phyllis found a house in Black Bottom: $30 a month, six rooms, no plumbing "except a faucet in the yard which we can hose easily into the kitchen—there's a hole in the wall of the kitchen into which to attach the pipe of a wood stove. The house is in fairly good condition considering those around it— it's right smack in the worst section. The people we met were very kind. Men walk around bloated with malnutrition. An overwhelming number of kids. I don't know why, but we have four outhouses in our yard. If we take the house, it will be with the understanding that work done will be mainly in the areas of health and welfare. It would be absurd to work on registration with most of these people. The way they are living is so much a day-to-day process of cheating death—human beings can take an awful lot."

But the idea was tabled, then abandoned, to her parents' relief, mainly because transport was costing us more than we'd thought. Originally, we'd imagined getting around in cars lent by northern friends or volunteered by locals. Elias drove one belonging to a Brandeis graduate student. Joe Bowman chauffeured for a while. Modjeska lent us her '56 Pontiac. Sometimes we rode the bus. We also spent $650 on several oil-guzzling heaps and $177 renting a Ford. Adam Stewart, a skilled mechanic, kept the clunkers running. He and his kin repaired them at night at his home eight miles north of town. Still, although the fleet helped us transport people to the courthouse for registration July 5-10, after that, says Phyllis, we were down again to one good set of wheels.

Independence Day fell on a Sunday. That weekend, James Brown did his thing at Township Auditorium. We were warned not to go because, Phyllis heard, "there are many fights at his dances—kids drink and whites and blacks dance together until someone picks a fight. Last year someone was knifed and another man shot. We worked at the office—us celibates."

Next day, on what was otherwise a public holiday, she manned a four-hour shift at the courthouse, where registration was open all week. Her main task was to help frightened people through the ordeal. From that day she still possesses a list of registrant names "that speak the time and place.... Sallie Mae Govan, Willie Mae Knowles, Sallie Mae Sulton, Jessie Jackson, Mose A. Diamond, ...among 41 registered so far in three hours. Three failed. Roman Dawkins, straight from a bar: 'Listen, I-I-I-I want to tell y'all somethin'. I love y'all.' Tears, very drunk"—but passed the test. People failed when they froze up. "We'll work with them."

Toward Phyllis the registrars were "fairly friendly. We even had coffee together." Toward would-be voters they could be hostile, making the literacy test hard and embarrassing. "They tried to frighten people constantly, saying such things as, 'You're an old man—why haven't you voted before?' or convincing them that they were illiterate even before they tried to read." One form of humiliation was presenting passages to read such as the list of crimes found at (5a) on the registration form. "One lady missed three words—sodomy, fornication, and adultery—or was it miscegenation—I was terribly annoyed—and then such humiliations as when a white woman came in, and her little girl came over to talk and took an *I Am Registered, Are You?* button. Her mother, gasping, seized the child, pushed her to the other side of the room and clutched her."

Another monitor on that shift was a young black Columbia woman. Sometimes Phyllis thought her "slightly impolite to the registrars out of annoyance. I found myself soothing both sides fairly successfully, but after my shift I was exhausted. I got out at 1:00, and at 2:00 met a gentleman, Louman Anderson, at the office. I'm reviewing reading and writing with him. He was 'gassed' during World War II [sic]—his nerves are shot and his eyesight poor. We bought some magnifying glasses, but what we really need is interpreting earphones."

Because it was a holiday, she'd expected less than thirty people. Still, when 58 registered, the turnout felt disappointing. She went back on Tuesday afternoon when the rolls reopened, but that day was even slower. "In an hour only six have come. Such a bad feeling waiting for people to come—please come—I keep on wondering if I belong in this phase of the struggle. Political strategy sometimes feels so cold.... A Mr. Nathan just walked in—he is so nervous—I'm afraid he may not pass—no! It looks like he's all right! Hurrah!"

When the rolls closed at the end of the week, 249 new black voters had registered. The number didn't seem impressive. Ish wrote home that the problem was "more with the conditions in Richland County than in the way we went about our work. Columbia is a slow, apathetic city, and to get grass-roots enthusiasm up is next to impossible." More hopeful Phyllis wrote, "The most important part of the 'success' is that we've got the communities we've canvassed to really take part in the drive. Especially those who registered for the first time—there's a new feeling of pride and interest." Rolls would re-open the first week of August.

Sparse records survive about our later weeks in the city. Along with canvassing, the general idea became to work in twos or threes on community projects in different wards. In early August Elias told KZSU that building a playground required the community to form a committee: "Far as I know, in Richland and Columbia, no committees have been established before that could work together in getting things done for the community. SCOPE members have essentially brought the people together, and they provided all the information that these people needed to go ahead and start the project."

Living out in Ben Mack's Ridgewood, David Jacobson steadily mingled at Ridgewood Baptist, a short walk from the Caldwells'. On an early neighborhood stroll, a white policeman cautioned him not to wander. David took this as an innocent warning. "In any case, the occasion was the only one where I had any kind of encounter with white people in the area. Once living in Ridgewood, I can't remember going anywhere that I could not walk to. Once established in the community, I rarely left it."

Highly musical Ridgewood Baptist was the neighborhood social center. July 1, fifteen SCOPErs joined David there to hear NAACP Legal Defense Fund lawyer Marvin Mainer encourage folks to file job discrimination complaints against Columbia Bell and other employers. Mainly, David promoted voter registration and set out to end the insult of second-class treatment of blacks at a laundromat: "I don't think it actually had any white customers. Nevertheless its African-American customers were not allowed to use the primary entrance; that was for whites only. They had to use a side door. The idea was to organize a group of younger people from the community to reject this kind of treatment."

Around early August SCOPE organized a picket and boycott. David says the picketing wasn't his idea and recalls no opposition to it. Phyllis reported harassment from a man in a sheet and pointy white hat. Police arrived, removed the spook, and left her wondering how long the owner would hold out. David can't remember the outcome, but since the business depended totally on black patrons, he thinks they won in the end.

Arthurtown was another place we spent a lot of time. On June 28 we began in this spread of sandy paths and houses. At least part of it lay outside the city's southeastern limits. We had no maps, just drove out and started. To Lynn it was "almost rural but the houses are in bunches…quite pretty, although in poor shape. Gardens full of bright flowers all over. Out of the sandy (or clay) soil grow huge, green plants. There were also chickens, hogs, horses, and mules. Many of these people use mules to pull wagons and plows.

"We gathered a flock of children around us. Bill [Greenhill or Kornrich?] and I had six, all about ten years old. They clung to us and insisted on holding all our possessions, such as pocketbook and clipboard. They knew the area, and helped us approach people. The people were all very friendly, and we were surprised that most were registered. Street lights had been obtained for one street (Sugar Hill Lane) apparently by petition of the high school kids. This poor community has real fightin' spirit."

Phyllis guessed Arthurtown must have been charming back in the 1800s. Here and now, "mangy, worm-eaten, flea-bitten mongrels" became her friends, and men sat around "chewing tobacco on the steps of sad little shacks—perhaps a filthy and enormous hog waddling in the mud puddle beside them. Kids and kittens. 'Hey cat,' say the little kids. 'Hey jitterbug. Hey catbaby, set y'self down a piece.' Little ones, five, six years old—fourteen per house at least. Fifteen-year-old girl living alone with two kids, a man coming in occasionally to let her earn a living. Corn planted all around. Grocery stores—shacks in themselves— where people sit around and play checkers with bottle caps. And always pups and chickens and more kids. Then an old fellow drives his horse-wagon full of manure, and in the front seat he's got peaches—two for a penny, watermelons for fifty cents, cantaloupe for a dime—and always more kids than you could imagine."

(Probably more so than up north, a lot of southern women—black and white—had a lot of kids back then, though on average black families seemed to have more. But family sizes were already shrinking and would decline even faster as black women gained more education, health care, birth control, and better paying jobs.)

"And everyone is called by their first name—Lillie Mae Hopkins is 'Lillie' to her peers and 'Miss Lillie' to us kids. Miss Blanche can tell you everything about everyone, and Eli Brown is a drunkard, but he'll register on Monday, and Haddie Grey is gonna drag out her man."

Here the vote took on new meaning. "It means that the Whites or Browns won't have to drag their water from the pump two blocks away, that garbage will be collected, that Mr. Human, whose arm had to be amputated after an accident in the butcher shop, will get more than $35 a month to support himself, his wife, and seven kids—that Emmie Lou will have shoes, and Robert won't have to wear four-year-old Mary Janes to school. The meat Mrs. Williams buys won't disappear on the wood stove, and when her niece gets hit by a car and needs attention in the hospital, that attention will be immediate rather than leaving poor Ada Williams to die of neglect. Her ribs pierced her heart during the night. She's dead now—a kid of sixteen. Everyone is sure that, if they had treated her last night instead of this afternoon, Ada would be alive. Life is so cheap here. People feel old so young."

In Arthurtown Ricky Schaffer continued to explore and enjoy the challenge of connection: "Yesterday I had a most exciting success with a 50-year-old man with a fourth-grade education who lives on his disability insurance. After talking with him and his wife for about a half hour, he asked me to come back the next day to answer a few questions. I would have preferred to know what he wanted then; but I promised to return.

"When I did, he first confessed that he had to go to work after four years of education and could not read so well. (Most people feign short-sightedness or something.) He went on to say that he wished very much to register, but was unsure of his ability to pass the test, so I went over the application with him. Then I discovered why he really asked me back. He had once served thirty days for beating his wife, and wondered if that disqualified him from voting. He said he'd liked me the day before and felt he could tell me this in confidence and receive an honest answer without any shame or embarrassment. I am not even sure his own children know about it."

Because the Bradley boarding house seemed pricey at ten bucks a week, Phyllis was staying now with five others at Dick and Sharon Miles' modest apartment at 1208 Harden Street, listening to Vivaldi and sharing a bed with Margot. The

Miles' place seemed unreal with its air-conditioning, classical music, and "books, books, books." Phyllis was bumming meals but also making dinners for six and baking cake for her hosts. Pregnant Sharon Miles was also doing movement work. In 1966, for example, she would be part of a lawsuit testing discrimination at the Little Joe's Piggie Park, which still refused to seat blacks.

On the weekend Phyllis, Ricky and Ish held a freedom sing in Arthurtown with twenty kids of all ages. Wednesday night after a long day in an area where canvassers had never been, five of us and forty residents met at Arthurtown's Zion Pilgrim Baptist Church. Its pastor was J.W. Mungin, a non-violent activist and one of the plaintiffs in the ongoing suit against Little Joe's. He'd delivered the scripture and invocation at our welcome at Second Nazareth Baptist. He knocked Phyllis' socks off with a Good Samaritan story in which, according to her report, "Jesus [sic] was riding along on some mission, and seeing a man in the road, hurt, stopped, nursed him, carried him to an inn and told the innkeeper to nurse the man—no matter what the cost. He told it with tenderness and strength."

Phyllis learned that Rev. Mungin was only 23; another pastor there, with his own church and congregation, was six years younger. Mungin spoke of "shouldering one's burden—and the congregation answered in chorus. It would build into a chant—he would begin a phrase—pause while the congregation rolled, 'Well?' and finish—pause for an 'Oh yes, Lord...Amen...Yes, He did!'

Between speeches we sang. Local people expressed welcomes, doubts, needs, hopes, past successes and failures. To our surprise, however, the real meeting began afterward, outside on the dirt main road. As the crowd shared punch and cookies, Phyl started playing and, "in its little-by-little way, a crowd encircled me and the place began to swing and sway. People joined from the tavern and neighbors heard us and came out. I have never, absolutely, felt the joy of last night's singing. People would call out verses—children, old men, young mothers, great-grandmothers, kids, kids, kids, perspiring, smiling, gleaming. I had to tell them how I felt and I didn't know how. We just sang of love and hope and 'I want my freedom—free at last! There is so much strength in people singing and chanting together— first time in such a long while that I wasn't afraid to cry. "

By late July, the community was picketing an Arthurtown store. Around the same time, Ricky moved in there with "a wonderful family. I do voter registration mainly in the city, but mass meetings and my beginning efforts at a literacy school have been here. The flyer on which I am typing is the result of a most rewarding, and inspiring encounter with the federal 'power structure'—the Richland County branch of the Office of Economic Opportunity, that is, the Poverty Program."

The federal OEO had granted $80,000 toward the creation of an Arthurtown daycare center that would soon expand to other services. Not overestimating his own role in the process, Ricky was helping coordinate different civic groups in planning the center. Arthurtown's part included repairing an old building: "We are planning an old-fashioned 'barn raising' and I am trying to get all the youth out on Saturday to build and paint. It is a fantastic project, the first in SC and a model and pilot for other counties. This could be the most rewarding part of my summer work. It also may provide the opportunity to organize the youth into some kind of active political force—not to mention the adults." Ricky heard it was the first real improvement there since the 1920's.

8. Rovers

After a week in Arthurtown, Phyllis, Lesley, Ish, and three other guys formed a roving team that moved north to Adam Stewart's Haskell Heights, staying there in side-by-side houses owned by Adam and his clan. Phyl reassured her parents we'd be under his "strict supervision. He's a really colorful, pleasant fellow to work with. We'll have walkie-talkies with us, since telephones are scarce—so don't worry, we'll be exercising maximum safety precautions and I'll not be alone for an instant. Of the six of us only two are girls, and the boys are careful to watch out for us." The rovers would stay there about two weeks, where the roads ate up their worn-out tires. "For a while," Ish scribbled home, "we were flatting tires as fast as we could fix them, ten in a week." Adam came up with a dozen replacements, and the cars found other ways to break down.

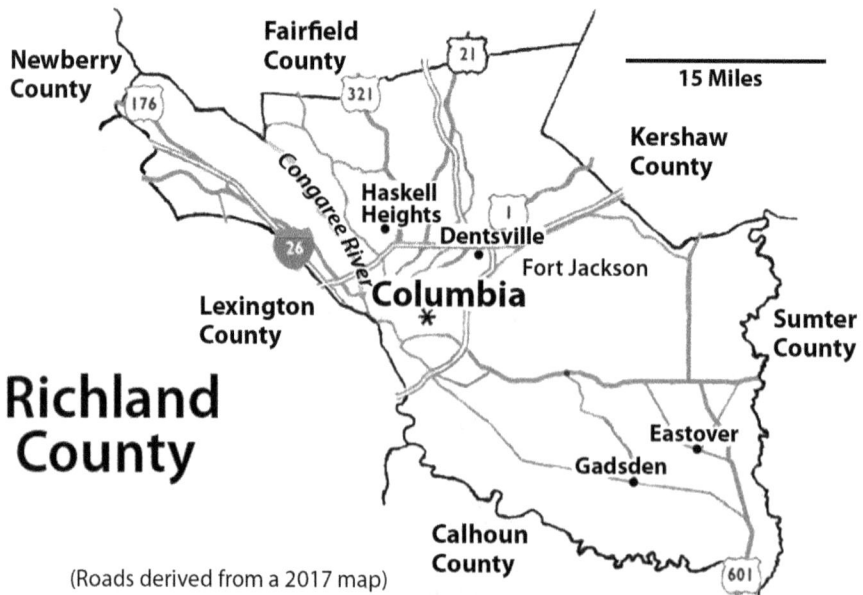

Newberry County
Fairfield County
21
15 Miles
176
321
Kershaw County
Congaree River
Haskell Heights
Dentsville
26
Fort Jackson
Columbia
Lexington County
Sumter County
Richland County
Eastover
Gadsden
Calhoun County
601

(Roads derived from a 2017 map)

Phyllis noticed the strain on Adam and found out about his heart trouble. She lamented his working from 7:30 a.m. past midnight.

She missed Citti and Margot, both now in Kershaw County, but loved the roving weeks with Lesley. "It's exciting seeing these settlements. It's funny what you find out about slums—no matter how poor, each one has real personality—even within a few blocks."

The walkie-talkies turned out to be mainly the latter: *talk*. Bought up north at $80 apiece, they were short on range and battery life. Another communication challenge was that we couldn't post letters from Haskell Heights and had to carry them into the city. But staying in Haskell made it easier to canvass there and in nearby Booker Heights and Crane Creek.

We had visitors in Haskell Heights. One was Father Troy, Brandeis' Catholic chaplain whose Bethlehem Chapel Phyllis had retreated to at times in her rocky freshman year, "the only empty place at Brandeis. Boy, was it great to see him—never thought it would mean so much." With him were Dean Zion and a young physics professor, Lenny Meyers, with whom the whole household sat down to watch televised fly-by photos of Mars.

Phyllis and Lesley shared a bed in the home of Mattie Friday ("Mama," *née* Stewart), Mattie's husband John ("Paps"), and Mattie and Adam's mother, Mrs. Viola Stewart ("Grandma"). "Mama worked once in a poultry factory from 4:00 a.m. to 7:30 p.m. for $20 a week. Paps works from 7:30 till 5:00 with a half-hour break for lunch. He comes home so very tired. He digs all day and comes home to wash in a tiny basin he can hardly stand up in—and this is not poverty, this is relative comfort." The comfort included a tandem outhouse: "Such convenience. Must be very aware of everyone. Mama has never had a toilet in her life. We get a pot at night in case, but Lesley and I took a moonlit walk in advance to avoid making music in that pot during the night. This morning while Lesley and I sat on those charming holes, poor Grandma couldn't wait.... we didn't know but we will next time."

She wished she could live in a place like this "where neighbors were neighborly and friends stopped by, and we could just invite anyone in, and even if we lived modestly, we could share all we had. We've always done a lot of sharing at home. But white or Negro people in our financial range just don't walk around the neighborhood at night—dropping in casually—honking every time they drive by, waving and calling out, 'How do?'—handing out sweet potato pie with raisins and singing all together on the porch." She clung to the music.

"There's a whole line of new-built homes here—all Stewarts of one relation or other. The house is spotless. We were up at 7:30 for breakfast of eggs, fried bologna, bacon, grits, toast, and coffee." She and Lesley were cleaning up after meals. "Mama cleans house for white folks all week—she needs a rest." Mama had been postponing the cost of seeing a doctor about her migraines. "You know how extreme these problems become as you get lower and lower on the income scale. Kids can't afford to get married. People live in black holes made of cardboard—fire traps, where old wood stoves burn their food—very, very little meat and if any it's fatback or pig's knuckles—stomach ailments are common and traveling cure-all men cheat these people out of every cent. A penny is a common offering in some churches."

For the migraines Phyllis thought Mama might need only glasses, and by the end of her stay, with Mama "staying home all day in bed sniffing some awful stuff," Phyl had arranged to take her to a doctor. SCOPE would pay for the visit "sort of as payment for keeping us—I'll try to do it gracefully."

As for what Mama really lacked, "To wash, we heat water and use a basin. The dishes get scalded after they're washed. But if Mama could only have a sink and a tub—if she didn't have to wash her clothes in a cauldron in the yard over a fire...." (Only in the past twenty years or so had many poor South Carolina women of both races been able to replace the cauldron with indoor tubs or machines.)

One night Phyllis was making supper with Mama, "chicken in grease, milk and flour; cornbread of grease, corn, flour and water; grease on some rice and on the cabbage; and believe it or not—it tasted delicious. 'It ain't good if it ain't good and greasy,' says Mama, pouring on the grease. I fairly slide off that outhouse seat."

Mid-July Elias came up to suggest Ish join the group in Calhoun County. Ish didn't know at the time that Ricky Schaffer keenly expected the next ticket out of Richland. He did know it was not a bad idea to make some space between himself and Phyllis. In fact, Ish thought Elias was moving him because of an incident some nights before when Phyllis and Ish were alone together at the end of an evening of paperwork at the office in Columbia. Ready to leave, they turned off the office light, which left the building in the dark. And there they were, by the open office door, together alone on a hot summer night. Well, what would *you* do? They'd only begun to embrace when someone entered the building downstairs, flipped on a light as he came up, and found them hastily emerging. Ish didn't recognize the man, who quietly, firmly told them to leave. This must be for the best, Ish supposed, remembering Judy. In truth the boy often felt alarmed by Phyllis' great intensity. Afterward, he imagined their discoverer complaining to Elias, though Elias tells him today that, whether they were reported or not, his transfer to Calhoun wasn't related.

For an evening meeting after he left, Phyllis worked with Larry Gilliard, a local piano-playing kid, hoping he would lead some songs. But a downpour that night with "thunder and lightning shaking the universe" made the clay roads impassable for Larry and most of the folks she expected. So by herself she tried to wake up the show-ups with song. Ben Mack and Adam spoke about how important it was for the church and its leaders to be a center for improving life on earth, not only in the sweet hereafter. In all, it was a rousing evening.

At the end of the week, she, Lesley, and Dinah Mae Dubard, a Bookert Heights teen, drove around confirming arrangements for driving people to the courthouse during the August registration week. Phyllis thought locals should do most of the transport. Other SCOPErs disagreed, but she felt that "even if it makes more work for us, we should let these people work—even if we make work when we can do it ourselves. I know no other way to involve us all together."

Mama Friday had no children, but by the end of the fortnight she'd adopted Lesley and Phyllis: "She was very protective of us. She filled us in on how to behave and cautioned me not to hang around with the husband of her cousin down the block, who had offered to show me his new 18-gear truck cab. She helped me see another way I was seen—as a white woman."

Mama had reason to worry for her. Phyllis was magnetic, though she seemed unconscious of her effect. One night she cajoled Adam into letting her help swap out a transmission. Ish remembers her dazzling exuberance and everyone's marvel as she scrambled down under the chassis in a borrowed men's shirt, greasy overalls and hat to hold her hair, and is not surprised how the evening turned out. Also on hand was Gareth, a young man with a troubled past. Phyllis wrote of him, "He works with us and happily, he softens up more each day. He shoots pool and goes to night clubs and beat a policeman for touching him during an arrest, but really this man-boy just needs someone to truly believe in him and he comes out fine." Sometime after the transmission job, she was dismayed to learn that Gareth had carved her name on his arm.

P hyllis had noted how "frankly" the weekends went. Paps "drank his beer, went fishing, read the paper and slept. Most of the men get themselves a couple of beers and maybe go out to a bar in addition." On Saturday they all sat out on the porch "and several friends—mostly at least slightly intoxicated— sat down to chat and sing. Many of these men have been so beaten down, the only time they have the courage to assert themselves as human beings, and speak what's on their minds, is on the weekend when whiskey breaks all those shackles.

"And that's when Jesse sits down and tells me he's not being fresh but he wants me to know that we're all together in life and even in death—and we're all one—and that he's not afraid of me because I'm a white woman but he'll respect me. And the tongue runs loose and chains of unhappiness come loose and all seemingly disconnected but, in truth, basically connected blues and troubles 'til you are reminded of the patchwork quilt Grandma's been making with all assorted colors and designs, all sewed into a simple, basic, ever-present order."

Mike and Sophie Greenfield came to visit their daughter in Haskell Heights. How could they not come down after reading how, one Sunday morning before visiting churches, she'd "washed me and my hair, peeled peaches and cut 'em up to freeze, brought water from the electric pump, had a few moments of meditation in the tandem, brought the slop bucket to the hawg, and all the time thinking—you all should be here"? She brought them down to meet Ish in Calhoun as he was settling in.

The last week living in upper Richland, the rovers canvassed Bookert Heights, a little further north in a fairly integrated area. "Each time we came to a Negro home we asked where Negro settlement ended and white began—people are more willing to live next door to Negro folks when their nearest neighbor is a mile away."

That day the cars went to hell: "two flats, a blowout (don't worry, they don't travel more than 35 mph so even a blowout is easy-going). As we drove, the hood unhooked on one side and whipped against the windshield. All's back to normal now with fresh spares and a wire on the hood. The station wagon eats oil—two quarts per day—and we fill the left front tire every few hours—but she's pretty safe and a panic to drive."

The rovers shifted to lower Richland, probably connecting with William Blakely's group. During Reconstruction, former slaves had obtained some land there, and a number of small communities had built up along a railway. For lack of local housing offers, Lesley and Phyllis stayed in the Miles' cramped city apartment, driving down on some days, on others re-canvassing parts of the city in heat and sudden rains.

Sharon was getting more pregnant and "Cat" the cat was going crazy being locked indoors because of fleas. "In the middle of the night he pounces on us in bed." For five nights the girls poured on the Dem-o-Derm, then shifted to the Williams family at Evergreen Court where Ish had stayed in June. The work was hectic and constrained by news of the beating of Mark Dinaberg, a SCOPEr in Newberry County. Security tightened around the girls, who were "not only not allowed to canvass alone, but also, we can't be together—must be with a boy at all times—this may sound good to you, and it may be wise—but I'm sorry for it. Every other hour we have to call into the home office, and doing work in pairs now consists of two people going to each house—half the manpower, twice the time."

On the 30th, with music in mind, Rev. Bowman took Lesley and Phyllis to a gathering in tiny Eastover, 25 miles south of the city. To their surprise, it was a revival where Bowman inspired the hall with a sermon about laying burdens aside "and joining the race—the human race—the 'Christian race.'" Phyllis doubted her songs would go over there. "But I was wrong—people sang more than before, and I could feel tears streaming down my cheeks as we sang, and my head splitting from tension." Though more people had stood for the revival, still, half of them stood to sing "O Freedom" and "This Little Light of Mine."

Riding back she was glad to learn how closely she and William Bowman agreed on issues such as capital punishment and homosexuality. Regarding the latter, our Alan Kern was in the throes of working things through, and Phyllis writes about his confiding personal problems with her. Alan tells Ish that he was sorting things out, still enough in doubt that near the end of August, as restrictions loosened, he and David Kricker double-dated two young black Columbia women.

Lesley, too, was just beginning to gather such insight into herself. She says, "At the time, I was just realizing that homosexuality (or any kind of sexuality) existed. And I did not want to be gay at all, so I was in complete denial. At Brandeis (probably after SCOPE), I went to a performance of 'The Maids' by Jean Genet and heard the word 'lesbian' for the first time, and thought with horror, 'Oh no! Why did my parents name me Lesley?' 'Lesley Lesbian! Everyone will know.' And then immediately, 'But I'm not, I'm not!' It was quite a while before I acted on it."

Apparently the revival with Bowman wasn't Phyllis' only collaboration with traveling clerics that summer. By mid-July she'd been "bringing the message to people by traveling with a preacher, billed as a 'traveling saviour,' to his evening prayer meetings. The first time I went, I sat in the back of the room transfixed. I was unprepared when, after everyone rose and sat down again, the preacher announced, 'And now, I have a little Jew-Girl here, who can sing just like us.' I stumbled to the front with my guitar, but as I sang the people joined me, clapped and swayed, and one by one rose to their feet."

More alarming for her, most likely, was a remark that Adam Stewart made at the end of the evening they were working on cars: "Adam looked up at me quizzically and said, quietly, 'But y'all killed Christ, didn't you?' It was the only time I felt like an outsider with Adam whom I had come to admire and care for deeply. I said something simple like, 'No, no—I didn't kill Christ.'"

On August 1, the Richland SCOPErs and friends drove to the coast for an integrated day off on Pawley's Island beach. Then followed a week of getting people up to Columbia to register and covering Gadsden in lower Richland. In Gadsden Phyllis visited a new Head Start program, "virtually segregated, though open to whites—they gave me 31 youngsters for twenty minutes, and it was a challenge. As they got a little restless, we made a circle and I plagued my memory to recall the song games of Bronx House Camp III. I was moved and distressed to see how much was needed by so many of the children to establish even basic communication between child and teacher. The teachers seem well-equipped, but the job is mammoth."

Only a score of whites lived around Gadsden. Of a potential 650 black voters, about 250 weren't registered, and canvassing seemed encouraging, but the area already had good precinct organization and people interested in working, so the team shifted a few miles to Hopkins. The work was less strenuous there because houses were farther apart and could only be canvassed by car. By that time Phyllis had a sore throat, headache and stomach problems. Still, when the registration week ended, she and Liz Hafkin procured a nine-hour overnight lift to DC for a weekend movement conference. Then Liz decided to remain there the rest of the summer doing legal research for the Mississippi Freedom Democratic Party. For unhappier reasons, the quick dash up would also abruptly end Phyllis' weeks in the South.

9. EVERYONE OUT

Phyllis documented her experiences in Richland County through the first week of August. Besides Lesley and Elias, others staying Richland were Kathy, Davids Jacobson and Kricker, Betty, Ricky Schaffer, Bill Greenhill, and Alans Segal and Kern. According to Elias, each decided how much to take on. In general, he said, "After canvassing a ward, we don't send an entire group back. We assign one or two to the ward for mass meetings, literacy schools, any kind of project they want in the community. It's up to them. Some of the members are doing a very, very fine job. Other people, you know—it takes different minds."

Ricky Schaffer, Kathy, Betty, and possibly others tutored in literacy schools. Alan Kern searched the outlying county for pockets of potential voters. From Atlanta he'd contacted Eric Heymann, his best friend from home in Miami. In effect a 24th member of Brandeis SCOPE, Eric joined Alan and may have brought a car.

Left to Right: Unidentified, Phyllis, Kathy, Alan K., Eric Heymann.

Elias singled out Alan *Segal* for organizing a youth group. This Alan is heard in one early August evening session with KZSU, in the company of one or two local kids. Besides canvassing, they were working toward integrating Columbia's central YMCA. There was a Negro Boys Club at Howard School, but it had no gym, so one of them had gone to see if he could use the basketball court at the central Y. First the staff refused to let him in, then asked him to pay $40.

The youth believed the girls' Y was less rigid, telling KZSU, "The Y lady told me today they don't have to integrate. The way they get around it is that every time a Negro calls the YWCA Central, they refer her to the Phyllis Wheatley branch." (Phyllis Wheatley YWCA was a parallel, black-oriented Y institution, founded in 1905. Its first branch was in DC.)

But the boy added that if a black girl applied to Columbia's all-white YWCA and lived closer to it or wanted to take part in a program there that the Negro branch did not have, she wasn't turned away. The boys wanted the YMCA to at least do the same, and Segal was trying to talk to its administrators about fuller integration. Failing that, he'd turn to established leaders in Columbia to see what they could do.

Though the two Alans, Ricky Schaffer, David Jacobson and others overcame their frustrations well enough to carve out constructive roles in town, others became more discouraged. In late July, some of the dozen still in Richland proposed unsuccessfully that the entire chapter might leave for some needier county. By that point, returns on canvassing seemed thin. One evening in early August, the KSZU reporters sampled the flagging spirits of a handful of Richland SCOPErs. As one lamented, "You have to search in Richland County.... to get people excited enough. When the courthouse opens extra weeks, people don't feel right away that they're going to be suppressed from voting, and they don't get excited. Things are slowly getting integrated and there's no big form of oppression for them to jump against."

To his roommate up north, Ricky Schaffer mused, "The Jim Crow signs are quickly disappearing. There are some exceptions, of course—the medieval conditions of the Negro mental hospital. The entire mental hospital, Negro and white, has lost its federal financing and is making plans to desegregate."

Speaking separately with KZSU also early in August, before the passage of the *Voting Rights Act*, Elias suggested that SCOPE's frustration stemmed from the reality that most "motivated" people were already registered. The remainder was the poorer, more reluctant, less literate, county-wide pool in which previous canvasses had also fallen short. That potential registrant pool was still large—about 29% back in April—and we weren't making much of a dent. Elias also noted the frustrations of trying to transport people to the courthouse even from inside the city. For example, one afternoon we'd had eighty commitments from one ward alone, but only 25 showed up.

Basic problems were endemic, worse in some ways than in other cities all over the country, but not entirely different. Plans were under way for various acts of urban renewal—a mixed proposition both north and south. From at least 1955 Columbia had been attempting to deal with sanitation problems (toiletless homes), enforce existing codes, and "fight blight"—which often came down to clearing blacks from blocks that were coveted by USC. Still, from what Ricky could see, there had been little or "no attempt to enforce the minimal housing code...no housing code outside the city limits. This means that anything goes, and believe me, it does. I have walked into houses where the smell was so bad that my eyes watered and the heat so great that in five minutes my clothing was soaking.

"I guess that a third of the Negro males are unemployed. There are no minimum wages [still ain't], no unions, few pensions. Men work 45 hours per week at a semi-skilled job and bring home $30 to a wife and six kids. I met a woman who, in order to get a laundry job, had to sign a contract to work as many hours per week as is necessary to finish the job (sometimes sixty or seventy). She was being paid $14 dollars per week."

Meanwhile, he wished he could hold the middle-class blacks to a higher moral standard than he could claim for middle-class whites. A major challenge of ward-level work was engaging local power structures. Ricky saw black middle-class families striving "for no more for themselves. ...It seems to me the [middle-class] Negro's aim must be some kind of transformation of that class, and of the economic, political and social forces that embody it."

So others among us also looked for social redemption through blacks.

Still, Ricky didn't "wish to tell people what to do with their freedom.... I hesitate to say that to strive to become a member of the American middle class is unworthy...if the middle class could accommodate all those who strive for it. Perhaps I have no right to expect more from the Negro middle class than from the white. But there are still many degrading and de-humanizing signs of segregation that strike at the wealthy Negro as well as the poor."

For Ricky at eighteen, equality boiled down to equal opportunity; but the system undercut what equal opportunity could yield. White power brokers in the South had no need to "actively persecute. They need only maintain the status quo—actually they need do less. They can simply maintain the current trend—a worsening in the Negro's economic position." This was different from how things stood up north more in degree than kind.

Ricky wondered what real change could happen "without the rage, without the conflict," the marches and fight he saw back in New York. How honestly could he believe that voter registration and political education would bring about change? And how could he "convince a lower-class, libido-filled Negro teenager" of something he sometimes doubted himself? Others among us felt the same.

In all, how much did we increase black registration in Richland County? As of June 1, about 17,000 were registered, 24,000 not. At the end of the year, the VEP posted the following totals.

June	N/A
July	404
August	298
September	78
October	71
November	73
December	74
Total	998

The VEP showed no entry for June but probably added 150 from that month to our July tally of 249. If that is so, registrations rose in July and August (our watch) by 547. But September-December numbers suggest a monthly baseline of more than seventy, so the actual effect of our canvassing (combined with that the NAACP and possibly CORE) was probably more like 400. Some Brandeis SCOPErs retain the impression we accounted for many more than that, but that lingering sense may be based on July-through-September running *estimates* passed on to SC-VEP by SCOPE, CORE and the NAACP. Those estimates totaled 1,743.

Numerically then, our effect in Richland County was modest. Was it larger for other urban SCOPE groups? It seems likely that SCLC's urban SCOPE ventures were not much more successful. But in a *mitzvah* you do what you can. In the long term, black registration did grow on the wings of the *Voting Rights Act*. In Richland County as of 2015, Elias informs Ish, out of a total of 226,891 registered voters, 114,301 are non-white, greater than 50%. Prior to the act, he notes, there were no non-whites in the South Carolina General Assembly. From a recent census he found there are now eight black senators, 23 black representatives, and 99 blacks among 334 members of South Carolina county councils.

What had become of Dean Zion's vision of linking Brandeis University with a local school of higher learning—the reason for choosing Richland County? In April Margot and Professor Long had reported that Allen University president Howard E. Wright was "particularly interested in establishing ties with Brandeis." But by the time we arrived he may have moved on to his work in the fledgling OEO.

In early August Elias told KZSU about prospects of faculty or student exchanges. He favored the latter. None of the Columbia schools allowed students to choose their own campus guest speakers. Elias felt that the freer environment of Brandeis could help expand the students' minds. But he also thought more could be gained by stimulating cooperation between *local* white and black colleges than by connecting them to Brandeis. By early August, apparently Brandeis faculty had talked only separately with faculty members on different campuses. Elias noted that before our arrival a USC student had organized groups at Allen and Benedict. He probably meant Peter Lee, a white Columbia 19-year-old who'd been active in civil rights since high school. Peter and a few other whites had joined 500 blacks in the April protest march. On the march he'd been singled out and beaten while newspeople watched nearby.

In late May, three white students at Columbia College had disseminated information for us on their campus, and Brandeis SCOPE was seeking student allies through the SC Student Council on Human Relations. This interracial discussion group had begun in 1961, and members had been penalized by loss of academic fellowships and other repression for expanded activities and training at the Highlander Folk School in Tennessee. As of 1962, the group involved 280 members from numerous black and white SC schools. In 1965 it included Peter Lee among other college and high school students. Some had taken part in voter registration drives. In the spring we'd imagined doubling our number by working with them. Had Peter not been deployed that summer in field work for the NAACP, he might have opened up this channel. (A book by Sears describes Peter's later activism in gay rights, health and AIDS.)

Several young whites had been at our welcome at Bowman's church, but in subsequent personal contact with high school students from the council, according to Lynn, Terry found them "very mild, timid." After reading *Rebellion in Black and White*, Ish wonders about that as a generalization, but apparently nothing more developed.

In early August, Betty still thought we could have made more campus contacts if all of us had stayed in Richland, despite the fact that the schools were on break. At the risk of losing draft deferments, David Kricker and one or two others considered staying on in the fall to pursue such connections. But no one did stay on in Richland.

"And that's the way it goes," Elias concluded for KZSU. Interscholastically he was hoping the Brandeis administration would make "a more definite statement of what exactly would be involved." He excused the vagueness as a necessary "testing period," but probably sensed Waltham's withdrawal. In late August the SCLC executive staff was still imagining that "an exchange program between Allen University and Brandeis is planned," but nothing came of that. Still, that's how movements are: well-meant but tentative plans that grow or filter and thin out according to facts on the ground.

10. JUST STARVING

Now to summarize our summer-long efforts on behalf of the infant Phyllis and Ish had heard about on their first June day in Black Bottom.

Tuesday night August 10, Phyllis was back from the conference in DC and starting her last letter home. She'd gone right back to canvassing and had just talked with an advisor to the superintendent of schools about designing a proactive monitoring system for families in Head Start. Monday or Tuesday she also attended a meeting about a federal day care center project (perhaps in Arthurtown), speaking to mothers who were forced to quit work to care for their infants; to children forced to quit school to care for younger siblings; and to elderly people without children who were disturbed at the number of ill-clothed, ill-fed children running unsupervised through the neighborhood.

Within a week, she was so sick that Elias flew her home to Teaneck. She didn't think this illness was a continuation from a previous week, but the psychological outcome of a harrowing incident during the night ride north (see "Change Gon' Come"). Her worst disappointment in this was losing touch with Sylvia Rashonda, the starving infant in Black Bottom that Mrs. Bruce had directed her to in June. All summer, Phyllis had been leading other SCOPErs in trying to help both mother and child.

Seven-month old Sylvia Rashonda was the daughter and second child of 17-year-old Clayvon Drayer. Clayvon herself had been in utero back when her mother's husband came home from the service, and the pregnancy had led to their separation. Neither Clayvon nor her slightly younger sister had gone beyond a first year of schooling. During Clayvon's first pregnancy at age fifteen, her mother had died of cancer hastened by starvation. Now the first child, Willy, was two years old and, according to what Mrs. Bruce told Phyllis, living "in absolute filth" and "has never had a real bath—even in a sink." Mrs. Bruce had been trying to convince Clayvon to take Sylvia Rashonda to the Columbia Hospital clinic. The baby, according to Mrs. Bruce, was so thin as to be "unrecognizable as a human being." Even just hearing about the infant, Phyllis wanted to take her home. She told her parents, "Ish's presence was the only thing that gave me any self control—he kept on looking at me with 'buck up' in his expression, and I felt bad that I couldn't look at the problem objectively."

Shame on Ish.

Phyl called the welfare agency. Next day she and Citti returned to Mrs. Bruce, who steered them to a rickety, two-room, broken-screen-door dwelling. The floor was dirt, with a hole in a corner for a toilet. There was no electricity, no water except from a hose out back. One room held a chair and had flypaper hung from the ceiling. The other held only a crib. It was, in all, "a really dingy shack, flies all around, several mangy kittens and naked Willy, walking, falling, clinging to a bottle."

Outside the house, Clayvon's grandmother, Mrs. Drayer, talked to them, mentioning the baby, "'such a little thing.'" Phyllis replied how much she loved babies. The old grandmother "smiled…blinking her mostly blind eyes, waving away the flies—she wore two different, very worn men's shoes—she has no bed and wears an old black dress on top of a T-shirt. But nothing was more pitiful than Sylvia Rashonda—seven months old—so small you could fit her in the palm of your hand, flies matted in her ringlets, an empty bottle stuck in her poor little mouth…not moving, barely breathing, so sound asleep I thought her dead. I rubbed the little head caked with dirt—no response—her belly was swollen, her thighs the size of my thumb, her little wrists limp. She was lying on a filthy mattress with a plastic bag on it, her head in a hole in the mattress. I couldn't stand it."

At first Clayvon "didn't care to see us," but came around to letting Citti and Phyllis take her and the baby to the hospital. Mrs. Bruce realized what Phyllis did not, "that Clayvon would feel compelled to go along with me because I was white. I bought some diapers (she had a tiny rag around her bottom, and she was red and chafed and had rickets), and a little blue cotton blanket, and we wrapped her up. While Clayvon got dressed I sang to Sylvia 'I love you' in a million tunes." (Phyllis' mother had done that with Phyllis.)

At that point Phyllis knew little about the city's general pattern of medical segregation. She did know that CORE had led a march a few weeks before our arrival demanding compliance with federal laws requiring that public hospitals integrate. According to Moore, in 1921, all-white Columbia Hospital had become the county's first all-white "public" hospital (there was none for blacks). In 1934, the black community (including its doctors) opposed the creation of a segregated wing for blacks. Beyond the segregation itself, they objected to the fact that all black "charity" cases (almost all patients—white or black—were unable to pay), were designated as training material for white interns, off-limits to black physicians. In response the black doctors boycotted the place, sending their private patients to one of two small, black, Waverly district hospitals called Waverly and Good Samaritan. These private institutions were largely funded by northern foundations, especially that of Sears Roebuck magnate Julius Rosenwald. By the end of the 1930s, however, foundation money was shrinking. In the early '40s, Columbia Hospital opened what must have been a larger (165-bed) wing for blacks, with black nurses still under white supervision. Around that same time, Modjeska Simkins began door-to-door, black neighborhood fundraising to combine Good Samaritan and Waverly into one improved fifty-bed facility that opened in 1953. Financially and in terms of equipment from then on, Good Samaritan-Waverly barely hung on, in part because it was expected to serve seven surrounding counties that often welshed on reimbursements.

In 1961, a Benedict College student, Bennie Glover, was rushed to "Good Sam" after being stabbed in a lunch counter sit-in. On recovery he began to lead a campaign for hospital integration. In 1963 the Fourth Circuit triggered change by deleting a separate-but-equal allowance from existing law through which hospitals got federal funding.

Although CORE had just staged a peaceful march for Columbia Hospital's true integration, as of our arrival the facility was still isolating most black children in a separate ward, now and then sending overflow to "white" pediatric beds. At the emergency room, Phyllis and Citti met Dr. Hann, a Quaker pediatrician who'd come down that summer from Philly in order to treat black children. Dr. Hann had "a most wonderfully, refreshingly, pleasantly friendly way of approaching people—we had a good talk this afternoon that hurt in its graphic aspect but felt good in the way she offered me her confidence—I'll see her often since we'll be working to get as many mothers as possible to bring in their children.

"Dr. Hann checked the baby—7 lbs. 4 oz., temp 97 degrees. She told Clayvon her baby was very ill—malnutrition—so much so that the baby might have brain damage—she told Clayvon the baby would have to stay in the hospital for at least two months. ...I tried to save Clayvon as much as possible from those nosey nurses, treating her as if she had no feelings—'Guess that fella who gave you the baby was no good, eh?' Meanwhile, Dr. Hann told me a hair-raising tale about a little girl brought in this morning, three months old, her feet chewed nearly off by rats."

Relieved when Dr. Hann told her Sylvia Rashonda would be all right after some hospital time, Phyllis gathered information on things like schedules for shots and Planned Parenthood that she wanted not only for Clayvon but for other young mothers. "The immunizations are free, so we'll try to get the children there."

But the Columbia Hospital admissions process turned into a nightmare: "Clayvon being nervous, I suggested we go to the john. And there in the city hospital: 'Colored Women,' 'White Women.' All right, I thought, perhaps since the *Civil Rights Bill* of '64 the signs haven't been removed. We used the "colored." She can't read but if she had known, I'd—It was terrible. She calls me ma'am.

"When I presented the papers to check the baby in, the lady said, 'Honey, you don't want to bring your baby here—this is the colored.' I thought I would die—I felt like such a traitor—and Clayvon didn't even know the humiliation I'd submitted her to."

The admissions lady had assumed that Phyllis' unseen baby must be white. Phyllis tried politely to question the head nurse about the policy. "She kept staring at my SCOPE pin and said very harshly, 'Don't give me any of that stuff.' She went over to talk to the other nurses and I was afraid she wouldn't accept the baby and hastened Clayvon to the 'colored ward'—Pediatrics Room #196—

so many children. 'Oh, we're not segregated—we have places for them, and if there are too many babies in the colored ward, we send 'em to the white—it's larger, you understand.' I couldn't help hating today. Such a tiny, helpless baby. There was no attempt to make Clayvon comfortable. One nurse kept saying, 'just plain starvation'—no feeling for this poor unhappy 17-year-old mother crying, carrying the stench of that shack."

Clayvon had no money, no credit, so Phyllis signed for complete charge and responsibility. Then came some relief. Within the crowded ward for black children, "all the nurses were Negro women, and that poor dirty little baby got bathed and placed in a clean diaper—she never had a bath before—and in a clean crib by the window. That Sylvia Rashonda, skinny and bloated as she was, made Mama proud—she has the largest most beautiful black eyes peering almost unseeingly out of that little skull—cheek bones so pronounced, ribs almost outside her body."

Next day, June 24, a young white USC student stringer for UPI came around to learn about Phyllis and Sylvia Rashonda. Phyllis found him "a pleasure in his own way—he was so delighted with the baby. O! She gained a whole pound!—8 lbs, 4 oz.! And today when I held her she actually smiled—a toothless, old lady's grin but a happy grin. The reporter has decided to work with us in his free time. Great. Welcome aboard, Jim Singleton!"

But the piece Jim wrote was disappointing. Phyllis wanted much more about Mrs. Bruce. Years later, she reflected, "Mrs. Bruce introduced me to the way that women in the black community took care of each other, and this became a theme for me throughout my time in the south." However, though Jim seemed sympathetic, he "wasn't interested in writing about Mrs. Bruce and how the community cared for its members, even though two infants were found dead in the bushes the day of his arrival. He was unwilling to communicate that Sylvia's story was just one of hundreds of cases of starvation in a community where premature death was commonplace and suffering was hidden."

To Phyllis' dismay, Jim's angle was "white civil rights worker saves black infant." By mail she warned her parents about what might show up in *The New York Times*. She felt bad because, after Dr. Hann had spoken with Elias, Elias quoted the doctor to Jim as saying, "That girl saved this baby's life." To Phyllis it sounded melodramatic, making her "look like an exception to the rule, which would obliterate any value for the article. Emphasis should have been on Mrs. Bruce. Without her I'd never have found the baby. Ah, the whole deal is so frustrating. Only thank goodness Sylvia is alive."

At the mass meeting on June 24, Phyllis persuaded some women to visit Planned Parenthood. She hoped Clayvon would come to a picnic on Friday in order to take home some food, "but no luck. I only hope she claims Sylvia Rashonda. I'm sure she wants to, so put down and afraid. She hardly knows her own mind."

In the ward for eight or nine days, Sylvia improved slowly, with frequent visits from Phyllis, Citti, Margot, and others. By the 29th her skin was softening "and her belly has an almost normal consistency—tiny little girl she is. Countless Negro ladies have offered to take her. None can afford it, but she's so helpless." Clayvon had yet to visit.

Then Dr. Hann took a week off, and a Dr. Hardwright took over the ward. Around July 2, he discharged Sylvia Rashonda as "another starving kid—we can't feed them all." Ricky Schaffer's letters describe an evening confrontation with Hardwright in which Ricky took part: "We found out that the child was back in the mother's care (rather lack of it) in the same wretched conditions from which it had been taken. Several of us went to speak to the doctors. Citti (in the ten seconds before I could cut her off) all but accused the doctor of malpractice. This bastard of a doctor got furious and nearly threw us out. Another doctor explained that the child needed care and feeding, and that the hospital could not keep her for that. He had therefore discharged her and given the mother a prescription.

"In a sense he is right. If the hospital had to feed all the starving infants in the city there would be no facilities for treating those who were ill or injured. But that mother can't afford food, never mind medicine and vitamins. There are some welfare agencies that could help her, but without our help how could she ever have found them?

"How can people be so indifferent to such happenings? And they are indifferent if they only help to perpetuate a system that blames an individual for his failure and calls federal aid paternalism (which in a sense it is in its present form) but at the same time forbids the radical changes necessary for elimination of poverty, disease, hopelessness. Who does not close his eyes to all this to find some peace and sanity? Yes, but too much of this nation has them sealed tight."

Phyllis arranged public nurse visits to Clayvon twice a week as long as the nurse deemed necessary, "a long time, I hope." July 4 brought some insight into why Clayvon had not attended the picnic. "Today we were to meet Clayvon and the kids for church. She couldn't come: no shoes or dress. I felt sick at being so blind. Margot and I took her home with us. I scrubbed little Willy's panties and diapers, bleached, washed—such an odor—but what happiness to see them white, fresh, hanging on the line in the sunshine! Same with Sylvia's clothes, and after Clayvon bathed both kids and put on fresh diapers and a little pair of shorts on Willy and a funny pink dress on baby, I put Mama into a bubble bath and let her soak for a good twenty minutes—washed her dress and gave her my yellow seersucker, the dress I could most practically give up.

"Then—the big splurge! We went 'out' to lunch at a coffee shop. We even played the juke box. Clayvon cracked a few smiles. We talked about getting her into night school and her plans about marriage. She doesn't want to marry Willy Sr. We're working on welfare right now; meantime, she had a chance to be with some kids her own age—us and Rina—I hated to bring Clayvon home to that awful shack. But she agreed, it must be cleaned—we'll see."

Later on, along with arranging appointments for her at Planned Parenthood and the Well Baby Clinic, Phyllis and Lesley talked to her about working and took her again to lunch. "Gradually we began to get it—or to wake up to how much we didn't get. On one visit, for example, Lesley brought her wrap-around skirt for Clayvon to use at a job interview. Later that week, we returned to find the skirt hanging as a curtain in the front room."

Margot recalls visiting Clayvon as well, perhaps on her own, and spending "many an hour sitting on Clayvon's porch, listening to her dreams of one day coming North to the Promised Land." Although Phyllis had reported that Clayvon couldn't read, Margot remembers exchanging letters with her that fall from Brandeis until suddenly there was no reply. Maybe someone else had been corresponding on Clayvon's behalf.

August 10 found Phyllis still researching services for black orphans and unwed mothers. There were almost none, although "the social worker in the Children's Bureau was sympathetic and said they—she, I think—were urging token integration." Two days later, shortly before her return to Teaneck, Phyllis reported that Willy Sr., Clayvon's only source of money, was "in jail for tearing down someone's house while he was drunk—six months to a year. She had no food in the house other than half a box of grits."

They went shopping for groceries, a pack of cigarettes, and a 29-cent imitation wedding band. "I don't know what else to do but buy. She's having difficulty with welfare because she's not disabled. She can't join any part of STEP [a training and employment program] except chamber maid school and she loathes that prospect—I'm teaching her how to iron, make a bed—me the domestic one? She has an appointment with Planned Parenthood for a fitting on August 29. Will we ever know if she goes? Can't be earlier because it must be immediately after her cycle is finished. The baby seemed cleaner and perhaps 8½ pounds."

Years later as a professor of social work she reflected, "My relationship with Clayvon and tiny Sylvia woke me up to the shame and isolation of people living in poverty. When I met Clayvon, I assumed her situation must be an exception: surely, children were not starving to death in Columbia, South Carolina. Surely, if anyone knew of these conditions, they would act immediately. But our work together initiated me into the everyday world of human indifference in the face of suffering."

There was another resident of Black Bottom that summer whom we should have but may not have met. At the age of seven, Lugenia Key Hammond (1897-1991), eldest of thirteen sharecropper children, had been hired out for $1 a month as a maid to a plantation owner's wife. Half a century later in 1953, she and her husband bought a home in Black Bottom where she began helping neighbors with food, clothing, and advice. At some point she founded a preschool for children of working mothers. In 1966, with OEO assistance she started a community center in a small, former junk store near her house. It's possible SCOPErs assisted in early stages of this effort. Later Lugenia helped expand it in larger quarters, supported by volunteers from white Trinity Episcopal Church, where a priest encouraged civil rights efforts. An online tribute (*scafricanamerican.com*) says she helped bring about the 1971 annexation of Black Bottom by the city and its receipt of a HUD urban renewal grant that replaced dirt-floor homes like Clayvon Drayer's with public housing, a clinic and an expanded community center. Who knows but Phyllis' vision of a SCOPE house in Black Bottom might have linked us up with this remarkable grass-roots leader?

Lugenia Key Hammond
Courtesy United Black Fund.

Soon after finding Sylvia Rashonda, Phyllis also had taken up the broader medical segregation in the city. She met with NAACP Legal Defense Fund lawyer Marvin Mainer and came away with the impression that NAACP legal priorities were elsewhere, but it's likely the NAACP was and had been doing more than she understood, based on Bennie Glover's case and the NAACP's own range of tactics. Marvin referred her to the American Friends Service Committee and Salvation Army, but nothing further seems to have come of those connections. However, within a few years Columbia's public hospital was desegregated and, in some way, Mrs. Bruce had played a part.

A year or two after our project, Richland County treasurer Tom Elliott began hiring blacks for positions higher than custodian in county government. His first move was to recruit Ben Mack.

KERSHAW

11. Swanky Camden

Brandeis SCOPE spread out to Calhoun County in June, to Kershaw County in mid-July, but we'll follow the Kershaw group first. The girls who finally went there were Margot Thornton, Thais Courts, and Citti Allsup. The boys were roommates Bill Kornrich and Ricky Gurbst.

Two-thirds of the county's roughly 17,000 adults were white. Most of the 7,000 people in Camden, the county seat, were white as well, but the town had a longstanding black community, much of it "middle class," including a small cotillion/debutante level that paralleled white gentry patterns. Of about 5,900 potential black voters in the county, 3,600 were still not registered. Most blacks in the county were rural, and a sizable registration gap existed between them

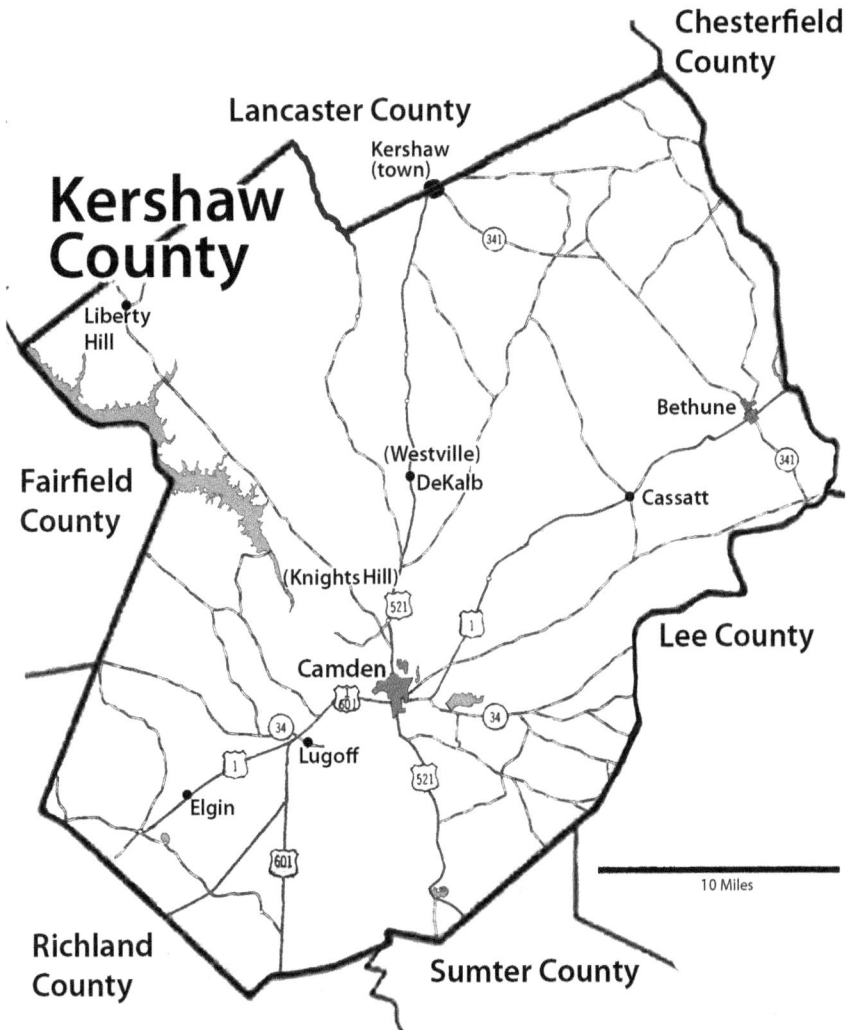

and blacks in Camden. If Bill Kornrich's information was correct, the Camden area and an outlying town called Kershaw were about the only town-like places where blacks were living.

The Congaree-Santee river system feeds that part of the state, and every county we were in had swamps. Kershaw County was the hilliest and must have had (still has) the largest stretches of woodlands and brush. In addition to farming and logging, the county had a long tradition of resort hotels for northerners lured down in the cooler months to pretty Camden's steeplechase, polo and thoroughbred racing. The town's main streets are broad, and there's lots of evidence of its role in the Revolutionary War.

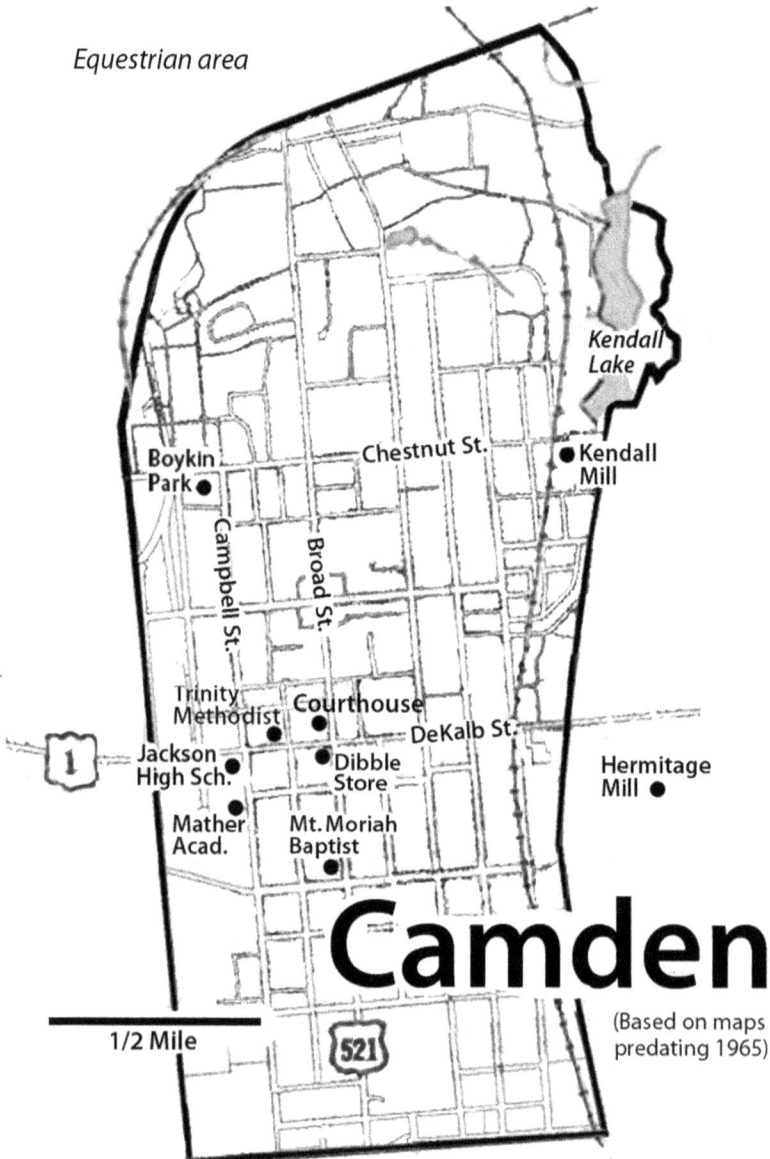

Equestrian area

Kendall Lake

Boykin Park ●   Chestnut St.   ● Kendall Mill

Campbell St.

Broad St.

Trinity Methodist   Courthouse

DeKalb St.

Jackson High Sch.   ● Dibble Store

Mather Acad.   Mt. Moriah Baptist

Hermitage Mill ●

Camden

1/2 Mile

521

(Based on maps predating 1965)

The masthead of the thrice-weekly *Camden Chronicle* boasted serving "South Carolina's most progressive area." Of course the paper also featured Sen. Thurmond's weekly column. Outside a small section for "Colored Citizens," the paper did not much specify race except when seeking "Colored newsboys to deliver the Chronicle." In all it was a reputation-conscious county paper reflecting Camden's genteel image.

Besides horse-breeding and tourism, the Camden vicinity had mills of various natures, mostly still textiles, and was working hard to attract more industry. The *Camden African-American Heritage Project* (quoted below) dates modern industrial Camden from 1950, when DuPont brought a synthetic Orlon fiber factory to nearby Lugoff. Hiring 1,300 workers, it became "a top employer in Camden and brought nearly 1,000 new residents to the area in the early 1950s." Its opening was "one of the most significant economic developments in the history of Camden; and one that directly impacted African Americans."

DuPont wages flowed into local business. "The city met increased housing needs by creating its first apartment homes and new housing developments. The growth also stimulated improvements such as paving the streets and creating sidewalk." With DuPont nearby, "Camden was no longer a small quaint town. It became more industrial and much busier. Several people remember DuPont workers acting amicably towards blacks, at least in comparison to other employers in the area."

Black economic conditions varied widely across the county. Around Camden it must have been better than in most any other town-sized Southern city. For decades, blacks had largely owned and occupied what is now called the Campbell Street Corridor on the west side of town. In antebellum Camden, several hundred residents had been free people of color, out of whom and postbellum freedmen, a substantial business district had grown, extending into the proper downtown. A leading black family, the Dibbles, had come to own extensive properties tenanted by whites or blacks, and filled business and professional roles beyond its two-story downtown general store, E.H. Dibble and Brothers. In 1965 Campbell Street also boasted a private black elementary and high school, Mather Academy (founded 1887) that still drew boarders from outside the county. Seventy years before us, I.S. Leevy had studied there on his way to college.

For sure DuPont's arrival bettered blacks, though it's doubtful that many of the "thousand new residents" it attracted were black or how many blacks got DuPont jobs in the 1950s. The *Heritage Project* says DuPont was "one of the first major industries in Camden to employ a large number of African Americans in non-service oriented jobs" but concedes that "due to the law prohibiting blacks and whites from working in the same room, they mostly worked menial jobs outdoors." Dupont's grounds crew was mostly black. The Heritage document doesn't say when the law against the mixing of races in indoor jobs had ended, but by 1965, DuPont was employing a sizable number of blacks "at its facility and surrounding grounds." Other corporations had also come down.

The founding of Camden NAACP in 1945 stirred up several years of KKK arson and armed attacks. Beginning in the 1950s, Camden NAACP had gone quietly door-to-door expanding the number of registered voters. In 1956 in the small town of Kershaw, after large rallies led by the Klan, a black family's home had been torched. Heavily white Kershaw County had been the only county in its congressional district to vote for conservative Republican Sen. Barry Goldwater for president in 1964. Goldwater had shared his campaign stage in the state with the South Carolina United Klans of America Grand Dragon, Robert Scoggin. Though Camden was hardly a stronghold, in the 1960s the Klan may still have been rallying on the east edge of town, near white housing for its cotton mills.

Bill and Ricky were buddies; the girls were not. Thais was much more adept socially than Citti, more at home in her body and aware of personal effect. Margot was more reserved than either, and her race would make her less of a draw for local black youths. As hinted some pages ago, there was also something going on between Thais and Bill. In young Lynn Goldsmith's view, these upperclassmen were an enviable couple, and she worried about their working together.

Elias faulted the five for choosing such a "middle class" county, though the "choice" had resulted mainly from aggressive recruitment by the reverends, endorsed by Ben Mack and Pat Gandy. Around June 25, Lynn Goldsmith and five others had attended an eight-hour picnic in Camden, mostly likely in Boykin Park on Campbell, sponsored by Gadsden's impressive Trinity Methodist Church. Lynn (whose words inform the next page or so) understood that the park—named after an admired black minister—was one that blacks were supposed to use. "It may not have been pretty there, but did we have fun!" she wrote. "Talk about Jewish mothers! The Negro mother beats her hands down. They make you eat it all."

It was chilly and windy; the music blasted. "Many girls danced together when they weren't doing line dances. We played games, and ran around entertaining the kids. My back ached from the piggy-back rides. As it turned out Rev. Curry's smaller Mt. Moriah Baptist Church in Camden (founded 1866) was also having a picnic, so we got to know some of the mothers." Also at the picnics were some students working with the NAACP, but plans fell through for a dance with teens that night.

On June 27, the Sunday of our leadership meltdown, Ben Mack drove Lynn and five others back to Camden for services at Curry's church and another chance to meet the congregation. Around then, Lynn understood from Ben that Kershaw was one of three counties "set up and ready to go, with a lot of work to be done." Overall, Camden struck her as "quite rural and nice. We were finished with the service so early we decided to go to another."

Left: What was then Trinity Methodist is now Camden First United Methodist. Right: Mt. Moriah Baptist. Its brick veneer postdates 1965.

At a following feast, "the kids all came to us and asked us if we wanted to integrate a place down the road called the Sandwich Box. They are all ready to go. Someone must come there to help them."

Things were looking good.

Later back at Gadsden's Trinity Methodist yet another picnic followed, interrupted by black clouds rolling in. "Buzzards wheeled in the still air, and we sang freedom songs on the porch. Suddenly we heard the giant drops falling, then pounding us as we hurried to get everything inside. The water dropped down like an ocean. The red clay was so rutted that the water immediately became rivers."

As things played out, Lynn didn't end up moving to Kershaw. Of the five who did, Phyllis was especially sad to see Citti go: "I canvassed with her today just to be with her a while before she leaves." Citti struck her as "an exceptionally warm, sensitive person with a lot of friendliness that seems able to penetrate further than most any I've seen—I would have loved to work with her in Black Bottom, but she wanted to desegregate restaurants, etc.—that kind of work is in Kershaw" (we thought). It was "not enough for Citti, but a challenge all the same." The likely truth is Citti still would rather have landed in Alabama.

Decades later, Kershaw SCOPEr Margot recalled being "the only African-American among white students in racially charged South Carolina. I felt safer, freer, and more at home when I worked alone. But that isolated me from the possibility of support from my peers. Moreover, there were some painful instances of racism among the students, some of which I brought up with the particular individuals but more that I kept to myself. I am thankful I was part of SCOPE, but it was challenging in ways that may elude the white participants." In reaction to Ish's questions, she asked, "How can we possibly write a single, truth-filled narrative when there are so many different voices, heard and unheard? This includes the people who lived in the communities where we were guests."

She's right, of course, and Ish lacks knowledge of the summer from their points of view. Most are now gone, and aging memories are hazy.

In an unreliable donated '55 Chevy with Massachusetts plates, SCOPE arrived in Camden the afternoon of July 12. By chance it was the monthly voter registration day; the next would be August 2. According to Bill's information at the time, six or fewer blacks had been registered in June. According to minutes kept by Margot, straightaway Rev. Curry took the SCOPErs to the courthouse to meet Sheriff David "Footsie" Hilton, who assured them of the town's full cooperation and doubted there would be any incidents. (He probably refrained from mentioning the hiring of two black deputy sheriffs, the first since Reconstruction.) The three registrars, added Margot, "were cautiously polite in the beginning, but as conversation continued they became warmer; I feel they shall be quite cooperative with the project." Thais remembers them seated at folding tables outside the courthouse.

The courthouse in the 1960s.
Courtesy Camden Archives.

For July '65 in Kershaw County, the VEP year-end tally shows no entry for black registrations, but a narrative from Bill at the time strongly implies that some folks registered on SCOPE's first day, and in 2015 he recalled a subsequent registration day for which they had time to canvas, saying the registrars were "generally pretty cooperative. There were a lot of people waiting in line outside the building for it to open."

SCOPE set up an office in Rev. Gadsden's church. The boys were housed by Rev. Curry, Margot by a Mrs. Kennedy, Thais and Citti by a teacher we remember only as Miss Dibble. NAACP leader Rev. William B. Gaither (with SCOPE that summer in North Carolina) says her first name was James, affectionately known to her friends as "Jimmie." Then in her sixties, she was a well-respected figure. Gaither says Kershaw SCOPE also had the support of Rev. George Wilson and his Camden Second Presbyterian, and Rev. Judge Clark and his St. Paul United Methodist in the Knights Hill area north of Camden.

SCOPE called an evening meeting for Thursday, July 15. It attracted about seventy kids who embraced ideas of canvassing and integrating various places. This led to a core of several dozen students regularly working with SCOPE. About half could canvass on their own. From this point, Kershaw SCOPE would experience an unsettling divide between eager support by black Camden youngsters and distanced caution from worried adults.

In the first few days, canvassing touched most black parts of the city. Margot recalls many years later, "Our days began early. We would get up and knock on every door and listen to what the people had to say, and we would encourage people to register to vote. We would hold mass meetings in the church, where the ministers would be in the leadership. It was very powerful. Religion and faith were such a strong part of the movement."

Thais remembers canvassing "down the road through the black community, house to

These Campbell Street homes look much as they did in the 1960s.

house. Sometimes it was rural. I'd be watching out for white people. And I was the color of the enemy—first time I realized that. When we approached a house, that's how they were looking at me. So what were we going to do?

"I needed to do more listening. I remember sitting on the porch with a lady in her fifties or sixties, talking about voter registration—how in the white parts of town all the streets were paved because they could vote their people in, while the black community didn't have paved streets and so forth. She said she would go, and I knew she was saying that because of who I was—this young white person who didn't even belong here and she was going to obey. That was a very strange, world-shifting feeling."

Thais, whose mother had grown up Christian in small-town South Carolina, also remembers the feel of churches she attended. "People got beyond themselves because they'd found the spirit, and I became really frightened because that's not something I'd ever seen before—that religion could have that kind of effect on people. Frightening but exciting. My experience before of religion had been that you kind of endure it. Since then I've met a bunch of people who have the black church in their background, including my husband. And I was amazed at the power of that church and at the bravery of the people."

The next week, while the boys were elsewhere, Margot and Thais and numerous young volunteers visited the homes of all unregistered blacks in Camden. Meanwhile Citti worked four days in a plantation area called Knights Hill a mile or so north of Camden, where she and Margot would also attend a revival. Citti also covered Westville, about fifteen miles up Route 521 from Camden, five miles short of the county line. Was she working alone up there or together with people from St. Paul United?

Together the three women canvassed Lugoff, about ten miles down Route 1 from Camden. They also covered Elgin (formerly known as Blaney but

Thais and Ricky. Photo Bill Kornrich.

renamed in honor of the watch company that had opened a plant there in 1963) and the small community of DeKalb about twelve miles north on 521. Around this time, Margot also started tutoring mornings at black Jackson High. By December, about a hundred of the county's 4,000 black students would be attending schools with whites, so Margot had joined two northern AFSC teachers, Margaret (or Margrit) Meyer and Sandra Fisher, to help them prepare.

Margot, Thais and Citti worked on other issues as well. One visited the Camden Head Start program and prepared a report for federal investigators. The program had been ordered to integrate by July 23, but as of the 22nd, it was still completely segregated by location and races of children and staff. One teacher had heard nothing about any plan to change that. The only sign of mixing was that on the 23rd two white teachers would begin weekly visits to the black Head Start for art and music. The SCOPE report noted so many books at the white Head Start that an overflow was parked in the hall, but few at the black one. It added that while the white children's library trips included the town's white-only public branches (there were two), the black children's trips were only to the much smaller Negro branch. (In some towns around the state some public libraries had already integrated, including Greenville in 1960, following arrests and lawsuits there. Kershaw's libraries would merge officially in 1973.)

Margot on a day off.
Photo Carol Sable.

12. BETHUNE

Meanwhile, during that same week Bill and Ricky took the Chevy north to farmland around the all-white town of Bethune (pop. 500). Quotes below come from a journal Bill kept of the week. In the 1940s the town had been a Klan stronghold, and most likely still was. It kept itself entirely white by now and then redefining its boundaries. Camden's HP Kendall textile company had built a scond plant in Bethune in 1956 that it had recently expanded.

Ricky and Bill stayed about four miles outside town with L.D. Mungo, a savvy farmer, illiterate beyond signing his name, and his wife Ellen. Their area had one of the lowest registration rates in the county, and Bill took delight in beginning something that sounded like the kind of work done in Mississippi the previous summer.

Along with two teens from Camden, they reached the Mungo farm about 10:00 a.m. "We pulled into the sandy driveway. I asked Ricky whether the white painted house was the one. It wasn't. We continued on a few hundred yards to a house of weather-beaten wood, rusty metal, and surrounded by farmland covered with cotton, tobacco, and beans." As they jumped out of the car, four or five young kids came to the door. They were frightened when the guys approached and introduced themselves, claiming they'd be staying there a while. Then Mrs. Mungo and the eldest son appeared, straightened things out, and settled Bill and Ricky in a large bedroom with double bed. As in many black homes, on the Mungos' living room walls hung a color portrait of the late John and Jackie Kennedy, a picture of Jesus and a china-plate portrait of Dr. King. The kitchen was about the size of Bill's family kitchen back home. Another room contained a TV, crib, bed, and stove. A bedroom had two double beds; another had three plus a single.

Ellen and L.D.
Courtesy of the Mungo family.

It took several days to learn all the kids' names. Nine children and four grands still lived there, ranging in age from months to 23. Three daughters had left the state. One son, Joe, lived nearby and worked a few days a week as custodian in the Negro schools, paid by federal money. Joe drove Ricky and Bill around, pointing out other black dwellings. Few blacks around Bethune owned land beyond what lay beneath their homes. The Mungos owned twenty acres on which they rotated cotton, beans, tobacco, potatoes, and black-eyed peas. They grew tomatoes, greens, and other vegetables for the table. L.D. kept chickens around the yard and "always at least one hog to provide meat for the family."

One afternoon Ricky and Bill tried plowing: "It takes a lot of practice with the ropes and plow before you can begin to keep a line straight. Mules are incredibly stubborn things. To me they are also ugly and smell bad." The Mungo boys laughed at their efforts.

The morning they arrived, Ricky, Bill and their co-workers from Camden began work near George Washington Carver Elementary, just outside the town. Their reception was "mixed, much different from that in Columbia or Camden. There had been no advance publicity. None of us had yet been to church there, and we were clearly white. People did realize we weren't from the South from our accent.

"That afternoon we put in a few more hours canvassing. People wave when you drive by. We feel a connection here more vital than in the urban areas where we had worked, a real sense of community; we are happy to be welcomed as much as we have been. We drove down the main street of Bethune, about three blocks long. We received some very inquisitive and piercing looks, most likely due to the presence of the two black teenagers in back. Can't please everybody."

They didn't like driving at night but had to return their co-workers to Camden, passing a café marked "Private Property Whites Only." Returning on US 1 was terrifying with dead give-away Massachusetts plates. They sweated as vehicles came up fast behind them, passed with their brights on, swerved toward the Chevy. The only security they imagined they had was a fake walkie-talkie with cord attached: "From behind, it looked exactly like a police or cab—a psychological plus for us. At least it could do us no harm."

En route back they were stopped twice by Highway Patrol for a missing tail reflector. The first trooper gave them a warning ticket; the second told them to fix it soon. Next morning in Bethune, where not everyone yet knew who they were, they were able to get that done.

That night and nights to come, they watched the TV news of riots and burning inner cities. "Along with that, and more so now, the disastrous news from Vietnam. Perhaps the reserves will be called up. All I can imagine is another Korea. God help us, because LBJ sure isn't. When will we ever learn?"

Tuesday they headed north a few miles and down a secondary road of about ten black homes. This took all morning. "We explain who we are, what we are doing, and why. We mention Dr. King, as this is an SCLC project."

Otis J., about 45, was working out in a field. They found him after going to his dilapidated, weather-beaten house where a 12-year-old girl was in charge. The mother was out working as a maid at $15 a week. Otis was a tenant farmer paying $15 a month for the house. "He was working about an acre of depleted land using a hand plow, not even a mule. His aged shoes were cut open to accommodate his toes. He was trying to cultivate corn, but it was dry and only about a foot high. There was no external water source. We couldn't see how anything could grow in that so-called soil. It appeared to be almost pure sand. Mr. J. was not aware of the concept of crop rotation."

Mr. J. could not read, write or sign his name. "He knew that there was something wrong with the conditions under which he lived, and he wanted to do what he could to improve his situation. Since he had almost nothing, he seemed not to be overly fearful. As we stood in the fields, a black VW drove by. A few minutes later the car returned from the other direction. After we left, we drove past his boss's house. The VW stood in the driveway. I hope Mr. J. doesn't have any trouble because of us.

"Later that morning we walked about a quarter mile into a cotton field and giant watermelon patch to an older woman working there. She earned $40 a month, with which she had to support herself and her 17-year-old grandson. The county health agency would not give her assistance for glasses or medication. The people at the agency told her she earned enough money to take care of that."

That second afternoon, AFSC tutor Margaret drove four kids out to work with them. "On our way to Margaret, our Chevy broke down, just stopped. We got the Mungos' car, and Joe pushed us along until Ricky could jump start ours. I made a running leap into it, so we wouldn't have to stop. We drove back into Bethune, but as soon as we stopped the car it would not start up again. Although we were hesitant about going to a white service station, we had no choice. They charged us $3 for some new wires and connections on the battery." Then, in pairs (Ricky and Lionel, Bill and Bill Sheppard, and Jessie Sutton and Nisi) they worked along Road 28-111 (Youngs Bridge Road) where almost no one was registered.

Meanwhile, "Margaret was driving around talking to parents of first graders about sending their children to previously all-white schools. This is in itself a large problem, with many arguments on both sides. By pushing integration, the federal government has caused problems for Negroes as well as whites. Some Negro kids, like John Mungo, are entering white schools in twelfth grade. This will be very uncomfortable for them. Margaret makes decisions on an individual basis as to whether parents should send their children to formerly white schools. Some factors are economic status, academic skills, available parental help, and distance.

Hungry, they walked into Truesdell's Drug Store on Main in Bethune, which had a lunch counter. Six seats were empty. Unfortunately, the group was made to understand that the counter did not serve Negroes, despite the suggestion in Margot's weekly SCOPE minutes that it had been serving Negroes the previous two days.

"As we sat down, the girl walked to the other side of the store. On her way back, the lights and fans started going off. A few white customers asked what was happening. The girl told us that the store was closing (4:00 p.m.), and we had to leave. We didn't argue. We walked outside and stood around until they locked the front door."

Still hungry, they drove a few minutes outside town on US 1 to Flynn's Truck Stop, which advertised itself every five miles from at least twenty miles away. Margot's minutes say the place had been recommended by a Negro. Bill thought they'd have no problems at this interstate business saying *Welcome Truckers*.

"We pulled up and, through the large glass windows, saw people eating inside. We walked to the front door to find it locked. We learned later that Flynn's is a 'back door' type of restaurant. I proceeded to frighten a few of the customers inside by whipping out a pen and paper and writing down information.

The people inside stopped their laughing. The 'segs' like these don't understand that we have the last laugh on them. All that is needed is a federal court order, which is easy to get. Non-compliance with this order results in a fine of several hundred dollars for each Negro turned away.

"We returned to town to buy something at a Piggly-Wiggly grocery. As we pulled into a parking space, the chief of police of Bethune pulled in next to us. He is a man named Faulkenberry who evidently had been thrown off the Camden police force. He wanted Ricky's license, auto registration, ownership papers, and more. He asked whom we were working for. Answer? SCLC, which he had never heard of." When asked for their address, Ricky or Bill gave "Camden, Trinity Methodist Church," since SCOPErs weren't supposed to reveal host names or addresses.

Bill out in the county with Mr. and Mrs. Gant. Courtesy Bill Kornrich.

"What were we doing here causing trouble? Answer: We aren't causing trouble, just getting people to register to vote. His response was, 'Well, those who look for something usually find it.' Why did we force Negroes to go into the restaurant? Answer: They wanted to go in to eat. He wanted to know if Pat Gandy (owner of car) was white or black. He told us to get out of Bethune and not come back. We yessir'ed him repeatedly. He followed us four miles out of town toward Camden before turning off."

Unfortunately, they'd been talking with Officer Faulkenberry on Main Street where whites could get a good look at them. "We drove a bit further and turned off on a series of back roads that bypassed town to get to the Mungos'. We decided never to go through town again." They also decided never to turn off Highway 341 into the Mungos' road if another car was in sight.

"Tuesday evening we drove to Camden at 7:00 for our second youth meeting. By about 8:00 there were almost a hundred kids inside. We sang a little, spoke about our Bethune experiences, and told the kids to wait another week before starting any direct action such as sit-ins, picketing or marches. It was so difficult for me to restrain these kids, to tell them to hold on; but we can't do anything without Rev. Curry in town. He wouldn't want to miss anything." A plus that night was Rev. Mungin's visit from Arthurtown: "a great speaker, reading his own poetry, telling the kids about non-violence, leading freedom songs, and speaking about standing up for one's rights. A lot of new kids attended."

By now the troubling pattern had crystallized of support from the kids, reluctance from most elders other than Curry and his preacher brethren. Later, after a surprise birthday party for Ricky at Trinity church, they moved over to Mather Academy gym for a dance and basketball game. Bill "had to be in charge of the dance, keeping all kids with shoes off the floor. There were more than a hundred. We are riding high with the kids."

"We left Camden at 10:45 p.m., a long ride home along dark US 1 with John and Willis Mungo in back. There were still a few establishments along the route with signs reading 'Whites Only.' We bypassed the town as usual."

Throughout the week, Bill digested his thoughts: "The key to getting people here to open up is using words that resonate with them: *Martin Luther King, JFK, civil rights worker*, and *Negro*. Emphasis on the last is important. The people have a deep, unspoken understanding of the racial suppression with which they have lived for generations. Some do not understand why we are involved in this voter registration work. To some it is a very radical idea and potentially dangerous. Yet they know the reality of their lives and that the winds of change are in the air.

"At first people are frightened. As they open up and determine that you are friendly and intend no harm, there is a bit of embarrassment. After a while, people invite you into their homes, regardless of the condition it is in. Most are quite willing to listen. At this point, the conversation becomes more open, and there is often an occasion to share personal stories. When you return for a second visit, acceptance and commitment to register are close to 100%.

"For some it is extremely difficult to have anything to do with us. As we walked up to one older home, we saw two elderly people out back. By the time we went around back to meet them, they were inside, doors and windows shut tight. I knocked and started talking, but gave up after less than a minute. We later were told that the woman was old, quite deaf, and very set in her ways. Maybe during another visit we will have more luck.

"We went to the home of another elderly couple who were sitting out front. Here we ended up talking for over an hour about all kinds of things. The man was illiterate, but his wife managed to fill out a registration form quite well. They gave us a large watermelon we shared with half a dozen Negro children who followed us around. At first the kids had mocked us a bit and laughed at us as a group. After we introduced ourselves and two teenagers from Camden working with us, they walked around with us and eagerly volunteered to show us where Negroes lived and told us their names. We had to harass and pretend to smack them a few times before they were able to call us 'Ricky' and 'Bill' rather than 'Yessir.'"

Bill found the adults friendlier than people in Columbia or Camden, but most knew little about the movement and especially the tenant farmers were frightened. "If we say something about how the Negro should be a first-class citizen, an automatic chorus of 'Yes, man!' or 'You're right! You're right!' erupts. We have spent several hours trying to think up questions that require 'No' answers. Many relegate everything we've said to an unconscious zone within minutes of our departure. One man's 'yessir' scenario and promises to register ended up by his throwing the form out the car window when he drove down the road and left our view.

"With persistence and enough visits, we may be able to get large numbers of people to the courthouse in Camden. Unfortunately, I am sure that if one local white person went around telling people not to vote in an election, even without threats, many would not. This is real fear, difficult for Ricky and me to comprehend, based on generations of experience. Both of us get so aggravated when we hear people say, 'Things are all right,' or 'I don't care about voting.' It makes us want to scream.

"Many people here are sharecroppers and maids working forty hours a week for $15. I have heard dozens of stories from women who never have enough to eat and work for a white woman for little or no pay. This is a totality, an integral reality. Growing up in a servile position with no opportunity can poison the mind and corrode one's ability to decide what options might be available. In fact, there are not many at this time.

"The mentality manifests itself in so many small but painful (at least to me) ways. An educated woman says she doesn't need to register because she has electricity, running water, and her kids are all up north. A man in his forties says he won't register because the whites don't want it. Another man works from Monday morning to Friday evening shining shoes, cleaning spittoons, and sweeping floors for white men. From Friday night to Sunday night he is drunk and lashes out at white people and how badly he is treated. I think of this in some ways as a 'newspaper boy' mentality, as so many Negro boys and girls deliver papers as their first job. They learn to 'yessir' and 'yes, ma'am' at an early age. Obsequiousness is a survival skill."

With John Mungo on Wednesday they visited shacks around a hamlet called Cassatt, driving "all over God's country—through forests, over sandy road, past swamps. We stomped out into cotton fields and watermelon patches searching for people. A lot of folks here don't understand why they should vote. Some feel hopelessly disconnected from the world around them.

"We spent our lunch topping tobacco. People driving by stared in amazement at whites and blacks working together in the fields. Good suntan weather for sure. You feel like honest-to-goodness civil rights workers out in the fields trying to make people realize an opportunity is available, making friends, and evading all contact with local whites.

"We returned home for another great southern supper, talking, watching TV and playing with the kids. I spent more time talking with John. He wants to attend Penn State, but it is doubtful he could be accepted. John is a thinker and a talker. He showed me a very creative piece he had written on tolerance of other people's beliefs, religious and philosophical. I thought it was extremely sophisticated considering the educational opportunities he has had. I think he will do okay next year when he integrates Camden High."

Thursday they followed mail routes for Kershaw town, Bethune, and Jefferson. "You get to feel really at home talking to a woman peeling peaches for canning or shelling peas or even just sitting around. A lot of older people never get to relate much to others. Often they live alone. Civil rights workers are perfect 'targets' for stories about World War I, slavery days (from their grandparents), trips here and there, or grandchildren and great-grandchildren.

"Martha Lee J., on Highway 341, was outside waiting for the mail. Practically illiterate, why was she waiting for the mailman? She has a 12-year-old grandson who stays at her house during the school year. The boy and his family are from New York City, and they want their son to go to school in Kershaw County rather than New York. She has received one letter from them all summer. She had recently received a form from the county school system for her grandson, but she couldn't read the form and answer the questions. She was waiting for 'Mr. USA' [the mailman] for help. We went through the form with her, assisted her in completing it. Now, whenever we pass by, she smiles and waves. She is invariably sitting in front of her little house.

"We also met Mr. G., a wonderful veteran of World War II. He loves to joke and laugh, has a great sense of sarcasm and can catch you off guard. We spent about an hour with him. It's hard to tear yourself away from people like him, and there is no reason to hurry off.

"Thursday evening it happened again—the car stopped. We pushed it to a friend's house a quarter mile from the Mungos. Mr. M. and Joe fooled around under the hood but couldn't get it running. It was already 8:00. We couldn't get in touch with any Negro mechanics that late, so we left it in Mr. Mungo's driveway, went home, and spent a quiet night. Friday morning we woke up with the roosters and the Mungos at 6:00. Joe, who lives a half mile up the road, had already left home so we went towards town to find a mechanic. Mr. _____ is about sixty but in great shape physically and mentally. He spent an hour exploring before he found the cause of our most recent problem: a wire from the battery to the generator had been cut. He taped it together.

"You could tell Mr. _____ was an old timer. He pretty much took the car apart with a screwdriver and a wrench. He's been a licensed mechanic for thirty years. He told us about his bootlegging days. He stopped because he could no longer outrun police cars after they installed radio-telephones. One of his comments, between much swearing and muttering, was that the car was 'makin' more noise 'n a noisy preacher.' A really great guy, and he fixed the car. He drove us back into town and picked up a white guy he knew. It was a tense situation for us, but nobody said anything. I'm sure the latter knew we were civil right workers. I didn't want to go into town, but we had to get permanent tape at the gas station. Mr. _____ charged $3.50 for over an hour's work. Hopefully, the Chevy will decide not to quit on us again.

"As we had awakened so early (for us), we headed out by 9:00. Willis, Ricky, and I canvassed north off SC 341 to the outskirts of Kershaw town. There are mostly tenant farmers in this area, most of whom open up wonderfully after ten or fifteen minutes. We came upon a family in a brick house. They were quite unfriendly. We berated them a bit. I don't know whether we aggravated them enough to get them to register. There were four adults in the house. Two had previously registered; the other two weren't interested.

"One close call. Not knowing exactly where Negroes lived, we drove down a typical dirt drive and arrived at a typical old wooden house. The doors were open. No one was around. We paused to enjoy the beautiful landscape of fields, trees, hills, valley, and sky. We took photos and slowly drove back out to the road. As we began accelerating, a car pulled into the drive, no doubt the occupants of the house—white. We felt quite lucky. You can never tell what will happen.

"After lunch we decided to help work the Mungos' tobacco, a new experience for us. Out in the sandy fields, five of us took off between two and five yellowish leaves from the bottom of the stalk. We piled them up in our arms and dropped them on a cart-like sled the mule pulled around. Back at the house the whole family helped tie the leaves in groups of four or five onto poles about a yard long. We took 24 of these long sticks, piled them into two carts, and drove them to the shed where we hoisted them onto hanging racks. In this shed the leaves are heated and dried. We closed all the doors and hatches about a minute before it started to pour.

"Since it was raining so hard, we decided to stay home. It would have been foolish to drive on the wet dirt roads and catch a cold or pneumonia (this from Mrs. M.) going house to house. Nature is still the ruler, even for civil rights workers. We wrote, talked and watched TV.

"Friday evening we drove into Camden again, this time to see Dean Zion who came to visit. We dropped off John and Willis at the Canteen, as we wanted to see the dean and Elias alone. They had brought three [real] walkie-talkies, some money, sample forms, and note cards. So, we are KOY 2111 for the rest of the summer. We demonstrated the walkie-talkies for the kids. Some went in a car with Ricky while I stayed inside. They were really amazed at the equipment. Great playthings—too bad they are completely useless. The late ride home was rather nerve-wracking—John and Willis with us—but we made it with no trouble. When car lights came up from behind, it was always frightening." He was thinking of Goodman, Chaney, and Schwerner.

Early Saturday morning they picked beans for an hour or so, then shelled them inside while watching ridiculous TV quiz shows.

"About 11:30 we left to recanvass a few houses. Mrs. _____ yelled out, 'Hello, Ricky and Bill,' as we passed her house. We lined up a few people for the August 2 registration. Mrs. _____ called me away from another woman and asked if we were going to demonstrate in Bethune. I reassured her we wouldn't. You could see the fear in her eyes. She thought that the Selma march was wonderful, but too much was at stake to do something similar in her home community." She was asking because Hosea Williams had announced on TV that there would be demonstrations in the seventy counties SCOPE was in if the *Voting Rights Bill* wasn't law by August 1.

That same weekend afternoon Kershaw SCOPE paid a social call on the group in Calhoun County. For Bill the drive back home was beautiful. "The scenery down here is great. There is growth like crazy all over the place, advancing as far as the edge of the paved highway and occasionally over the edge. Saturday night we spent with the Mungos as usual. We brought two presents: a can opener and the 'Beatles IV' album. They were overjoyed with the latter—the kids, that is."

On Sunday they fanned out to revivals and churches, including one just over the border in Lancaster County. "The preacher was fantastic. His language was incomprehensible, but his gestures made his message obvious. John and Willis said that he often goes through six or seven handkerchiefs during a sermon. I was asked to give a speech on behalf of our group. People clapped, but I don't know how much they understood." Bill guessed he'd find out on August 2.

Sunday afternoon they also attended a wedding—"a beautiful affair in Chesterfield County" in the groom's parents' home. "Mr. M. looked quite calm, as usual. This was his fourth daughter married, so he probably was becoming accustomed."

Bill's presence at the wedding was good. From that summer on, he and his own future family would be considered a branch of the Mungos. Mid-August when the new *Voting Rights Act* made it possible for L.D. to register, Bill would find him first in line.

13. MELTDOWN

After Bill and Ricky returned to Camden, the week with the Mungos must have seemed like a dream. The week of July 26, the reunited five resumed canvassing in Camden and elsewhere preparing for August 2. A meeting for Camden adults on the 29th drew only fifteen, but most were "quite enthusiastic." So there was a range of opinion of SCOPE in adult Camden. Meanwhile, the AFSC tutors were winding up and shortly heading home.

Then on Saturday the 31st, Citti and Thais were deported back to Columbia at the insistence of Camden blacks. KZSU tape from August 6 captures the two guys' summary of what had gone down. The taping went on when Margot joined them but ended soon after Elias and Rev. Curry walked in.

On the tape, the boys largely agree. At the outset, Bill explains that in Camden "the white people, the police are on our side. You know, they just don't want any trouble. They'll arrest anyone who gives us trouble. The county clerk, we sort of have a standing agreement that any day we can get fifty people to register, he'll keep the courthouse open. They don't want any trouble."

The skyline of old downtown Camden today is about like it was.

The three were struggling to mobilize older Camden youths. In Bill's view, "The more intelligent kids and the ones who would be more interested in what we're doing here this summer have gone north to get a good job. The kids that are left are mostly younger, fifteen and sixteen—almost no older kids—and they don't have any conception of what the movement is. It would be unfair to expect them to. We have meetings every Tuesday night, about a hundred at every meeting. But as far as expecting concrete work, you know, it's their summer, and they're not interested. They want to have fun. They want to go swimming, play games and mess around. Quite often we assume the position of camp counselor rather than civil rights worker."

Short two of its members, Kershaw SCOPE had also run out of cars. They'd had two, but the Chevy had broken down on registration day; another had been wrecked accidentally by young, well-meaning Jessie Sutton. "We had commitments all over the county," said Ricky. "We put 250 miles on the car. The last trip coming back in, at a quarter of five, we had three ladies. About 700 yards from the courthouse it stopped (laugh), and the ladies ran. They got there about 5:03"—too late.

Since then, Bill continued, "We've been re-canvassing the city again and again, and trying to get hold of a car." The community wasn't forthcoming, he thought, "because they're reasonably well off, economically, and have most of what they want in a way. You know, they have a beautiful park out there," he said, probably referring to a different one than Boykin. "Their park's much better, so they never go to the white park. They have it good. They have their own restaurants, and Miss Dibble owns several stores downtown. We had another mass meeting for adults, and we had twelve people there after passing out 800 handbills."

Ah, youth! It was much as Ricky Schaffer had found in Columbia, and Kornrich and Gurbst were at least as eager to make something happen faster than the adults would allow. Bill said it was "really hard to get anything moving."

They were thinking of demonstrations but feared the effect on a registration day coming up August 16. Ricky agreed that any disturbance before then would frighten most people away. He cited Newberry County where, after the SCOPE volunteer had been beaten, only 22 people showed up. "Demonstrations have to be properly planned," he said, "and about the right thing. Elderly people don't want any trouble. They don't like the idea of kids running around, and anybody getting hurt."

Ricky went on, "And how do you tell a 75-year-old woman—there's a lot of them here—with granddaughters visiting her for the summer and they're working with us, how do you tell her that her house isn't going to be burned down by the Klan? It's the whole way they've been brought up."

Ricky had wanted a haircut. The town had "four barbershops with Negro barbers, on one side of the street. One of 'em cuts white hair, so no Negroes go into that."

He entered a less-crowded shop for blacks and sat down in a chair: "A guy walked over and said, 'You want a haircut?' I said, 'Yeah, I want a haircut, please.' He looked at me and said, 'But you're white!' 'Yeah, I know, but I'd like a haircut.' He said, 'Well, they won't like it.' I said, 'What do you mean they won't like it? The law won't like it? It's against the law to cut my hair?' 'No, but they won't like it.' I said, 'You mean, the white people won't like it.' 'Yeah.' So all of his friends in the barbershop told him to cut my hair. I said, 'Are you afraid that something's going to happen to you? If so, don't cut it. It's up to you.' He said, 'Well, I'd rather not.' That's the kind of thing that runs with the old people. They told me to go next door. When I went next door, a young kid was going to cut my hair; he just said he was busy."

A third dwindling resource was ministerial backing. Suddenly, "Now we're only working with one minister because the other one threw us out of his church and the other one's out of town." And though Rev. Curry was still in the game, his deacons (his employers) were not.

What had happened? Why, after two weeks, had adult support dropped away and Thais and Citti been expelled?

One factor was a restless, premature move by the SCOPErs a few days after July 20. Their target was a Camden movie house where blacks had to sit in the balcony. On their own, the SCOPErs decided to quietly integrate the ground-floor seats. In 2015 Bill remembered how he, Thais and Ricky went to see "The Great Locomotive Chase," taking along David Lennix, a big kid about age thirteen whose parents had given permission.

"We sat halfway down on the main floor, Ricky and I on opposite ends, figuring that this would give the most protection to David and Thais. Perhaps that was not the best thought, as it put a white woman next to a black male, but I don't think any configuration would have resulted in a different outcome.

"There is some murmuring and laughing as we sit down. The movie goes on for a while. A few pieces of popcorn are thrown at us from behind. More murmuring. Then down the aisle comes a very large white guy, furious and hollering at us to get out. At first we pretend to ignore this, but he gets right next to the row and appears prepared to come towards us. As it is clear he wants us to leave, and as we feel very responsible for David, we decide to go. As we do, people laugh and some clap. The guy stands there. We get out of the lobby to the ticket booth to get our money back. There is no one in the booth or anywhere else. So we go to the police and tell them what happened."

The police did nothing. At first Rev. Curry wanted to return in greater numbers. On second thought he realized, says Bill, "You don't go back when you know that you're standing alone and you may lose your congregation, and you'd have no one else in the city with you. We're paralyzed. Here's a guy who wants to lead but doesn't have any followers."

They weren't faulting Curry, "who has entered restaurants, and has guns put to his head, and is ordered to leave and keeps going back. He's not afraid of anything. Like he said to us when the trouble was in Allendale County [where Wayne State University SCOPE] was working, 'Let's go and help them out there,' but he just can't, here; he's put us in his church, never asking the congregation, and Bill and I live at the parish house. He's stuck his neck out plenty. He just can't do it alone."

They did fault leaders outside the clergy. At the meeting that had drawn twelve adults, attendees had included a dentist NAACP precinct leader for registration. There also were the mother of three boys working with SCOPE, her friend, and three elderly people "who live around here, who just happened to come." Arriving late was a funeral director (almost certainly the head of Collins Funeral Home, a Camden landmark). According to Ricky the director had run for city council and lost by 200 votes. Sometimes SCOPE could borrow a car from ordinary folk, but this man was "the biggest disappointment we've met. Absolutely doing nothing, won't get us a thing. He has nine cars in his funeral home. We asked him for money for gas; we've asked him for a car, and he just doesn't do anything. The dentist, too, just won't go any further."

Bill isn't sure what happened at the theater after their challenge over the seating. He thinks it reopened a day or two later with open seating. Whatever the outcome, the incident heightened fears among Camden's adult blacks.

Thais and Citti's expulsion was fueled in part by Miss Dibble's disapproval of the action at the movie house, but more by mounting sexual rumors. Some versions alleged misconduct in SCOPE's office in the church. According to Lynn, "No incidents have happened between Bill and Thais except one. The rumor that they had been making out in the church was false. It stemmed from some Negro kids being out in the field behind the church. The one incident was one time when Bill and Thais happened to be in a room together. No one knew about it except Rev. Curry." Thais told Lynn the reverend may have been "a little angered that the girls have not yielded to him."

Based on experience, Ish can imagine how Curry might have stumbled on Bill and Thais less than vertical in the parish house. Frankly, where else could they relax? For ten weeks, privacy was rare for anyone in Brandeis SCOPE,

Collins Funeral Home today on West DeKalb, across from Trinity Methodist.

though some seized moments when they could, as Ish and Phyllis had done. Living outside churches, Elias and Kathy must have done, too; at the end of July they announced their engagement.

But it wasn't just that. By separating from the girls for a week, Bill and Ricky had probably raised risk to Thais and Citti's reputations, and the two girls had not shied away from talking with one or two local youths who were viewed askance by some black adults. In Margot's distant recollection, one of the young men had been accused of rape; Thais thinks this was not the case. But in any case folks were noticing. Maybe Citti's going alone to Knights Hill and beyond also raised talk. More scandalously, one night at a revival she caught a ride home to Miss Dibble's with a young black guy. Pulled over in front of or standing on Miss Dibble's porch, he and Citti talked for several minutes. Next morning, word was they'd been making out.

According to Lynn, rather than confronting Citti, Miss Dibble complained to Rev. Gadsden "who told Rev. Curry, who told Thais, who told Citti she was upset." Gadsden's Trinity congregation then pressured Gadsden to remove SCOPE from the church and distance himself, leaving all the weight on Curry. "Then Citti went out canvassing alone and got picked up by the police—stupid!" Also, at some other moment, when confronted by a white man she thought was police, Citti revealed Miss Dibble's address as the place where she was staying.

The SCOPErs thought the lurid rumors had to do with both fear of reactions from whites and jealousies among black women.

Thais' view of these events has changed over the decades: "Lynn is right: we were incredibly naive, so this didn't really sink in far enough to make us more discreet." However, she adds (in line with Bill's reflection on SCOPE), "A big part of the value of SCOPE was introducing local black people to whites who behaved like friends."

According to Margot's minutes, on Saturday July 31 Miss Dibble "became very disturbed because it wasn't safe" for Citti, Thais or Miss Dibble, and asked them to leave. At stake was reputation. To Miss Dibble, wrote Lynn, the girls were like daughters, but she lived alone, had status in the community, and wanted them to uphold it." Near the end of the August 6 KZSU tape, Rev. Curry enters and supports this general account, adding that he had not been able to find anywhere else for them to stay. Pressured by the fear around him he agreed with a subsequent order by Ben and Hosea that either Citti and Thais return to Columbia or all five SCOPErs had to go.

On the tape Ricky speaks for the group in still admiring Miss Dibble, who had tried to help and continued to be "active in a way; they had their first biracial committee meeting in Camden history last week, and she's on this committee. Very nice lady; very nice. She housed the two girls, worried about what would happen if the whites found out they were living in her house, the trouble that would come of it. She'll give you food and take you around to people. She's interested, and she has sympathies with us, and she's registered and votes. She teaches school and does her part."

As an elder now herself, Margot laments our youthful brashness and our inability to recognize that leadership takes many forms. Our perceptions, she sees now, were "clouded by our being outsiders and unaware of the nuances in the community." In retrospect she considers Jimmie Dibble "a radical fighter for human rights." Incidentally, within a few years a younger Dibble would become a trustworthy investment advisor to Muhammad Ali, and to the Nation of Islam.

B y August 6, Bill and Ricky felt a need to do more than register voters. Now Bill saw direct action as the only way to "get the community organized." There were things in town that might inspire a demonstration. For example, no swimming pool was open to blacks, and the YMCA was white. Tony's restaurant on DeKalb was still not serving blacks. When the owner had been fined $300, he'd put up a sign saying, "All money received from Negroes will go to the Ku Klux Klan." Pines Drive-In also still held out into 1966, when both places yielded to federal orders. Ricky said the Piggie Park on US Route 1 down at the Richland line was also still segregated, though concessions had been made at some other Piggie Parks. The SCOPErs had been prodding Camden blacks about slow implementation of the 1964 *Civil Rights Act*. "About half the people" didn't know about it, didn't "know what it did in opening up chances for employment, against discrimination—that you can't deny a colored person what you give a white."

Thais and Citti had visited the county hospital and seen it still placed white patients in a better section than blacks, but from the US attorney general they learned the case was already in court and federal examiners were coming.

But other things should happen. Bill understood that two large firms didn't employ any blacks at all: Jaclyn Hosiery Mills (founded 1947) and McLean Trucking Company. "Negroes have applied there, and we're waiting to see the result." He and Ricky regarded black DuPont employees as apathetic because they thought they had it good. Margot, who entered the room about then, disagreed with that characterization.

Ricky lamented black acceptance of inferior schooling at Jackson High compared with all-white Camden High. "We tell them how important it is, on and on. And the thing you run into canvassing, they just say, 'Yes, sir, yes sir, yes sir, yes sir,' and then you close the door and they go back to watching television. It's unwillingness to change and push. We get upset; we yell at people and tell them how rotten things are."

He found some blacks "just as dead set against sending their kids to integrate the schools as the whites. 'No, I'm not sending my kids there; I'm not going to have my kids going with white kids.' And it's completely in the mind. It'll take a really long time. The problem in the movie theater will be solved; but I doubt if any summer project like SCOPE will ever solve this."

Bill and Ricky understood that, a couple years back, the Junior NAACP had "kind of broken away and tried their own boycotts and things." But right now, in their opinion, the NAACP was moribund apart from "little meetings in winter. They could do a lot more during the school year, when there are many more kids here, two or three times as many as now."

The awkward but positive truth behind our short-run project seems to have been that NAACP legal efforts and moves by white authorities to keep Camden a reputable town were in fact churning out a measured progress on key things like the integration of public schools, which would begin that fall. Near the end of their radio interview, Bill or Ricky conceded that things were changing, "and really not so slowly."

Still, it was hard to let go the hope of speeding things up. They still thought the younger kids could push more boldly. The younger kids were great, said Bill. "They won't stand for anything. Of course, the way they don't stand for anything is violence, usually. There's a lot of fights between whites and Negroes. We've been trying to explain nonviolence to the kids. We can get them to sort of understand how it will be against their interests to start fighting with whites if they were to hit us while demonstrating. But so far, in a demonstration [if white kids hit them] we know they'd go for the white kids, summarily beat them to death if they can."

In a street conversation with Ricky, "This Negro kid says, 'Okay, say three white boys jump us here. Would you fight back? Or would you be nonviolent?' Tough question. I said, 'Look if a guy jumps us and there's a cop standing there, I'd be nonviolent. But if it's an alley, and three against three, maybe I'd hit back. Otherwise I'd get killed.'

"This didn't get through because they can't figure out about cops yet. So they'll say to you, 'Why? I agree with your nonviolent ideals, but if anybody ever spits on me, I'll kill him.' And the other kid says, 'Well, I don't mind spitting, but if anybody ever kicks—I hate being kicked. Then I'll hit him back.' And the third guy says, 'I don't mind any of that, but as soon as they hit a girl, I'm going to hit back.' Each one will take so much, but they don't understand it and they haven't been used to using it. And even the leaders, one carries a gun if he ever goes down anyplace."

Bill was willing to bet that "if some kind of project would stay all year round, you could get somewhere. I mean if you could get anyone white to stay and work this thing like we're working this summer." Bill wished he could do that, but the draft stood in the way.

"What we try and do with our Tuesday night meetings is explain to the kids how they can organize. We delegate as much responsibility as we can so that when we leave it won't just end. We take kids out canvassing with us and show them our filing system, and maybe teach a few how to type. Rev. Curry will let them use this office."

Ricky would have liked to spend a whole future summer there just with the kids, not doing any kind of civil rights. And he wished there were some way to "get the adults to look at the kids as people who are capable. They say, 'Oh these are kids and won't be able to do anything.' We try to explain that *these kids* do all the work and are good. They know what they're doing. They come and tell us how they can't get into this restaurant and this lunch counter, you know.

"I don't think these kids can handle the leadership by themselves, but if the adults would help out, maybe you could get something going. We just can't get 'em together. You can't have kids at this meeting if adults are there, because kids are kids, and that doesn't go. It's this crazy kind of thing. 'No, you can't do that, because they won't like that,' or 'you can't have too many meetings because my deacon board won't like that, and you can't have just kids because the kids make too much noise.' Every way you turn you get blocked."

Overall, the guys told KZSU, Camden blacks had it "very well—not equal but you drive around and see houses getting painted, people building new ones to replace the old wood shacks. Downtown is still pretty segregated; you get glares when you walk in, and at some counters they just won't serve you. If three of *us* went in, they'd serve us because they're afraid of us. But it's a town that's changing. It really is much more the changing South than Columbia." Then the boys confessed to the radio team, "You hit us on our down-in-the-dumps day. Today and yesterday we've been so terribly depressed. Monday we were really high." Ricky ended, "I do think the goals were a little high."

14. HOLD ON

Monday, August 2, had been their latest registration day. With the courthouse open from 9:00 to 5:00, more than fifty Camden public school students had canvassed door to door. Almost all of the forty registrants who'd requested rides showed up to take them. In all, by SCOPE's count, 110 blacks and one white registered. The front page of *The Camden Chronicle* reported 105 including two whites. The article mentioned county clerk Ed Ogburn's saying this was the highest number in about eighteen months.

Inside the *Chronicle*, the community section by and for blacks thanked the registrars and credited Rev. Curry and SCOPE for most of the turnout. Per Margot's minutes, local adults and young people drove people in and encouraged more to register. The registrars were "extremely co-operative; they were lenient, pleasant and processed six at a time." Fifty years later she doubts she meant all that: "If I said 'extremely cooperative,' it was because in those days I often said what I thought people wanted to hear." Still, some people the SCOPErs had thought unlikely to pass the literacy test did pass. Not transporting people whose chances were slim had kept the success rate high, though seven failures were brought in by one of the reverends, who hadn't checked them out beforehand.

A day or two later, Bill and Ricky relaxed with "an act of reverse integration," swimming in a nearby mud hole with some of the kids. They also tried to talk with the Camden YMCA about its membership policy, but the director was away. By Friday they were back out canvassing for August 16, hoping that even if the registrars didn't remove the literacy test, as required by the new *Voting Rights Act*, if they found a car, they might be able to bring in another hundred.

"That means, I guess," said Ricky, "about August 14 we'll go back again to remind these people. I guess it was worth the three of us plus about six kids going house to house yesterday." The three would hang onto the plough.

The August 6 tape ends with the arrival of Rev. Curry and Elias and some dispute that is hard to decipher. Bill and Ricky complain about once again having no car; Elias replies that, though cars do not rain down from heaven, he will provide another. He also warns them to stay in closer touch with Rev. Curry.

With the next car, Margot, Ricky and Bill had surprising success not only on the 16th, 21st and 22nd, but also in an early September legacy effect. On the 9th the trio canvassed Kershaw town, each paired with a local youth. "We covered much territory and were well received in the city which has a reputation for being quite backward in race relations, getting many transportation commitments." The police detained but found no cause to hold them. Next day, the team was out again.

The Kershaw SCOPErs themselves have left no record of what they did after that, but Lynn recorded her impressions on driving up from Calhoun County on the evening of Friday August 6 to haul them south for a Saturday holiday on the coast. She was glad to see Ricky and Bill, who were staying in Rev. Curry's "beautiful, wall-to-wall carpeted house." But she wasn't allowed to linger inside with them: "Gee, they have a tense situation. They can't do a thing. I see why Citti and Thais were such a problem. Every move they made would be suspected. They couldn't be in the house alone or with someone."

August 16, Lynn drove up again with Ish to help with registration. She found "excitement even as we got there, ten minutes after the books opened. The *Voting Rights Bill* was effective. No one filled out a blank—the registrars did them all! People didn't even have to write their names. The line was moving right through." By now registration was inside the building (most likely in the regular basement registration office) rather than at tables outside. "The line waits outside, and each person enters through something that can't quite be called a door."

Bill sent Lynn off with "an incredible old gentleman who talked my ear off all morning. Mr. Sasportas appears to be white but is Negro—I noticed a very large number of people who could pass as whites. It must be very disconcerting when canvassing. I learned Mr. Sasportas' family history—he's French—and listened to history and poetry. He knows a poem for everything. I must say, he's very obnoxious—nice though, and bought me a Coke while we went around fetching people. The car crept along while Mr. Sasportas talked and pointed things out. I didn't think we should be sightseeing, although Camden is pretty."

"At noon I was separated from my dear friend—thank God! Next we took a cavalcade of cars out into the county. The Kershaw group uses a different method in picking up people. They go into an area and prepare the people, and then go back and pick them all up. This eliminates sitting in a half-full car waiting for someone to get ready. The people in Kershaw are ready and waiting when we come to pick them up. They even wait patiently for hours when we are late. They dress in their Sunday best to go register. We got three carloads of people.

"I began to take people home. The last load was so full I had to take them by myself to the town of Kershaw, twenty miles away. Everyone waited for me to get back." The Kershaw trio "bragged as we all left the courthouse that they were going to Columbia for a picnic—and all I had all day was half a root beer and a Diet-Rite Cola. Damn them. However, the day was most successful, and couldn't have been done without the help from Calhoun: 213 people were registered!—double last day's figures." Of that number, 205 were black.

Lynn helped out again on August 20-21, Kershaw SCOPE's last registrations. Late Friday afternoon she made it to Camden "in record time," bringing two others including an Orangeburg high school student, Gerard Williams. Registration was going fairly well. "Our first mission was to go downtown and pull people off the street. Pete, Gerard and I parked the car. The two boys wanted to go to a pawn shop—they needed some money—which ended in nothing. It wasn't hard to locate the Negro end of town. Friday evening (about 5:30) brings everyone out on the streets. We stopped for some slush and talked to a man who had just been to the courthouse. Gerard and Pete didn't want to talk.

"Bill was at the courthouse by the time we got back. Gerard and I went with him to get people. Again we came back with an empty car. Some kids came by with the news that they had found a great place to get people. They jumped in the car and directed me to a little 'joint' with blaring rock 'n roll, and people oozing out. The car was surrounded, and all we had to do was pull some in. They kept eyeing me, and the men told me they would register if I was going down there. I was glad to get away."

A little before seven that evening Lynn and Gerard drove several ladies back to Kershaw town. Returning after an hour, finding no one waiting for them at the courthouse or Rev. Curry's, they headed home nonstop.

Here's a summary of the summer SCOPE project in Kershaw County. It had been started by two courageous local ministers without real support from their deacons and flocks. Lacking that, SCOPE had turned to the kids, in keeping with the idea that it was really black youth making things happen. But Camden was no college town, and it was summer, so the group never found a core of older students to work with. They did gather a large, contributing younger set.

As of June 1, 1965, about 2,400 blacks were registered in the county. At the end of 1965 the VEP reported the following monthly additions.

August	596
September	228
October	11
November	7
December	5
Total	847

The August number must include July and maybe also June. Does September show "pent-up demand"— people formerly held back by the literacy test? But in that case, we should have seen pent-up effect in Richland County, which we didn't. To Ish, the Kershaw numbers show that in only seven weeks, the small SCOPE team and their counterparts brought home about 800 new voters. But it's sad to see how things petered out by October. Things really would remain in the hands of the NAACP.

Banished at the start of August, Thais and Citti returned to Richland County where Elias recalls telling them that Brandeis SCOPE had voted for their withdrawal, and so he was sending them back to New England. Phyllis wrote that the vote went the opposite way, at least about sending them home. When they balked, Elias told them they couldn't stay in Richland; nor in Calhoun, it being, he told them, "an independent unit altogether." Then he passed on a modified order from Hosea that disassociated Citti and Thais from SCOPE but allowed that individuals could do as they pleased. So Citti and Thais migrated to Orangeburg and the Columbia University gang. At least once, they also returned to Camden. Their moves boosted cooperation between Kershaw, Calhoun and Orangeburg SCOPEs for canvasses and registrations.

Citti, 1968.

Of the 23 veterans of Brandeis SCOPE, Citti is the only one Ish couldn't locate. He does know that by 1968 she was deeply involved in resistance to the Vietnam War through the New England Committee for Non-violent Action. In that year she was part of a group of six women burning the draft cards of male war resistors, as a way of sharing their legal peril. The last Ish saw of her was in Pittsburgh in 1969 where she'd come to win over white blue-collar workers.

CALHOUN

15. UNITER

Remember Hope Williams Jr., the 55-year-old farmer from Fort Motte. Ish should call him "Mr. Hope." That's what South Carolinian Elizabeth Robeson calls him, referring to conversations they shared in the 1990s when she was researching the life of Julia Peterkin. It's a common form of respectful address. But Ish started out in Pennsylvania and wound up in California, so formality doesn't dance off his tongue.

Maybe the five SCOPErs who got there before him learned more of Hope's past that summer than he. Most of what Ish knows about it comes from a tribute by Congressman James Clyburn plus memories passed on by Hope's son Abraham, now retired in Fort Motte.

There have been at least three Hope Williams around Fort Motte since the late 19th century, but if we have the death records right, Hope Jr.'s grandfather was known as Hardtime Williams, and Hardtime's son as Hope Williams Sr. (1888-1949), a strange and often cantankerous man who found his peace spending weeks at a time by himself in the woods. They say his eyes were like a tiger's—six or seven colors—and that he

Mr. Hope. Photo Lynn Goldberg.

never bowed to a white man. Probably in the early '20s when Hope Jr. was about age twelve, Hope Sr. was chained to a road gang for defending himself from a white man. That's when Hope Jr., the youngest son, left off-season schooling and took over as head of family, building a place for them to live while the father was in prison.

Hope grew up and married June early on in the nightmare Depression. Abe, first of their fourteen surviving children, was born in 1938. When World War II began, a federal Resettlement Administration program placed Hope and other poor black farmers on state-owned land growing cotton and soy for the war. At the end of the war, South Carolina passed the land on to white men, some of them vets, whether already farmers or not. Black veterans need not apply.

The betrayal left Hope owning less than three acres, plus tilling rights to two or three more abandoned ones he obtained by paying back taxes. Back to survival. "Trying to get by, that's all it was," says Abe. To make ends meet, Hope took over managing nearby black sharecroppers of a powerful extended family of white men who knew him as a gentle, respected man of his word. Abe was

111

Calhoun County

10 Miles

Richland County

Sandy Run

Lexington County

176

Hampton area

Congaree River

Fort Motte

Sumter County

601

Caw Caw

✳ St. Matthews

6

Lone Star

Clarendon County

Creston

Orangeburg County

Cameron

Elloree

Orangeburg ✳

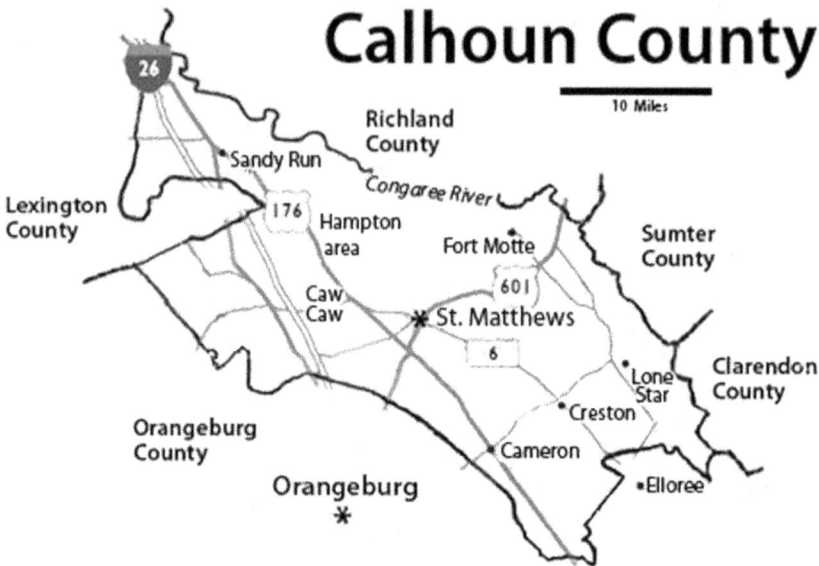

placed in charge of the younger siblings in farm work on their own land and in cents-a-day labor elsewhere whenever the chance arose. These duties—plus driving the school bus to the tiny black high school housed fifteen miles away in a Baptist church in Cameron—delayed bright Abe's high school graduation until 1959. Then Hope asked him to forgo college at South Carolina State in Orangeburg so that thirteen younger siblings could also get their diplomas, and eventually all of them did. In 1961, Abe migrated north to DC. It was tough, he says, but gradually he carved out careers in small business.

Meanwhile Hope had never stopped reading nor taken his eyes off the prize. Along with lifelong devotion and learning at New Bethany Baptist in Fort Motte from age fourteen (Ish remembers a clapboard church), in the 1950s Hope educated himself by reading and finding folks outside the county who wanted to bring about change. By the late '50s he was criss-crossing the county in his beat-up, powder-blue pickup exhorting black folks to sign up to vote. "He was a uniter," says Abe. "People liked to be around him because he was a philosopher. He was always trying to build relationships and get people out of this poverty, if he could." Most people didn't comprehend very clearly what could be done, but Hope "spent a lot of time out there fighting that system."

Defying threats from whites, by 1964 Hope had started a small group, mainly in St. Matthews, called the Calhoun County Improvement League (CCIL). He'd gone as far as he could at single-handedly rounding up poor, often terrified, marginal readers, persuading them down to the courthouse to try their luck on the rare days one could attempt to register. The CCIL needed help: summer kids to prowl the county talking to people house by shack. To lay the groundwork for a canvass, the NAACP briefly lent Hope several young field staff, including Peter Lee.

On June 29 Pat Gandy transported five SCOPErs from Columbia, 35 miles south to the Williams farm: Lynn, Carol, Terry, Mary Ann, and John Babin. (Ish joined them in mid-July.) Of the five, Boston Irish Babin must have stuck out with his twang, his quick class-conscious patter, and labor union family roots. John had grown up fast in Somerville MA, which is next door to Cambridge and was then, in his estimation, headquarters of organized crime in the Northeast. The son of a disabled railway worker, from the age of ten he'd been selling newspapers, scalping tickets and running numbers in Boston. Despite hustling for years on the street, John still had a hard time talking to people he hadn't yet got to know.

John

In 1908 Calhoun County—named after the slavery era senator—had been carved out of rural backlands of Orangeburg and Lexington Counties. Its nearest big town was Orangeburg. On a road from Orangeburg to Columbia sat St. Matthews, the county seat, population a thousand, mostly white. Was it a stoplight along Route 601, or only a stop sign or two? It had a train stop, sidings, courthouse and weekly gazette. It had weeknight lodgings for a few black men who commuted by rail from an outskirt called Lone Star to work in town. The railroad bisected the town east-west, serving enterprises such as the wholesaler, lumber yard, coal depot, cotton and cattle feed mills. There were some beautiful old homes and, in 1965, perhaps a small, white-only inn.

County population was about 12,000, two-thirds black. Out of a black voting age population of 3,300, 487 were registered, many due to Hope. Of the 2,600 voting-age whites, about 90% were registered. "Not too bad," Ish wrote home wryly. "In some counties whites are registered up to 117%." Was that an exaggeration? In Wilcox County, Alabama, SCOPE volunteer Maria Gitin reported a mere 110%.

Agriculturally the county was mostly sizable white-owned cotton farms, or black sharecroppers on white-owned land; a few blacks like the Williams owned small acreage, much of it worn out soil that whites had left behind. In the 1950s black farmers had been shifting from place to place trying to upgrade to better land. Most working blacks were tenant farmers, field laborers at $2 per ten-hour day (a dollar higher than Alabama!) or maids at $8-10 for a five-day week. Cotton mechanization was starting, and many old shacks were abandoned.

A fundraising letter the Calhoun SCOPErs sent north in July mentioned other details about St. Matthews and the county: no black in public office; no sizable black-owned store; six black boys employed in white stores. Negro homes mostly "substandard," oftentimes shacks with wood stoves, no inside water, sometimes no outhouse. Store-bought food about as costly as in the North. Like elsewhere, the powers that be still ignored the 1964 *Civil Rights Act*, not to mention longer-standing provisions of the 14th Amendment that Thurgood Marshall had made applicable to civil rights.

Hope's Kids

Hope was that rare and unmovable tree, planted near the Congaree. Another active Fort Motte man was Abraham "Ham" Frederick (or "Federick," as we understood), a Second War veteran whose farm looked pretty successful to us, though Abe Williams doubts it yielded a living.

Earl Coblyn, civil rights lawyer in Orangeburg, was teamed up with Charles Thomas, an education professor at South Carolina State, in masterminding a list of things they hoped to accomplish in Orangeburg and nearby counties including Calhoun. (In *Out-of-the-Box in Dixie*, a vivid photo-narrative, historian and professional photographer Cecil Williams says "Doc" Thomas would be largely responsible for the peaceful integration of Orangeburg's public schools.)

Earl knew the large work Hope had done to get some people registered. He didn't know how much of an organization backed Hope up. He thought our presence that summer could strengthen the CCIL enough that by the end of the summer Hope might fashion "some semblance of a board" that NAACP chapterhood required. To this end, Earl would work closely all summer with us, most often through Lynn and Mary Ann. Freshly minted from Wellesley, Mary Ann was on a path to law school.

Riding into the county on June 29, Lynn saw it as "one enormous cotton field. I almost wondered if any people existed there at all." Her first impression of Hope was that of "the most wonderful man one could ever meet...hard to tell his age, by no means young. He works in the fields himself." She learned he ran citizenship classes, too. From the start she saw that people knew and respected him; the black community loved him. She felt "immediately drawn. He, his wife, and a swarm of kids (not all his) pack a small decaying house in the middle of the fields, and chickens and cats run around. While Pat went out in the fields to talk with Hope, we wandered around the house. Beds fill nearly every corner and wall, except where the TV stood." (Like these, most quotes on Calhoun are drawn from Lynn's summer-long diary.)

Calhoun cotton, then and now.

It would take some days to work out good housing, but Hope hadn't let that hold things up. The idea was to tuck the group into the northwest quadrant of St. Matthews. The area was almost all black, though a large white church and big homes of the Wise and Zimmerman business families were there. Lynn,

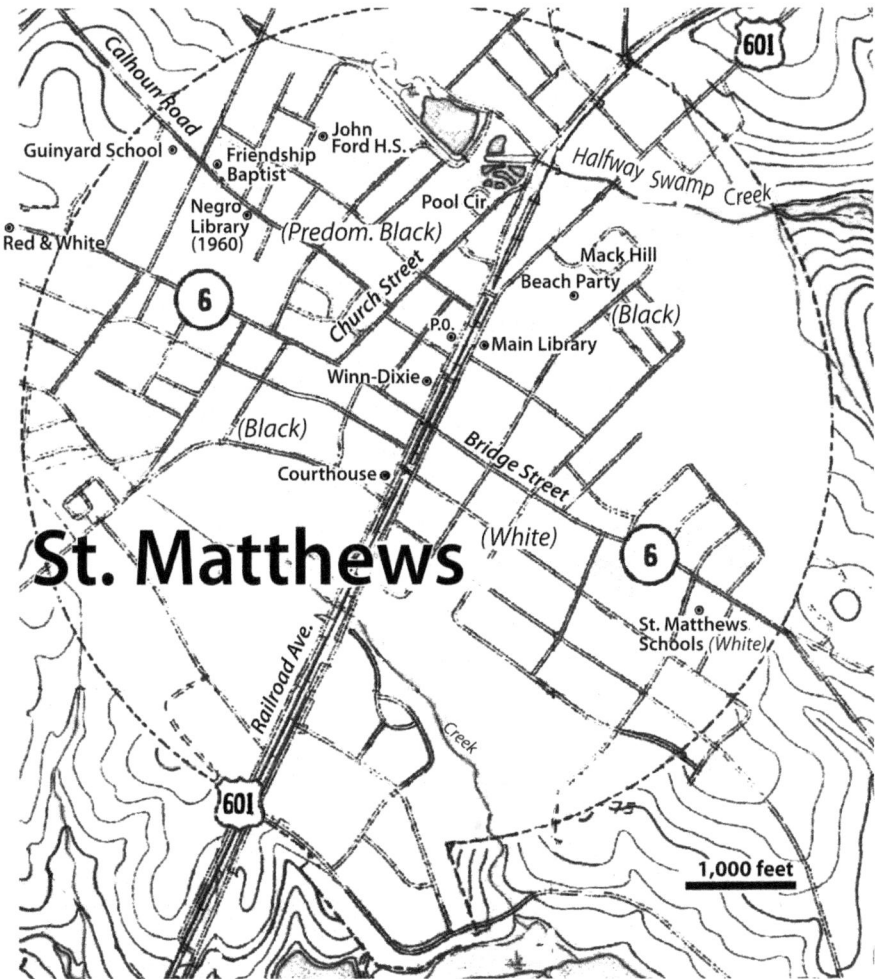

The main arteries (east-west Bridge Street/Route 6 and north-south Railroad Avenue/Route 601) were mostly white homes and businesses.

Carol, and Mary Ann were placed with an "ancient" (to Lynn) widower, Rev. Gus Howell—no inside water, wood-fed stove. Neighboring CCIL supporters included Furman ("Toot") Hart Sr., his wife Cleola and their kids. Toot had had to quit school around grade 6 and was a veteran of the South Pacific. In 1950 he'd been hired for construction work at the Savannah River nuclear bomb facility sixty miles away, and was still employed by that federal plant. That unusual type of employment afforded protection from local economic reprisal.

Near the Harts on Calhoun Road were also Reese and Geneva ("Miss Geneva") Floyd and their son Kenny. They ran a small grocery. Back of them was the family of Thomas and Lillian Murphy.

John and Terry found beds in a small, neatly kept, multi-room house at 403 Church with Arthur C. Johnson, who was mostly retired from his shoe repair business in town. In a tinier house next door was another CCIL fam-

Hope's Kids

Miss Geneva, age 96 in 2016, runs a laundromat now where the store was (photo Lynn). Son Kenny Floyd was 9 in 1965 (photo Carol).

ily, the Keitts—William ("W.M.") and Virginia ("Jean") and their kids William Jr. ("Junie"), Janice and Barbara Ann. W.M. and Jean were both toolmakers at Utica Tool in Orangeburg. Actually, they'd been occupying 403 Church but had scooted next door to make room for Terry and John. On Johnson's other side—across one end of Pool Circle, a horseshoe lane—lived elderly Mr. Haynes (perhaps Willie or Alton), whose activities, apart from bestowing fresh eggs on the SCOPErs, were a mystery.

The Harts' already full house on Calhoun Road became a temporary office. Lynn said they were "really nice about it. We type in their bedroom and spread our stuff all over the living room. Often we are there late at night. Someone is always home to take messages, and they put up with anything. After a morning of hard

Recent brick sheathes the frame house built by Furman Hart Sr. on his return from the war. Son Melvin stands out front.

work for us, Mrs. Hart came out with Cokes and homemade cake. The problem was, we couldn't really set anything up or invite other people in."

Concerns arose fast about the girls' safety at Rev. Howell's. One night they were visited by "a strange white man and a strange Negro." The white man did most of the talking, and the other they couldn't understand at all. The white man said he was looking for another lady. "We said something about Carol, and his reply was something about wanting to go out and look for a wife. Both men were obviously a little drunk. They left after a few minutes. Carol, who had walked up at the end, was very confused. Rev. Howell has no idea what is happening. We feel quite stranded here, and not completely safe. Mary Ann and I walked down to Eula's to take our baths with slight trepidation. We were thankful for two Negro boys who walked along with us. Because it is Friday night, there are many kids out walking around and riding in cars."

Lynn and a visitor in the temporary office at the Harts'.

Janice Keitt.
Photo Carol Sable.

During their absence, numerous cars stopped in front of Howell's house. Carol sat inside with doors locked, shades drawn. Voices outside made her jumpy. A boy came to the door and asked her for a match.

Apart from that, the group was warmly received in the neighborhood. "Everyone is so anxious to help us—it seems as though they are competing to see who can give us the most." The especially generous Floyds fed them breakfast from their little store and let it become SCOPE's temporary meeting place. Right away the group moved easily among their black neighbors and got in touch with Mr. Parker, a local teacher in charge of the newly created Head Start. Later that summer Terry would transport kids to the program when the school bus wasn't available.

The SCOPErs ran into Mike and Joe, two college-educated black NAACP workers from Orangeburg County who had done some work in Calhoun. Toward the end of the day, SCOPE caravanned with Mike, Joe and Hope on a brief tour of the county—"so spread out," wrote Lynn, "we must get more cars immediately. Canvassing will have to be done by car. We will also need to increase our number with Negro helpers." Hope and his erstwhile NAACP aids had already planned first steps for SCOPE, and "everything was arranged, even to the exact areas we would go to first. The books will open on the 12th, and we will be ready."

Mr. Hart drove the gang all around St. Mathews, pointing out white and Negro areas. Lynn thought it would be difficult to pull off any direct action here: "Whites own all the stores, there are no theaters, and the swimming pool will not come under any laws. There is no place [no pool] for Negroes to swim."

One possible target on the edge of St. Matthews was a beachwear factory called Beach Party. It was owned by Jonathan Logan, a New York corporation whose brand was "a name in many a girl's closet, the inevitable dress label for a junior miss." Blacks had applied there but none had been hired.

For an open meeting on Wednesday night, Lynn and the gang "hurriedly planned our little session as people began to arrive. We were happy to see four kids arriving, even a little early. Then people began coming in great numbers. Many we had never seen. We were astounded. Young kids and mothers were there, too! We just couldn't believe it. They all crowded into the Harts' tiny

117

living room, 25 or more, and all wanted to work. They filled out sample registration forms and were pepped up by Hope. The only one who can sing in our group, I was a little nervous about leading them all—no problem. They took over. I taught them some songs and sang out the verses. We ended with a beautiful 'We Shall Overcome'."

The canvassing plan was to start out the first few days along route 176 in Cameron—the county's only other incorporated area—approaching the farms mostly in the evening after work time, between 4:00 and 8:00. At the base of the rolling clay hills where the Low Country of South Carolina begins, white Cameron boosters described it as a pretty little town of "wide streets shaded by aging oaks, a scene of picturesque serenity." Though basically agricultural, the town's mattress factory dated from 1889. Picturesque as that may sound, its population—607 in 1960—would wither in ten years to 476. When we were there it was shedding young blacks who saw no future where they had grown up.

The morning after the first meeting, five volunteers showed up for the effort around Cameron, a fifteen-minute drive away. Terry ferried two carloads, setting Lynn, Carol and a girl named Blondie Haynes down by a house along the highway, promising to pick them up later.

For Lynn, "It was not too enjoyable after we had covered the couple of houses where we were. Fortunately Blondie knew every house in the area, so we did not expire walking down roads where there were none, but we walked many miles in the beating sun. Most of the people were not home until noon, but there were always kids sitting around outside who could give us some information. Large families are the rule on these farms, and eighteen kids is not uncommon. I did all the talking, though Blondie should have been trying at convincing people."

The former Beach Party as of 2016.

16. KINGDOM FOR A CAR

Ex-Pittsburgh barber Perry Como sang merrily about "finding a wheel," but from the get-go in Calhoun, as in Richland and Kershaw, transport was an enormous hassle. In Atlanta, SCOPE trainees had received many cautions based on experience in Mississippi. The advice about cars wasn't bad for Calhoun, as far as it went, though we didn't always obey it. For example:

- Drivers should have in their possession driver's license, registration papers, bills of sale. Project director should also have all this info. If carrying supplies, it's good to have a letter of authorization from a specific individual so as not to be charged with carrying stolen goods.

- Doors locked at all times. Gas tanks locked. Hoods locked. Windows rolled up at night.

- No one goes anywhere alone, certainly not in a car and certainly not at night.

- No unnecessary night travel. No objects inside that could be construed as weapons (hammers, files, etc.). Absolutely no liquor containers inside vehicles.

- Do not travel with names or addresses of local contacts.

- Know all roads in and out of town. Study a county map. Know locations of sanctuaries and safe homes.

- Make sure the car's inside light doesn't go on when people get in or out at night.

- Be conscious of other prowling cars. Write down make, model, year, and license numbers of suspicious cars. Keep records of when they appear.

What the list hadn't warned of: non-functioning gas gauges, empty tanks; broken hoses, headlights, taillights and gearshifts; mysteriously drained dead batteries; missing door handles; breakdowns, blowouts, worn-out bearings; sliding sideways in downpours into the mire off ubiquitous, slick clay roads.

For the afternoon of the first day's canvass there were eleven volunteers and suddenly four cars. One "animal," a donated '55 Ford, the SCOPErs nearly didn't take because of its condition and lack of registration or bill of sale. Lynn was "surprised anyone would give us such a bad car. It hardly has tires left, the emergency and regular brakes don't work, there are no handles on doors, and the gas pedal is disconnected. Yes, I drove it to town and back. (Terry got the flat later.)" A few days after that, Pat Gandy would deliver another car the papers for which sat back in Columbia.

One Tuesday, intrepid Lynn got up before her housemates and was on the road by 8:45, heading for some servicing at 48-year-old, NAACP leader James Sulton's Esso station in Orangeburg, twenty minutes away. (Besides owning and running the Esso, for a decade at least Jim had been leading the Orangeburg movement. In March 1960 he, photographer Cecil Williams and two other businessmen had personally attempted a lunch-counter sit-in at the Orangeburg SH Kress. In 1964—with help from Earl Coblyn and others—he'd unsuccessfully run for the state's still all-white assembly. For well over thirty years, Jim was a civil rights rock.)

It took Lynn almost ten hours to reach his garage: "First I ran out of gas. That wasn't bad because I coasted into a gas station—whew! I got into Orangeburg and followed the directions to the service station but drove past without seeing it. Well, I didn't have any reverse and I had to go out into the country in order to make a U-turn. I went back up the street and still couldn't find where I was supposed to go. I drove across town, getting myself completely lost. I finally got back to the right road, and stopped at a store to call Earl for help. His line was perpetually busy. At last I gave up and asked the owner of the store (a white man) where Sulton's service station was. 'That's a colored station,' he told me. His son (or helper) pointed it out."

Eventually Calhoun SCOPE would rent two cars from Charleston (85 miles away), returning them after three weeks of horrendous wear and tear. When Ish came to St. Matthews in mid-July, he arranged to borrow a black '56 Chevy in excellent shape (apart from a rusted exhaust pipe) from Ed Cahill, his family's minister in Pittsburgh. At the start of August his childhood friend John Cooper drove it down, bringing a box of Toll-House cookies that really turned Lynn on.

Ish recalls "Coop" being smitten by Lynn. In any case, he stayed a few days. He'd been born in Charleston in a navy hospital Quonset hut. His mother came, he says, from "ancient Tennessee evangelical stock, a curious mix of conservative (no stimulants stronger than water) and progressive (suffrage, racial tolerance)." Three years at Quaker Haverford College had cured him of any "southern reactionary heritage thing," but Coop's few days driving and exploring Calhoun County with us brought "a quantum leap" in his outlook.

According to Cooper, the interstate system was not yet completed, and "you couldn't get to St. Matthews from Pittsburgh by any direct route. So I wound up following whatever roads looked to be the fastest and most direct on the map. In the early afternoon, I stopped at a Rexall in Richmond. A couple of 10-year-old kids came running through the store wearing sheets and hoods playing KKK. I thought of how lions engage in roughhouse play as cubs to develop the attack skills that make them fierce predators as adults. I was used to getting rousted by small-town cops and the non-air-conditioned South in the summertime, but I wasn't prepared for sharecroppers still doing their laundry in a cauldron over a backyard wood fire. Schlepping around rural Calhoun County for SCOPE in an old Chevy pretty much turned me."

Another problem with the cars was that whites owned all the county's gas pumps. Though subject to the *Civil Rights Act* of 1964, most of them turned us away. The challenge of fueling compounded all others in those gas-guzzling days. One day Lynn, John Babin, and local teen Harold McKenzie were assigned to finish an area near Cameron. First they were going to test a gas station that had refused to serve us. To Lynn it was "rather disappointing that they had served me before, and I had no difficulty at all, although Ish had been threatened there. We test these stations and tell them that they are violating the *Civil Rights Act*. We warn them that we are writing to the main branch of their gas company. At Five Point Gas Station [near Lone Star], Ish was not served, and was informed that this man served both whites and Negroes, but not us, so was not being illegal."

In the past, Lone Star had been a stop on the Atlantic Coast Line railway, with two gas stations and a general store. It may still have been so in '65, though for a long time it hasn't, and to our city-hick ears, saying "in" Lone Star sounded odd. Driving past acres of cotton you'd notice a town limit sign. A mile or so later you came to an elbow turn with sheds and a few other buildings. As Abe Williams describes it, apart from some large white holdings, Lone Star was the area where black farmers had abandoned worn-out, leftover soil to move to Fort Motte where slightly better land had been left behind by black farmers moving to Columbia or further north. In 2016, Ish discovered, Lone Star is a good place to pull off a moment to listen to crickets as crows dismantle a road-kill possum. A peaceful spot. According to white St. Matthews native and attorney Martin R. Banks, Lone Star was "the closest thing we had to a western movie set." In fact, after the 1960s some of its buildings were moved to the town of Santee to be a "wild west" theme restaurant and country store.

Whatever Lone Star's condition in 1965, one Sunday a few days after filling up in Cameron, with tank almost empty again en route between churches, Lynn pulled into Five Point unaware that the Good Lord's blue laws forbade any Sabbath Day sale of gas. "We pulled in and I asked for a dollar's worth. The man said nothing, but shook his head. 'Don't you have any gas?' we asked him. 'Sure

Downtown Lone Star, 2016.

I got gas, but I told you before I don't got any for you.' We thanked him kindly, and cheerfully said good-bye. I almost had to laugh, because I couldn't believe it." But the joke was on us.

Eventually we must have learned about the Sunday prohibition, but on that occasion Lynn continued her quest. "We coasted, when we could, into Lone Star. Nothing was open. We stopped to ask some boys. One of them got in with us, and we drove across the tracks to Deacon Murry's house. We tried calling St. Matthews to have them come rescue us if we didn't make it back, but we couldn't reach a single phone—there was just silence." (More later about Southern Bell.) "Damn! The Murrys had a little gas, so we crossed our fingers and drove home."

Some gas stations, we discovered, welcomed our business. One of these was W.G. Smoke's Pure Oil filling station ("Be sure with Pure!") in St. Matthews on Bridge Street across from a Baptist church. White Fort Motte native Jeff Reid works on the staff of the Calhoun County Museum after a local high school career teaching history. Age fifteen in '65, Jeff recalls only casual interactions between himself or his father and Hope back then, when Hope stepped by the family's liquor, beer and snack store gas pump on the north edge of St. Matthews. Pumping Shell gasoline, Jeff knew him as a pleasant man, easy to get along with. He has no memory of Hope's involvement in civil rights at the time. He can't imagine his father refusing anyone a fill-up. Debbie Roland, director of the museum, says the same about her uncle, who owned a pump in Cameron.

On a late August afternoon when canvassing became unbearable, Lynn drove somewhere with John Babin and John Lee Anderson, a local volunteer. "I had to take the station wagon. This car is an unbelievable mess. It stalls every time you go slowly. Only a muscle man can steer it and the muffler is gone, aside from many, many other things. I gave up, and turned the heap over to John Lee to drive. We came in early—first stop was the Pure station. The white man who owns it [Mr. Smoke] keeps asking if there is any way he can help us. He has much Negro help, and they fixed up our car."

17. FIVE PLUS FOUR

The previous chapter mentions Harold McKenzie and John Lee Anderson, two of the four young St. Matthews men who worked alongside us through the summer, schooling us on what was what and placing themselves at greater ultimate risk than we. We would not have done much without Harold, John Lee, Everett "Butch" Jackson, and Furman Hart, Jr. (For clarity I'll call the latter "Junior," his family nickname, though we called him Furman at the time.)

Lynn felt Harold McKenzie was the "best and most dependable volunteer, one of the sweetest boys I have ever met." One of eight children, Harold had picked cotton as a kid. He and 75 classmates had just graduated from John Ford High School in St. Matthews, of whom, he estimated, five or ten were still around, the rest off on summer jobs or on to better prospects elsewhere. Harold was familiar with life in New Jersey where he had often visited an older brother. Thin, bespectacled, thoughtful, pithy, wry, and quietly affectionate, Harold's mantra was, "Some things change, and some things stay the same."

Harold a few years later.
Courtesy of Sonia McKenzie Rivers.

"Junior" Hart had graduated from John Ford High in 1964. He'd grown up in town leading what he says was a childhood much like that of local white boys: "I wasn't picking no cotton, tracking no mule. I did not live on the so-and-so place. I lived in *Mr. Furman Hart Sr.'s house*. I had clean dungarees and clean sneakers every day to go to school." He was, he says, "a very skinny guy, a *very* skinny guy." He had asthma that interfered with school but did not prevent him, while a student, from rising early to start the fire to warm Mrs. Parker's kindergarten classroom. Like his dad., he liked to dress sharp. Lynn found him "the funniest person I have ever heard speak—when I can understand him. He speaks so fast."

John Lee Anderson, 21, was more phlegmatic or maybe simply recovering from just having finished an army artillery stint. At the end of July Lynn would type up his request for an application for a job as relief policeman in St. Matthews. "The opening was announced in the newspaper, and we immediately decided to have someone apply. It would sure be great if he got the job. Otherwise he has a job as an interior decorator in New York. Like everyone else, he would just leave this unbearable place." Not surprisingly, he didn't land the local job.

Junior a year or so later.
Courtesy of the Hart family.

Lean, 16-year-old Butch Jackson made Ish a little nervous. Ish assumed he came from a rougher, more distant home. He hadn't. His family lived just the other side of the Keitts and belonged to the nearby Friendship Baptist Church

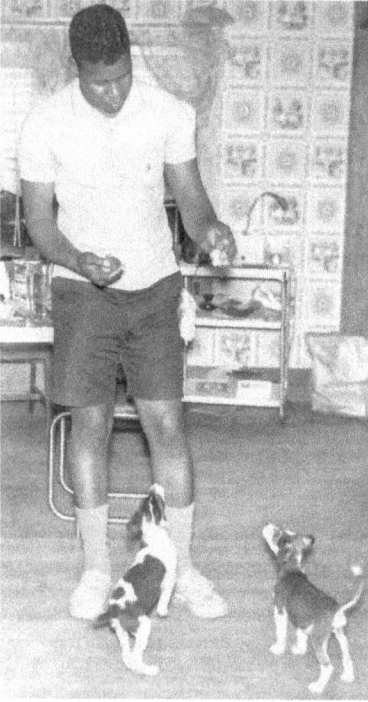

John Lee with adopted pups "Hope" and "Scope".
Photo Carol Sable.

that the Harts and Floyds attended. Junior recalls Butch's mother launching a restaurant at some time before '65. Butch was the youngest of five boys, athletic and good at baseball and boxing. His father worked in construction.

Looking back, Butch's older brother Freddie "Jumpy" Jackson describes him as having been an active churchgoer, "real Christian-wise." According to another ,older St. Matthews buddy, Charles Williams (unrelated to Hope), Butch "was a very nice guy but he had a quick temper. He didn't like to be pushed around." A high school make-up class took a chunk out of Butch's summer.

SCLC was granting $10 a week to up to four local youths per county to affiliate with SCOPE. Most likely Harold, Junior, John Lee, and Butch were receiving that. They should have been. Without them we were often clueless. Lynn recorded how she, Mary Ann and Harold "took the car down towards Cameron. An old lady, who had been too busy chasing her gobbler to talk before, was hanging out her wash. Harold got out of the car and began to help her arrange the ragged clothing over a fence. Slowly he began to talk to her about registering. Mary Ann and I also got out and pitched in. Mrs. Holman was glad for our help. When we finished we talked to her some more."

On a later outing, "Butch took over the hoe while Carol explained the sample to the lady. Butch hoed all the time we were there." ("Chopping" cotton was a back-punishing sort of hoeing, necessary for dealing with some kinds of weeds.) Later that day at another house, Lynn and Carol went up to the door and saw a girl "disappear suddenly out the back door. We started around the side of the house as the girl leaped over the fence and dived into the bushes. We sent Butch over to talk with her. He brought the frightened 15-year-old out so we could explain to her what we were doing. We climbed over the fence, and wound our way through the bushes to the field. Our approach caused everyone to run quickly into the surrounding forest. As we came back to the house, the mother, an elderly woman, was coming home bowed under the huge sack of wood she had chopped. Ish relieved her of the burden, winning her confidence in us."

For that first, end-of-June after-noon canvass, before which she'd stripped to her underwear (temporarily) to cool off from the morning effort, Lynn "went with William Mitchel (at 95 mph—we asked him to slow just a little) and Harold. We also dropped another group off to go by foot. For today we were sending the volunteers with each of us to learn the techniques. I found they were much better than I was in many instances, because they knew how to talk to these people. Canvassing here is no easy task. First two people we caught were farmers—we stopped their tractors in the middle of the field to speak with them.

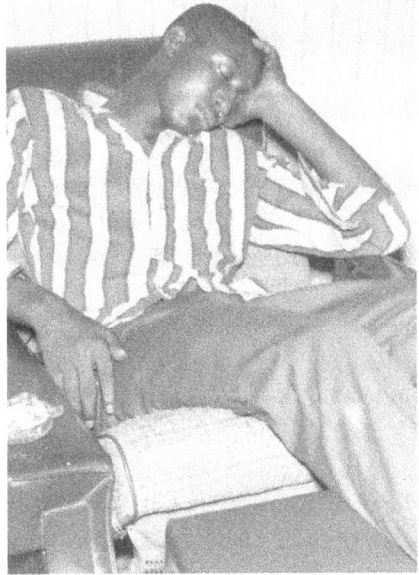

Butch napping at the SCOPE house. He had summer school as well.
Photo Carol Sable.

"Most people were hard to converse with and stubborn. They didn't like their shacks, and they didn't want to work all day for $2, but they weren't going to register. These folk require much more time than people in the city. They are more afraid of us and less trusting. Many are illiterate and have been well brainwashed. We came upon many families in need of welfare, especially child care. The majority are not even tenant farmers, but laborers living on the farms where they work.

"We finished our area and went to look for the other team. On foot they had covered about four houses in two hours, and were exhausted from walking in the sun. We took them to the rest of their houses by car. We stopped at dark, and returned exhausted and ravenous. Mrs. Bonaparte had kindly waited until 8:30 to prepare us dinner. [After that we] began our evening's work of fil-ing our day's canvassing. It was a very successful day, although everything goes very slowly. Hope came over and talked with us and told stories. At 12:30 at the poor Harts', we washed up in the back yard by flashlight, and dropped into bed."

July 4th weekend was coming up. On Friday the 2nd, St. Matthews policeman Ridgeway stopped Carol on the road and questioned her, saying the names of everyone in the group had to be submitted to the sheriff that afternoon. Lynn and Mary Ann watched her and John Babin, with whom Lynn was teamed, from behind a door "since we didn't think they should see any more of us than is nec-essary. No more was said, and we headed out to booming Fort Motte."

Of course, Fort Motte was a shell of its long-ago self. Lynn found one store and a population mainly of "ghosts in vacant houses. We left the cars and split into three groups. Only three volunteers had come this morning. Carol and I went with a Negro boy. It was a long ways between each house. We covered few—little accomplished except getting ourselves hot, dirty and tired. We walked down roads where no one lived.

The group returned to St. Matthews for lunch and to visit Sheriff Rucker's office. 'You have more guts than I do,' he said when we confirmed we were staying with the colored folk. He assures us that we will 'have our heads bashed in and we'll be raped.' He knew we didn't have the registration [for the Ford that Pat had delivered], and had not reported us, so we stupidly assumed he would let it go for a day or two."

After that they piled back into one car, along with three volunteers, to set out canvassing again. "Then what should we spy but the white police car that had been driving up and down the road constantly all day waiting to catch us. Terry was driving. He turned down the road to the Harts' and stopped in their driveway. The police car stopped up the road. We finally ventured out, were followed and stopped. Yes, we had no registration. Pat was stupid...should have known. 'Bring 'em in' was the order. Terry was put on $27 bail and asked to appear in court on Wednesday." He was furious with Pat, walked back to the Harts' and called Columbia, after many tries got Pat, who agreed to come out.

Then Lynn and Carol walked into the St. Matthews business district for office supplies: "While we were walking around and being stared at, we saw the blue truck and stopped to talk to Hope. There were three Negro boys with us. A white woman in a car stopped in shock and exclaimed, 'Oh! That is the most disgusting thing I've ever seen.' Many people were standing around and everyone burst out laughing. I thought I would die.

"We all walked back together. An enormous number of cars passed by full of gawking passengers. The word is getting around. Even when the five of our group are walking together, people stare at us in disbelief. It is really funny, and we are having a ball. All the time police cars and private cars are cruising up and down Calhoun Road [past the Floyds' and Harts']. I really admire the courage of the Negroes who have taken us in.

"One good thing about these episodes. Suddenly the volunteers, whose interest had diminished, were hit by the effects of what we are doing. They see now that it involves them, too. We expect they will feel more a part of our work. While our car is impounded we will have little trouble getting the boys to drive us around. Ever increasing numbers are coming around, and there are many we have on tap. A good place to find them is hanging around in town or at the Floyds' store."

Saturday morning for want of a car they canvassed again in St. Matthews. Lynn teamed up with Effie Lee Kimpson, around age twenty, a first cousin of the Hart kids (everyone seemed related). Most people were out visiting and walking around on the holiday weekend, "a big thing around here. The two of us came upon a house full of drunk boys. We may even have gotten some of them registered.

"We walked into town together. Although we were stared at, nothing much happened. We stopped at a drug store where Negroes are not allowed in the front, to get ice cream cones. Effie is well known and stopped to talk to everyone. She is a very opinionated girl and stands up on civil rights, was fired from a job for it today. She is in disagreement over the issue with her ex-fiancé." (Pressured by the ex- and maybe others, Effie's involvement would taper off.)

That afternoon a boy named Warren took Mary Ann and Lynn back down to Camerion to cover some unmarked dirt roads hidden among the cotton fields. There were very few houses and the people they did find were too afraid of the whites to agree to register.

"We find many more very old people than we have ever seen; 80-, 90-, 100-year-old people are common. No homes for the aged. They continue to live in the same place along with their children, grandchildren and great-grandchildren. However, most of the younger people are leaving. Almost everyone has relatives in New York and New Jersey. I even found someone who lived in Princeton.

"We had only been canvassing about an hour and a half when Warren found a hole in his brake line. That was the end. We picked up another team and returned to St. Matthews. Some of the SCOPE workers from Orangeburg were eating lunch in the store when we pulled in. They had come with a young Negro lawyer who works with them. He had come here because last night a 16-year-old boy had been arrested and thrown in jail. Walter Reilly had been working with us. The charge was partly driving a car with poor brakes. Both state and city police are hauling in every car they can catch. They check every detail."

The lawyer was Earl Coblyn, whose Babinesque accent blew us away. Like John, Earl was a Somerville native. On the young end of eleven children, his roots included maternal grandfather Eli George Biddle, a decorated survivor of the legendary, Boston-based Civil War regiment, the Massachusetts 54th, depicted in the film "Glory." Its demise had occurred at Beaufort on the coast about 75 miles from Orangeburg. A sign painter by trade and an inspiring part-time minister, grandfather Biddle lived until 1940, and as a small boy Earl watched his older brother George march proudly beside the old veteran in Boston Memorial Day parades. George went on to serve as an officer in World War II. As a high school senior, Earl was offered an immediate diploma if he'd enlist—which he did and was dismayed at the ruin he saw of Europe at the end of the war.

After finishing law school in the late 1950s, Earl had come down with his wife Donnessa and their young sons Renner and Wesley to bolster SC-NAACP, and especially the Orangeburg Movement. In court, he often teamed up with friend and mentor Matthew J. Perry (1921-2011), later the first black federal judge in the state.

Earl with Orangeburg SCOPEr Al Szymanski. Photo Dean Savage.

(According to colleague Judge Joseph Anderson, "To say that Matthew Perry was good in the courtroom is like saying Mickey Mantle knew how to swing a bat. Aristotle taught that lawyers and judges should be the very personification of justice. Matthew J. Perry Jr. comes as close as any person I have known to meeting Aristotle's ideal.")

Earl stressed the importance of county work because county officials controlled all access to federal anti-poverty programs Earl wanted to introduce. Always full of young people, his office would become a snack stop and hangout for Calhoun SCOPE. At work or driving around in his T-bird, Earl had an astonishing cool. Lynn learned that the Coblyns had "two very bright, sharp-minded little boys. Skipper is four grades ahead, because the Negro schools present no challenge to him. He is put ahead because he is bored. The Coblyns are very upset by this, and if they can't get him into his proper grade in a white school, they will be forced to send him to a private school. It was a pleasant time for all of us to be removed from the Southern atmosphere for an afternoon. The Coblyns are so New England!

"Earl sits all day in an air-conditioned office, talking on the phone. He was expecting a call from US Attorney General Katzenbach. He expects trouble in Calhoun. In fact, everyone we meet is shocked that we are in there. The Justice Department, the FBI, and the SC Law Enforcement Commission have all been contacted concerning us, and will be moving in as we approach the registration date. Earl is making all these arrangements. He also is insisting that the girls move [from Howell's house] or get a phone and possibly a dog." (Is that why the group would adopt a pair of lovable, worm-ridden puppies the girls cleaned up and John Lee sometimes fed?)

"Since Earl didn't want to leave his office, he had lunch sent up for us. It was very pleasant sitting and gabbing. Earl loves stories. He tends to neglect his [paying] work because he gets involved with things he'd rather do, like Civil Rights. He always is free if any of us need anything, and he's on the go all day. His cases can be done 'tomorrow.' There seems to be a constant stream of people in his room."

Another day, "Earl typed while we bothered him. People kept coming in and out. Donnie came to sit in his office because, she said, she never can see him any other way. She was extremely interesting to speak with. Donnie has been very observant of the Southern people, and really knows them. It was fascinating to hear her criticize the Negroes (and the whites)."

Through Earl, Calhoun SCOPE strengthened relations with Columbia University SCOPE in Orangeburg. In 1964 Orangeburg had been the site of intense demonstrations and, besides local summer efforts, eighteen AFSC college students had worked on registration. The challenge for 1965, said Earl, was expanding the canvass to more rural parts of the county.

After a supper of leftover sandwiches, the group sat around with Pat Gandy and Ben Mack, "mostly waiting to see if we could get our impounded car fixed. The sweet old policeman left the lights on and wore down the battery—it will have to be replaced."

The Ford wagon that Pat brought that day was now the group's one "good" car, good enough to drive to Orangeburg that evening to get to know the gang from New York and their local counterparts, and begin to coordinate for Orangeburg's July 6 registration.

"The kids took us over to see their freedom houses. Do they ever have a set-up, two enormous old two-story houses and a building with a huge meeting room and kitchen, all in a row. The five of us were jealous."

On Sunday the Fourth, the group split up to accompany various Floyds to five different churches where northern relatives swelled the pews.

"Everyone is wrapped up in prayer and communicating with God. There was a lot of singing—very

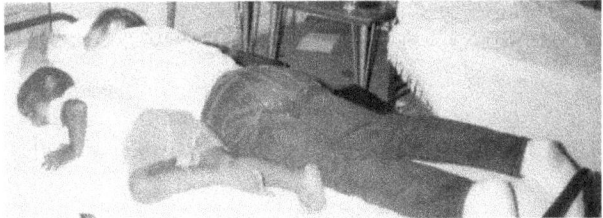

Nap time at Orangeburg SCOPE . Photo Dean Savage.

nasal voices. The sounds harmonize in weird chords. The minister leads some songs, and two choirs lead others. The sermon was danced in addition to sung. When the visitors from such places as Far Rockaway introduced themselves, I introduced myself and gave a little speech. I told them what we were doing and announced registration dates and our meeting. Next came the offerings. This is in addition to the collection they make. For an hour they collected and counted money. They read lists of names and contributions."

Late that Sunday afternoon, Lynn and others drove to Columbia to check in with friends, get materials, and request another male SCOPEr in Calhoun. Naturally, en route, the car with no reverse started to fall apart. "As we reached town, we couldn't stop without its stalling. I'm glad Terry can push."

As soon as they were back—without supper—Mary Ann dragged them to Friendship Baptist for a fundraiser performance of "The Slabtown District Convention," a spoofy play about old-time black Baptist women's conventions, performed in black churches in changing versions at least since the 1920s (see recent versions on *YouTube*.)

Then, wrote Lynn, Pat walked in with Jim Bowers, who had been one of the second small batch of students integrating USC in 1964, and "The bomb dropped. Without telling anybody what he was doing, Pat got up and made a fiery speech about Walter Reilly," the 16-year-old who'd been arrested for faulty brakes. Walter faced possible time on the chain gang. As Lynn understood things, "There is no juvenile court in St. Matthews, so he comes under adult trials and punishments. All this is due to police harassment which suddenly got unbearable at our arrival." Earl Coblyn had arranged for Walter's case to be heard after Terry's case for driving without registration, so that Terry's could provide a background of police harassment for Walter's.

"Anyway, Pat, without knowing the situation in the community, yelled about how some people may get hurt this summer and even killed, but we must get up and fight. He didn't inquire about whether this county was ready for direct action. In fact it is farthest from it. These people are scared. They don't want trouble. Pat stood in front of a crowded, hot room full of frightened people, and said he was ready to go out and die." Jim spoke in a similar vein.

"We nearly exploded!" she wrote. "Afterwards leaders met with us at poor Rev. Howell's to discuss what is happening. We all jumped on Pat, but Earl was tactful and kept us off." Toot Hart and Tom Murphy sided with SCOPE that this was not the time or place for stirring things up like that.

"We talked until late, very disturbed that Pat is going to continue these games. Plans were set for an eventual contact with SCLC on the matter, not Hosea Williams, but Rev. King himself. We were boiling mad, but still had to act rationally. Our side prevailed." Lynn also conceded "one good thing Pat may have done," which was getting the community behind Walter's case, to raise the money he'd need and couldn't pay.

A lot had happened in a week.

This seems to have been Pat's swan song with us. By early August, SCLC had dispatched him to Dorchester County. After that, they ordered him back to Atlanta where an angry Hosea called him and his memoir-writing buddy Dick Reavis, another white southern staffer, loose cannons and "rebels" (Ouch!) and reassigned them to Georgia.

With the waning of civil rights work in the South, Pat moved on to other progressive causes. Among other things, according to his daughter, in Seattle he helped create the nation's first 911 system and set up lesbian-gay support. Diagnosed as bi-polar later in life, he attributed his mental problems to head trauma he'd sustained in civil rights. He died in 1995.

18. CARRY IT ON

The group settled into a six-day weekly routine of canvassing as the heat and humidity worsened, in preparation for the few days when people could register at the courthouse. It canvassed early and late in the day with PB&J lunches and heat break, usually back in town. Canvassing ended at dark, followed by nightly compiling of data. Often all summer, the group would be invited out to supper by neighbors, though to be less of a financial burden, it begged off more and more. In 2016, the Harts' son Melvin (around age thirteen back then) told Lynn that at least one woman who worked and shopped for a prospering white family carved money out of the white folks' cash to purchase food for us.

Meals at home were covered by dwindling money for groceries, and dwindling interest in heaps of great summer tomatoes. Some suppers were burgers from The Jacket, a white-owned take-out place on Railroad Avenue that also served great fried squash and okra.

John Babin drew up maps that, toward the end of the summer, Lynn found incomprehensible. By the end of July at least, out in remote parts of the county, the group was looking for more local leaders: "We mark the cards when anyone seems interested and intelligent." At the end of the summer we handed all this over to Hope and the CCIL.

Saturdays also included grocery shopping (one of few regular contacts with whites), bumping into local friends, and maybe laundry: "While Mary Ann canvassed and did office work, Terry drove the rest of us down to the laundromat. We went in the back door to the back laundry room and did our clothes. While we waited, Terry and I drove to Cameron to finish my morning assignment. We returned, and hung around the laundry room for a while. We wanted very much to put the colored

Evening. John, Mary Ann and Terry do paperwork. Hope and Scope snooze.
Photo Carol Sable.

Pepsi signs in the white laundry room and the white one in the colored laundry room—we restrained ourselves." Sundays they fanned out to small distant churches, loosely attended in summer.

Hope's Kids

By July 5 Earl Coblyn was building a case about police harassment of black youth in Orangeburg and nearby counties, and Walter Reilly's arrest was added to that picture. The next day someone mentioned that Walter had just been seen: "Something was up if he was out of jail. A frantic call to Earl revealed that he knew nothing of the matter. Mr. Hart and Mary Ann went to his home and spoke with Walter's father, who had borrowed money to get him out. Strange— the trial had been postponed a week, without anyone's being notified of the change. The common opinion was that Walter might be framed, with us as the victims. Hope took charge of Walter for the night to avoid any trouble."

Our side had also postponed Walter's trial at some point when the arresting officer was absent. Eight days later, it was postponed again. "Great. Earl drove out to see Walter and found out that he was at the courthouse with his father. When he got there Walter had called another lawyer. The poor, mixed-up kid didn't know if Earl was still representing him. Who did he call? Gressette, the segregationist lawyer who runs all sorts of things in this area. Good grief, what a mess!"

It was less "mess," more like business as usual. The lawyer was the county's powerful State Senator L. Marion Gressette (1902-1984), known to his capitol colleagues as "The Gray Fox." Since the 1950s Sen. Gressette had chaired a state committee whose purpose was to hamper all moves toward desegregation. Through it, he'd been leading resistance to public school integration and staving off plans for desegregating state colleges and universities.

In later life Gressette would claim the committee was simply preventing violence such as occurred in some other southern states, but he was a key state segregationist. Melvin Hart thinks fiery Modjeska Simkins must have included him among those "few white folks that once they die...." But locally he was the fixer and safest bet to get Walter "off" with a fine and fewest days in jail.

(By the end of the '60s, Gressette was apparently shifting his shades of gray. One laudatory source says he was instrumental in drafting a 1972 law creating a permanent state Human Affairs Commission for eliminating and preventing racial discrimination. In 1978 he supported making the late Dr. King's birthday a state holiday. In 1981 he played a role in further desegregation planning for state colleges and universities.)

Actually, Marion's brother Bill was the man who, in the '50s and '60s employed Hope Williams to manage the extensive share-cropped farmland owned by the myriad Gressettes. Early August found us telling KZSU that Hope owned his own land, a "completely free farmer," but his Gressette gig must have been known in the county. Abe Williams looks back fondly on Bill Gressette—"a darn good guy, as a matter of fact. All you had to do was call him and tell him the problem, and he would take care of it. Him and Daddy was real tight."

Bill Gressette and Hope respected each other. Maybe that's part of how Hope survived in a county we'd been told was too dangerous to go to: The Gressettes ran it. Folks didn't inconvenience *them*. This helps make sense of a public honor and office bestowed on Hope by the senator later on. Then, too, all this was another way in which, as racist as the state still was, South Carolina wasn't Alabama. But about that Sherie Holbrook Labedis, who tells the story of SCOPE in Berkeley County, may disagree.

Tuesday July 6, Terry and Lynn helped Orangeburg on a day when "tons of people" waited to register: There was a line, and others were sitting on benches filling out forms. The registrars were "extremely cooperative," handing out applications to the civil rights workers, who could help registrants fill them out. Usually people were not asked to read the Constitution. The lines moved fairly rapidly. By end of day, 235 Negroes, eight whites, were registered. "Yahoo!" said Lynn.

Next day Terry was tried in St. Matthews, receiving "a suspended fine, thanks to Earl who explained that we couldn't pay right away. The police are catching on to the fact that we are here to stay, and won't be scared away. They haven't bothered us as much, and things are relatively quiet."

Back to cars for a moment: Have we mentioned mud? Next day Mary Ann and Lynn were covering "some scattered areas we had missed before. Looking for a small road, we turned up a dirt path through some fields. The houses turned out to be deserted, so we went on around the soybeans and cotton. I had just suggested turning around when we came to a huge section of the path that was pure ooze. Mary Ann drove straight into it, and we stopped in the middle. Ugh! We took off our shoes and stepped out calf-deep in mud. We dug the wheels out with our hands and rocked the car. After about half an hour and [the sacrifice of] two of our posters, we managed to get the car out of that mire and into another. At last we got out of that, too. We parked in the cotton, the only dry place. Mary Ann stepped out, and suddenly, horrible noises issued out of the car. We had run out of water.

"We hid the SCOPE material. With shoes in hand, we walked the half mile or so to the road, mud caked all over us. As it dried it cracked and fell off. When we reached the road no one was in sight. We started walking. Fortunately, Mary Ann had a white handkerchief and we flagged a car down after a while. The car was driven by a large white man with only one arm. Next to him was a huge shotgun. 'You never know what you might find on these country roads.' Mary Ann's answer was, 'Like a couple of stranded girls?' We played visiting vacationers, and he brought us to Creston, another booming town with all of one store. They were very nice (little did they know—I'm glad we weren't a mixed group). We were given a can of water. Mary Ann drove our car back onto the dry path (with some pushing). Thank God! I thought we would never get free! That was it for our morning."

Hope's Kids

Melvin Hart says the one-armed man was the most dangerous white in the county; had he already known who the girls were, the outcome could have been different. Or did he know and let them off out of respect for women?

A cleaned-up Mary Ann.
Photo Carol Sable.

Lynn, July 8: "Some of the kids are excellent canvassers—better than we—because they know the people and can talk to them. They know how to reach the people. I drove the car out (and ran out of gas) and worked with Betty, who was quite ineffective except in lessening the distrust of me as I explained myself. It is so nice to walk down these roads around here in an outer part of St. Matthews. Everyone waves and calls out our names. They all know us. So does the whole town. They are so anxious to be friends and for us to talk to them. It is a very strange thing for many of them to talk with a white person, and especially friendly ones.

"The rural areas are much more disappointing than the urban ones. In some we're practically closed out. Friendly and unfriendly people tend to be concentrated in sections. If we find a registered voter, we usually find others nearby."

That night was SCOPE's first community meeting outside St. Matthews. "We rushed through dinner at Mrs. Floyd's and drove to Cameron, Brown Chapel, a brick church far out in the country. We drove to this deserted place and went in. By 8:00, the scheduled hour, no one had shown up. What a let-down. We sat out on the steps while one or two other cars pulled up slowly. At 8:45 we had to begin. The discussion became better as time went on. More people showed up and things got livelier."

Mickey Shur, the young, guitar-strumming dynamo freshman from Orangeburg SCOPE (later to become a guitar-strumming rabbi), opened the meeting with freedom songs. After that "the meeting ran like a clock. People stood up and said wonderful things on our behalf. Our plea for support (especially cars) was answered. The leaders and others asked the people to take care of us while we do our work. Some really great speeches were made, and we know everyone was behind us. Some people were very concerned about what would happen after they register. What about voting? We were glad to see their concern. Hope encouraged them to set up citizenship schools."

R ev. Howell's place still wasn't right for the girls. July 10 Mr. Johnson moved out so that they could move in with the boys at 403 Church. From then on it was the SCOPE house, cementing relations among the SCOPErs, Harold, Junior, Butch, John Lee, and others, by having a place to hang out. It also nurtured a brother-sister sort of friendship mainly between the four and Carol and Lynn. The house was a place for work and play, and Carol was the playfulest SCOPEr. As tensions increased through the summer, in and around the house, she was still able to kid with John Lee and the others.

The former SCOPE house, 2016. The double window on the left was a picture window then.

Lynn related in a similar style. At one point she noted that "Mary Ann and the others get too involved with the grownups to develop any close relations with the kids. Carol and I played Tiddly Winks against Harold and Butch—the whites against the Negroes." Dancing now and then was another way to relate and "a way I was able to reach them better than anyone else in the group. Hurrah for the 'jerk.'"

"The volunteers can show up whenever they want to, and the work is waiting for them. They don't feel that they will waste their time sitting around. Harold and Butch (often John Lee and Junior, too) stay in our house most of the day and night as permanent workers. They go with us wherever we go, and participate in our discussions and arguments."

Musically, the location was also great. Sunday mornings meant listening as 13-year-old boy soprano Junie Keitt practiced beautifully next door for church.

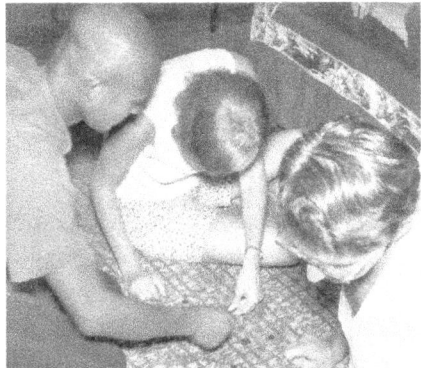

Harold, Lynn and Terry, squidging and squopping. Photo Carol Sable.

2016, from left: Formerly the Jacksons', Keitts' and Johnson's.

We've come this far by faith, leaning on the Lord.
We're trust-trusting in his holy word,
And he never, he never failed us yet.
I'm singing, 'Oh, oh-oh-oh, oh-oh-oh, can't turn around!
We've come this far by faith.

The SCOPE house wasn't far from the Harts' and, like all of St. Matthews, not a long walk from Bridge Street (Highway 6) in the center of town. The bridge carries traffic over the railway ravine through town. Narrow avenues flank the ravine. Bridge Street further divides the town north-south into quadrants.

The old Banks family home.
Courtesy of current owner
Richard Kline.

Bridge Street view of ravine
looking north.

Looking out from the SCOPE house one could think the area was solidly black, though the other side of Church Street was property owned by the Banks, a leading, extended white family, and nearby were several beautiful, large white homes and a sizable white-folk church. But the Banks' old mansion and others like it were down in the southeast quadrant where most white townspeople lived.

July 12 was registration. It was raining when the gang woke at seven. Dread of a washout grew when the SCOPErs got in the Chevy covered with signs, drove to the Harts' and saw no one there to help them. To get people out, Lynn,

Carol and Harold drove to the hilly Mack Hill Street neighborhood just off Railroad Avenue South. "The rain turned the roads into mires. The red clay road slopes into deep ditches. It wasn't too hard to get stuck—the car slid right into the side. The boys along in the car got covered with mud as they pushed me out. I went back to the courthouse with only one person—someone else could go out to Mack Hill, or walk the area. Mr. Federick offered to do it."

John Babin consults with men by the courthouse on a registration day. That may be Perry Bull and Harry Pierce on the right. Photo Lynn Goldberg.

At the courthouse the line wound up the stairway to the registrars. Lynn was elated: "At least thirty people were already there. Harold and I went out again to pick up some people towards Cameron. Each car as it went out received a map and cards. We picked up three people. Dirt roads had to be forgotten.

"Panic prevailed at the courthouse. Many more people were needed to stay there. Sample forms were filled out with most people. I went out to get gas and on the way stopped at the Harts'. Two FBI agents were there, to interview us of all things. They couldn't have chosen a better time—ha!"

Photo Lynn Goldberg.

Carol recalls thinking, "Wow, they really do look like their stereotype, wearing suits and trench coats." Lynn thought so, too: "Agent Friday brought me out to his car to talk in private. We lit up cigarettes and proceeded. He showed me his ID, then told me an assistant attorney general had requested the inves-

137

tigation for a possible harassment case." When Carol asked her agent why he needed all that information, especially about her family, "He said it was in case I got murdered, they would know who to notify."

Each of them signed multi-page, flowery statements and were told they might need to testify in court. The process cost them a precious hour. Back at the courthouse Lynn was glad to find that NAACP staff and Orangeburg SCOPE had kept things running. The latter called the girls naive to think the FBI was doing anything more than gathering information to pass on to local authorities.

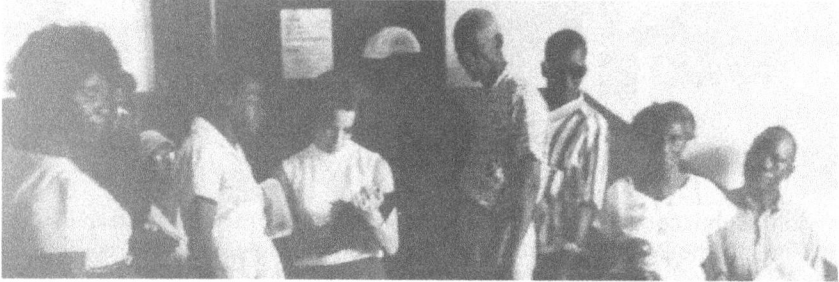

Carol checks names upstairs. Top of stairs may be Harry Govan. Fourth down may be Clarence Ziegler. Photo Lynn Goldberg.

At some point Carol was walking uptown with an Orangeburg boy named Freddie. A furious white man seized their forms, asking what they thought they were doing.

Lynn drove John back to the Harts' and picked up some pens. Dick Miles suggested she contact the federal DA about the slow-down. So back to the Harts' again, where she telephoned US Attorney Terrell Glenn how only five had been allowed to register in the first hour. "All sorts of illegal things were going on—even interpretation of the Constitution. Earl tried to stop it, but as soon as his back was turned they started again. Earl had to leave, telling us to ring Matthew Perry if anything happened." Later Orangeburg's Shelly Rosen got into the room to watch. "He had quite a time keeping track of them, and had a long list of complaints and names. Attorney Glenn said not too much could be done immediately, but apparently he received so many calls that word came down. He promised me he would call the county attorney to look out. The lines began to move a little. Earl Coblyn later said he had been in Glenn's office during the afternoon.

"Terry and I went back to our house to get a camera. At the courthouse, the line wound down the stairs and down a hallway. People stood all day or sat on the stairs. Almost all are older. An entire generation is missing—those in their twenties and thirties. We brought Kool-Aid in large jars and passed it out, and hundreds of candy bars. The workers had sandwiches on the job prepared by some of the women."

By 2:00 the atmosphere had improved when Lynn began helping inside the registration room: "The registrars found we were more help than bother, and we began the exhausting job of laboring with the people over the ridiculous form. Many people could barely write, and labored over each blank as we told them what to write; sometimes letter by letter.

"It was sweltering in the room as the sun came out. I was about to faint. The registrars were nice enough to finish all the people who were in the room at 5:00. The last

W.M. keeps watch.
Photo Lynn Goldberg.

people who got through at quarter to six had come at about noon. People waited hours and were not registered. I felt very distressed at these brave people, most of them hardly knowing what was going on, standing in that heat so patiently. They want so little. I wanted to cry. I have never been so pooped after three hours of sleep the night before, and running all day long."

Next day, *The State* announced results, saying that E.C. Morris, the county official in charge, estimated that about 110 blacks had registered: "way above normal. We normally register about twenty a day this time of year. There were so many applicants we didn't get to eat lunch. I went out one time to use the telephone, and I saw them lined on the stairs all the way from the second to the first floor in the courthouse." In what must have been the first time Hope was cited in *The State*, he said that the registrars "seemed fair" but also called on the board to open more than one day a month because, "At the present rate, it would take at least three years to register all the unregistered Negroes in the county." Dick Miles told the paper that about ten had been rejected. When the books closed at 5:00, we'd counted more than sixty still in line, and fifty more had needed to leave the line before it closed, after waiting four to five hours.

Earl stopped by at the end of the day. As usual, Lynn and Mary Ann gabbed with him for hours and asked him to join them for dinner. He led them to Quick Charlie's Dairy Bar, an Orangeburg hangout, noted Lynn, "for all the active civil rights people and intellectual, wealthy Negroes."

"Quick Charlie is a special friend of Earl's. We ended up going to Quick Charlie's house. He owns two—there are wealthy colored people. The house we went to, following his yellow T-Bird, was beautifully furnished with all sorts of extraordinary objects. We called the Orangeburg kids who arrived soon after with booze and spirit for the party I wanted. It was really fun, and I would have let myself go if I hadn't felt sick for being so tired. We left and I drove everyone home—to bed. Ah-h-h."

Next day the Brandeis five and Harold, Butch, John Lee, and Junior drove two hours to swim and picnic at a state beach near Beaufort. They would visit it several times that summer, having much less trouble than described by Sherie Labedis for Charleston SCOPE at Edisto Beach. From the beach they drove to Charleston to sightsee and visit SCOPE people there. The next few days, Harold and others in the Calhoun group began compiling a score of complaints on the registration day slow-down as evidence for a federal case under the pending *Voting Rights Bill*. The suit would need signed statements from people who had been turned away.

The group also began to document complaints from people who had been turned down at the Beach Party textile plant. After Earl stopped by and helped her type out the complaint sheets and statements, Lynn reported, "This comes under the 1964 *Civil Rights Act*, since there are over 100 employees in the plant. The land for this place was bought from a Negro with the understanding that Negroes would be hired—no one has. A couple of times people have been asked to report to work, then told there was no work. Something should happen here. We also found out that Brandeis trustees are large stockholders in the company."

Harvard also owned shares. Later, Ish and Ham dropped by the plant together. Mid-July another line of investigation emerged. A woman named Grace Brooks showed up to talk with SCOPE about the desegregation of St. Matthews schools. She said she'd be working with SCOPE.

19. HAROLD'S TRESPASS

On Bastille Day July 14 Elias moved Ish to St. Matthews, fulfilling Calhoun's request for an additional male. A new and compelling reason for this was that Terry had to appear in Baltimore at an army induction. Once there, he planned to "report" but not "step forward" at the risk of thirty months in prisonl. He'd be leaving July 19, not knowing whether he'd be back.

The group took Ish's arrival as a sign that Elias didn't trust them. In Lynn's view he'd been sent "to check us out... to investigate and take over. Ish is poking into everything, and I have a horrible feeling of being watched. I am afraid Carol and I are going to be considered insignificant, and will be ignored as far as responsibility goes. Our group has been functioning essentially without a leader. We each act according to our judgment. Ish began asking me and Carol, each time we did something, if we had told Mary Ann. I was quite furious."

She needn't have been, but Ish was probing about Mary Ann because Elias thought she had "taken over" and wanted to know about that. Later Dave Gelfand and Carole Estes visited St. Matthews from Waltham and also, according to Lynn, noticed Mary Ann's domination of the group. By that time Lynn herself sometimes felt that "Mary Ann doesn't like being bound to the group. I agree that it's nice to have some freedom, but she was wrong in just disappearing without telling us she was [going to Orangeburg]."

Whatever license she was taking, Ish could see that Mary Ann and Lynn were the sparkplugs of Calhoun County SCOPE. Fifty years later, Jean Keitt struggles to remember him, but Mary Ann she'll "never forget. We talked a lot! Mary Ann was a lot of fun." Ish concluded the group was basically consensual, though Mary Ann was its strongest influence and central to its coordination with Earl and Orangeburg. So he gladly settled into the team, as much as they would let him. They'd had cause to worry.

A day later Lynn was thawing out: "Our evening was fun. We invited some of the colored boys over, and Ish played his autoharp. Singing is so essential here. A couple of kids tried playing the autoharp. We sat around 'til late joking around—It's so good to have our own house." (A year later Carol went so far in forgiving Ish as to marry his college roommate.)

Money was a second sore point between Elias and Calhoun SCOPE. Until mid-July, the latter still depended on funds controlled by Elias. Three days after bringing Ish, Elias returned, accompanied by others.

Ish blended in. Photo Carol Sable.

Between him and Calhoun, "the battle over the budget began, and no agreement was reached," wrote Lynn. "The solution was our decision to pull out of the Brandeis group. We are now on our own financially. I hope we make it."

Elias may have understood differently, but Lynn's impression of being "on our own" was shared by the rest of her group. That night we began to write and mimeograph appeals to contacts in the north. Another source might be SCLC, via Bob Heard, a staff man for Hosea Williams who was visiting Orangeburg at the time. Lynn had befriended him in Atlanta. Their dealings started promisingly: "He is going to hopefully get us some money, since he is the one who cleans up dear Hosea's desk and finds all the forgotten SOS's. I am going to try to work directly through Bob. There are certain things a girl can do in such cases."

Two days later, however, "Bob had been kept at our house so he wouldn't mess up our meeting. Mary Ann was very intolerant of him, and had had a big fight with him. He was furious and about to retaliate by screwing our group. I was the only one who could talk with him, and I am a little annoyed at the way things were handled. I became his secretary, typed some of the large number of letters he was turning out, and corrected others. He was about to ask Atlanta to get rid of Mary Ann. Boy! Hosea is running around so fast that Bob practically runs the office. We had better be careful."

We wanted to buy at least one car because Carol didn't drive, and Lynn and Ish were under age to drive rentals, though they did drive them later on. Around July 21 in Charleston, we rented a pair of Rambler Classics at "fabulous rates," $25 a week for each. "So much better than buying a junk heap and paying outrageous insurance and repair costs," Lynn raved. "Dependable and luxurious. What a car to drive! It sticks to the road like glue and has power steering, air conditioning, seats that lie flat, and wall-to-wall carpeting."

Soon her parents sent $170 raised from a dozen Princeton friends and earmarked for cars. Local Rev. Milton suggested a two-day barbecue, record hop and mass meeting. The more modest result was a barbecue at Ham Federick's place in Fort Motte on July 31. Lynn and others drove out through a 3:30 a.m. fog to help with (or anyway witness) the start of the ten-hour cook.

Lynn described how "we sat with Mr. Federick. It was wonderful—the hot fire, the chill night air, the smell of the hog, roosters crowing. Everyone told stories, only like I've read in books. Mr. Federick gets the prize. He has seen much of the world, and has amazing things to tell. His style is so alive and simple. Day broke as we sat there, and we parted to go home."

Elias returned on the 22nd with Dean Zion to complain that he had not been informed that George Goldsmith had been sending out fund-raising letters. Lynn blew her stack, then made him realize "we really were going to insist that we be autonomous, so he said none of us would get the scholarship aid we needed. I fumed and paced during the whole meeting, but actually we got our way. Elias wants us still to report our actions, which is fine, but he will no longer accept collect calls."

To KZSU on July 30 she would confide, "Our dean of students couldn't understand our commitment to Calhoun County and the people that are working there, rather than to some deeper thing called Brandeis SCOPE, which means nothing to us."

The visit did not end supervision. Elias continued to appear and monitor, and Atlanta apparently continued to expect him to pass on orders.

Hope and Ham dropped in on us when they could. One evening Ham invited us to supper at his home. Lynn noticed when the group "began talking about southern sex codes. Amazing! It's a shame he never had much education, but even without it, he is a match for any of us in an intellectual discussion. He told us much about the South. He blames the Negro women who have children by white men. I find it hard to believe that this still is going on, and right here in St. Matthews."

Better believe it. Though we didn't know it at the time, chief among white men planting children in local black women was St. Matthews' scary chief of police, an extremely difficult man to refuse. That might be understatement.

Lynn noted a mother across the street who had come over to the SCOPE house. "The baby is very light skinned and has light hair, but is Negro even so. What a beautiful child! These white man's children have an even worse place in society than the Negroes. They are slapped by their father and ignored by the Negroes. I can't understand what kind of a father this is. Apparently, the more educated Negroes find the women who lower themselves to the white man in this way intolerable. White man can take a Negro girl, but Negro man and white girl are forbidden. Another thing I can't comprehend is that often white men live with colored women just as if they were married, and yet such a circumstance is forbidden by law in marriage. The southern white man is strange."

Ham talked with them about harassment: "Mr. Federick has been standing up for years for his rights. He and the other people laughed at the ridiculous behavior of the whites. The biggest source of annoying arrests is, of course, connected with cars. There is always a little something which can be jumped on."

Sunday July 18 Ham took them church-hopping in Lone Star, stopping unannounced at one where Sunday school and a business meeting were still in progress before the service. Ham went in to talk to someone. Lynn found some boys who said they were willing to work with SCOPE around Lone Star. After half an hour the group asked a deacon to go get Ham. They knew that once he started talking, he had a hard time stopping. Ish and Mary Ann stayed at this church and the others moved on.

"The next was a poor, cinder-block building with few people in attendance. We were greeted by uncomfortable stares. It was fortunate that Mr. Fed was along. He spoke to the pastor who was happy to have us, and John Babin and I remained as the last two went on. The church had pews of boards thrown carelessly together. A large, pot-bellied stove stood in the center. The shabbily dressed people were obviously bothered by our presence." Lynn and John each spoke but couldn't decipher people's "That's right" response.

The preacher gave a sermon on registering, quoting every other sentence from the Bible. Outside afterwards, an 80-year-old woman stopped them, saying she was 'wored down' by pushing forty years for Negro education. "She wanted someone to help her now. She was 'too old to vote, and to do any more.' We asked her just to push and we would do the rest. Her feeling was that she had never seen the Lord help her, but the minister said we were sent by God."

After churches, some of the group attended a party including the Coblyn family at the Orangeburg County home of Earl's co-conspirator, education professor Charles H. Thomas, Jr. "Dr. Thomas has a beautiful house. What a bourgeois afternoon!" thought Lynn. "We were all so excited by it, we went running through to see it." Most impressive were three separate phone lines, each with three extensions. "We had great fun calling the Liberty number in Orangeburg, a five-minute recording about a communist organization called SCOPE. The 'poor brainwashed students' are required to read books by such known communists as Howard Fast. 'This is Liberty Bell.'"

Southern Bell installers from Orangeburg had come to the SCOPE house July 19 to put in a phone the group had requested. As they worked they stared at the mix of blacks and whites around them. Our number, 5543, was not a "party line" but somehow, more and more as time went on, strange male or female voices broke in to rant and threaten. Clearly the line could not be used for confidential calls. For those we sometimes used the Harts' phone or, later on, the one in Earl's office (undoubtedly bugged more discreetly).

By mid-August, a day before someone opened fire on the SCOPE house, the threatening calls would arrive more than daily. Lynn, August 17: "Last night while Ish was alone he had a frightening conversation with someone who ended with 'I'll be seeing you, you mother-fuckin' bastard.' Today a phone call of ours was interrupted by a male voice saying, 'you n____ lover.'" August 19: "Late in the afternoon we got a call saying we would all be dead tomorrow. Ish called the FBI, hung up, and directly following we got another call—we had better get out of town, or we won't be alive. Then for over half an hour we had constant threats, most from a woman with a husky voice. We were actually having fun—six kids standing around the phone and answering it by turns. Strangely, the phone rang immediately after we hung up. We left a message with Earl and told the St. Matthews police as they circled past the house. The police informed us they would watch our house, and that they had increased their force (probably added one man to their 'enormous' force)." Too bad John Lee hadn't gotten the job.

But August was still a ways away. On July 20, Lynn felt tensions heating up in the sticks. Four people drove to Lone Star, four to Caw Caw township, about six miles west of St. Matthews. "Something is getting done finally. The only problem is houses. We have maps of the roads with the houses, but often houses aren't marked, or else they are all white houses. Sometimes we drive for miles only to find not a single house. We can only cover a few each trip because of all the driving. This is especially true in Caw Caw with its beautiful dense forests and rolling hills—the only pretty part of the county that I've seen.

"Incidents are getting more numerous. Two possible reasons. One is that the areas we are entering are more difficult, the other that the whites are getting more annoyed with us and are becoming more active. Lone Star is especially bad, and the Negroes have, in many cases, been frightened into saying nothing to us."

Revivals were heating up, too. Each lasted several days. From a tent pavilion down the road, electric guitars sang out. Churches were stuffed every night and SCOPE was granted time to speak. Also gearing up for some SCOPErs was the party scene in Orangeburg. The evening of July 21, while the boys attended a CCIL meeting, Lynn and Mary Ann drove there to look at the kinds of cars we might rent next day from Continental in Charleston. At that point, Orangeburg SCOPE had fanned out in the county. Its precinct groups were coming in to pick up new cars, so Mary Ann and Lynn saw lots of people and "had the greatest time. The Orangeburg gang has delicious liquor—wow! I couldn't have much because I was driving, but Mary Ann and the others got very high. I couldn't believe the foul jokes that were coming out of everyone, especially Earl Coblyn who kept falling off his perch on the car. Al Ziegler told amazing yarns about his family in the mountains of Tennessee."

(Alan Conrad Ziegler [1926-2003] was a 40-year-old zoologist and ex-Freedom Rider who had spent his early years in Texas and Georgia. He was working with the AFSC. According to one obit, he was a great one for humor and "almost a trickster." According to another, "His Southern background was apparent in a lingering soft drawl and gentlemanly ways." In later years he became a leading conservation scientist.)

We continued to learn how essential were Harold, Butch, John Lee, Junior, and the others who worked alongside us. After a meeting "to come closer with our coworkers," Lynn felt gratified "to see that some of the kids are beginning to feel our purpose. It was their suggestion that we take only one hour for lunch instead of two to give a longer afternoon. They will have to partake of peanut butter and jelly with us, and help us map-make and organize to get out more quickly. We asked for more people—I fear, in vain—and discussed the non-violent philosophy once more. The greatest part of the evening was the singing—we covered every freedom song in the book, and more. We made up verses, and had a gay time. Afterwards we worked 'til late."

A day or so later in a newly rented Rambler, Harold, Carol, and Lynn canvassed Lone Star until 2:00. "Almost all of the people are reluctant to have anything to do with us, and our contact with the whites makes it obvious why. Although no measures have been taken against the Negroes, severe threats have been made, which are very intimidating. We even came upon a strong Negro segregationist—a little old lady very annoyed at Carol and Lynn for working with Harold: 'He should at least be our chauffeur.' She wouldn't let us leave a sample application. We kept driving down roads that disappeared into tracks through a field—very annoying when you can't turn around. We kept doing this all morning—great for the car!"

Later that day, they and Effie Kimpson were out again. "We were heading merrily back when we spied Sheriff Rucker by the road. What *hadn't* we done now? He followed us for a long time, I suspect hoping to catch us for speeding or running away. Boy, am I glad I was driving a car with a reliable speedometer! At last the light flashed and I pulled over. Our smiling Sheriff stepped out and approached us."

Sheriff Rucker had stopped them to accuse Harold of trespass and order him to trial in Lone Star the next Monday night. There had been a complaint. That morning Lynn had been driving a small dirt road to some Negro "habitats—what more can I call them?—around a plantation field. We stopped at some, then stopped again to talk to some Negroes in the field. Harold asked them if they could talk for a minute. He spoke with them while Carol and I waited by the car. As we drove off, he said he had seen a white lady drive up behind us, stop, and turn back. Neither Carol nor I had seen her. She got our license plate number and reported us."

Next day, Ish would return to the farm, not stepping into any field, to talk to people whose homes were on white-owned land. The owner appeared and warned him not to trespass. Ish was civil but resolved, saying he believed he had a right to approach the homes as a 'business invitee', as Earl Coblyn had assured us. He wrote home that we'd "have to go back to the farm Monday to pick up the people we promised rides to."

Lynn and others met Earl at Quick Charlie's to fill him in on Harold's arrest. In Lynn's understanding, the arrest was complicated by Harold's being on probation for receiving a stolen can of beer, and the collateral covering his probation was the deed to his parents' house. (Jo Freeman points that it's odd legally for collateral to be attached to probation. Was he out on bail?)

Monday July 26 Lynn wrote, "Everyone came in around 6:30 for a quick dinner before the trial. Each group had a story to tell. Mary Ann had driven into a ditch. She and Gwendalyn had been helped by lots of white men. They were a little scared, but made it home. We had dozens of people in our house, and were rushing madly around in the short time before the trial. There were hamburgers to make. I dashed out to pick up Harold so he could discuss the trial with Earl. Earl, Harold and Mary Ann went off to the trial, and I left soon after with the Chevy filled with people. Mr. Hart and Mr. Murphy came with us, and also a boy from Lone Star who Carol had brought back to dinner, Jake Ellis. I was driving along when I noticed bright lights close behind me. I was about to comment, when I saw the flashing red light, and the car beeped for me to pull over. I thought at first I had been speeding because the Chevy has no speedometer, but Patrolman Lloyd Ayer began inspecting the car. Everything!—lights, brakes, turn, signals, etc. Good ole Chevy!—passed with flying colors! At the end, we got a sticker for our car, proving that we had passed. We thanked him politely and drove on."

Back safe in St. Matthews, Earl explained what had happened. He had not already been told the exact charges and therefore had asked for a continuum to the following evening. Earl looked them up. "He had fun tossing all his legal terms at us. We were all hacking around and having a good time. Ish pulled out his autoharp and we sang. It's such a blast thinking up new verses. While Earl talked to the men about a surprise election [more on this, next chapter], I danced and joked around with the local boys. The kids stuck around until late."

Next evening for Harold's continuum she and others sped to Lone Star in Earl's T-Bird and got there as a big crowd gathered. Everyone was nervous. She went into a store to buy a pack of cigarettes to share. They stood around for a while before going in.

"The court scene was hideous. The room was a large one in the bottom of a seemingly deserted building—the 'big' brick building in Lone Star, someone had told me. Behind a counter on one side stood a line of huge, nasty-looking white men including the judge [a local magistrate], Sheriff Rucker, a couple of policemen, and the owner of the field. The owner testified—and said nothing. He had not seen Harold; he did not know if Harold had, indeed, been in the field. The colored woman testified Harold had told her he had to see her. He'd said he was a civil rights worker. He talked with her for an hour. The poor lady had been so brainwashed, she didn't know what had happened. She had also been given something to drink. Sheriff Rucker testified the owner had told him that Harold had been in the field. He arrested Harold. Harold testified he had asked if he could talk to the woman from the edge of the field. She told him he could, and walked toward him. They'd spoken for several minutes.

"Earl attacked the case from two angles. First, Harold had not done the act willfully. In other words, as far as he was concerned, he was not trespassing because no one had informed him he was. Also, the complainant had not seen him. [Therefore,] Harold had the right to pay damages and be cleared of further penalty. The judge said, 'I don't understand what you're saying, but I overrule your motion.' When Earl asked him what motion he was talking about the judge said, 'I overrule both your motions.' I couldn't believe how stupid this man was. Harold lost and was fined $20. Earl paid $10, and the rest was due later.

"We moved the crowd over to the church. It was packed and they were really in the mood for a meeting. We sang with a lot of spirit. What was amazing was that our volunteers began standing up and speaking on their own initiative. I was so excited to see them taking up the words we had been saying for so long. A collection was taken up, and the entire $20 was given for Harold's fine. We paid off Earl and gave Harold the rest for Sheriff Rucker."

Everyone got a kick out of knowing that the white community would know where the money came from. As Ish summed things up, "Lone Star is a place where both whites and Negroes are convinced that things are toughest, but the meeting had a good turnout and lots of spirit—should help in getting people down to the courthouse Monday."

But the rest of the night was not so comforting. Back at the SCOPE house after we turned in, something—the Keitt family dogs?—made Lynn aware of a prowler outside. "We were up and down for a couple of hours, turning lights off and on, dead tired by 3:00."

20. Elections & Palaces

The previous chapter mentioned a surprise election. Shortly before July 25 we'd learned (perhaps incidentally, even a little abashedly, from W.M.) that three days after our next registration day on August 2, there would be a St. Matthews town council election. Caught by surprise, we met with and urged the town's CCIL leaders to consider running for seats. Three agreed: W.M., Toot and Thomas Murphy. Voters could approve up to six candidates, so the three men chose three white nominees to support as well. Keitt, Hart and Murphy were putting themselves and their young families on the line, and were wisely frightened. Lynn wrote, "Mr. Hart almost backed out. But they are each pushing each other, so they can't back down. The community is doing all the work, and we are providing the guidelines. Earl is helping with legal aspects."

Interviewed later by KZSU, three of us reflected on the weirdness of out-of-state white kids pressing these men to run. It made Lynn feel bad "that we're so important—the ones that have to provide this impetus. Three men that are going to run for council come over here and ask our advice. You wonder how a 40- or 50-year-old man can come to you for advice in his own home. They're the ones who know what it's like to live here."

We consoled ourselves with the value of creating situations in which blacks in the county could engage with us as whites who regarded them as equal and would act that way. Sunday the 25th SCOPE and the candidates planned and laid out flyers. Then Lynn, Mary Ann and Carol took off to meet Earl at Quick Charlie's at 9:00 p.m., which led to an evening of mimeographing, drinking and socializing with Earl and "Al." (This was either Al Ziegler or sociology grad student Albert Szymanski who, along with Mickey Shur and Dean Savage—another graduate student—formed a leadership trio for Orangeburg SCOPE.)

Terry returned on July 28. Next day, along with a visit from Elias, Geneva Floyd came over with the week's *Calhoun Times*, showing us articles on the approaching election and an advertisement for voting. Unfortunately, one article cited a law that said a voter had to be registered thirty days before an election, though we didn't think it applied to municipal votes. That may be as close as the county paper of record ever came to acknowledging our presence.

In Cameron we'd been disappointed by the results of a previous evening meeting. On July 29, at a second one planned by Rev. Milton, we focused on getting people involved. We spoke a little. Mainly, local people stood up, each adding encouraging words. John Lee, Butch and Junior stood in turn to add their own perspectives. "They were really prepared," wrote Lynn, impressed.

After the meeting, Lynn and others followed Rev. Milton in "a wild chase" to Orangeburg. "Furman was a riot in the car. We got to Quick Charlie's and had a squabble over money. We found enough, and each ordered something. Charlie drove in but we had to leave because we had work to do and didn't want to go to bed too late."

Next night after supper Lynn, Butch, Junior, John Lee, and maybe others fooled around. "We all have so much fun now," she mused. "We accept each other completely and play pranks on each other—I fear I am bound to lose my hair to a stray pair of scissors before I leave here."

For the election coming up on Thursday, more voters could still sign up on Monday August 2. Sixty people lined up by 9:00. When Lynn ferried 72-year-old Carrie White in nine miles from Creston, she estimated something more than 150 in the line that wound down the stairs, down the hallway, and in and out of various places. "Not one place to sit. The registrars had known this was going to be the situation, and still had refused the extra days or a switch to the courtroom so there would be more room. We are the only county around here which didn't get the extra days."

We ferried more people, searched desperately for more sample forms, and supported the line again with Kool-Aid. Earl helped us address a slow-down, alerting federal officials. Later the courthouse was not as jammed. Things went slowly but smoothly. The line became shorter and shorter until 5:00, when thirty people were turned away. According to Ish, 143 were registered. About 300 had been in line. The last person Lynn took home, Carrie White, had stood for seven hours.

After supper, most of the gang collapsed, but John Lee, Terry and Lynn drove to Club 4000, a ritzy place near Orangeburg, listened to music, had gin and 7-Up, got very high, and enjoyed it immensely. But it didn't look like Senator Gressette would increase the number of open days.

The day after that registration, the VEP petitioned the US attorney general to send examiners to South Carolina to witness continuing obstacles. In St. Matthews that day, John Lee, Junior and Lynn sat down for lunch at Mac's Grill, a small, white-owned, burger restaurant on Railroad Avenue near Mack Hill Street. Toot Hart had previously sent Junior and one or two others there to ask for sit-down service, per the *Civil Rights Act*, and they had been served. But Mac's had then closed for a spell. This time, they found it closed before they got there, "though, strangely, people still eat there."

Later, as the crew in St. Matthews compiled a list of people turned away at the courthouse, Ish and Mary Ann called from Orangeburg on a second consecutive registration day there. An Orangeburg city council election was looming that Earl thought—with support from whites associated with the recent influx of northern businesses—could bring in a black.

The court room was open for people to sit and wait in cool comfort. But after a record registration of 350 the day before, the registrars had slowed down, rejecting many after asking them to read, then halting the distribution of forms. Then, though there had been only two registrars, one left at 3:30 because (quoting Lynn) "he didn't want to register any more n_____s" and was "tired of having his picture taken." Now for lack of a quorum the process stopped.

Mary Ann and Ish asked the others to get there by 4:00, ready to demonstrate inside the court room. The St. Matthews gang tried to reach Ben Mack. Failing that, they left a message at Hope's farm about what was up. Meanwhile, Mary Ann and Ish were probably dodging instructions from Atlanta—relayed by Elias to Orangeburg SCOPE—not to get arrested.

Orangeburg SCOPE wanted registrars for tomorrow and more days in August. Lynn wrote, "The people had to be urged to stay. We told them they had to stand together for their rights. Most of us went around, sitting with the people and talking to them. At 5:00 the books closed." People's hesitation to stay might seem odd in light of massive demonstrations and arrests in Orangeburg as recently as two years before; but then the demonstrators had been local students mainly, not rural adults expecting to get home before nightfall.

Orangeburg SCOPErs told KZSU that about 250 people were inside the courthouse, including 200 "mostly mothers and grandmothers" from rural areas. Earl Coblyn told KZSU, "It was the first time I had ever seen the people in the rural areas really rally. It was very encouraging. There are, you know, very elderly people, mostly women. It's a good sign they can be rallied if someone provides them with leadership."

The Orangeburg courthouse, 1965.
Photo Dean Savage.

On advice from Earl and others in the court room after it closed, all but one of that group left to avoid arrest. We and the others remaining "sang songs and marched around the court room when the officials left. We opened the windows and let the city hear us. There were posters with slogans up on the windows." All but three of the non-student adults left. About 53 people remained—a dozen or more from Orangeburg SCOPE, a large contingent of Orangeburg kids, and seven from Calhoun: Butch and the six from Brandeis SCOPE. "Our decision meeting was short," Lynn wrote. "We would stay until 9:00 tomorrow or be arrested. The arrest was our own decision. Earl was there and told us everything. Sheriff Dukes came in. Suddenly, on both sides of the room, husky men in uniform poured in. They stood on each side as we announced our decision. They rushed us, jumping over the seats as we sat and sang."

To outnumber the protest, ar-resters included sheriff's deputies, SLED (the State Law Enforce-ment Division) and highway pa-trol. Lynn didn't feel scared as she was picked up, thrown and dragged out. As she passed Earl, "he en-couraged me to try to walk. I cried when a two-ton policeman stood on Al Ziegler's neck while hauling another limp body. In front of me John Babin and Al were dragged by the hands down the stairs and thrown into the car in a heap. My picture was taken. Al's hands were bent 'til they almost broke. Of course there was no medical aid,

The arrests. Photo Dean Savage.

and people had raw, bleeding burns from being dragged by their hands and feet along the stairs and cement sidewalks. The officers did all they could to hurt us, and enjoyed it thoroughly. Dozens of cars pulled up to the courthouse, with all of us singing. We were piled, pushed and thrown into the jail. We stood and sang songs while we waited for them to get our names."

Phyllis wrote home that Ish had "walked but when he slowed down he was prodded with a painfully twisted arm." Ish's only certain memory is embarrass-ment when Earl scolded him to hold his head high on the way out.

We were taken around the block to Orangeburg County jail, a.k.a. "the Pink Palace" ("pink" for its outer color, "palace" for its notorious filth) which was big enough to cram about fifty. Subsequent charges would be trespass and disorderly conduct. Donnie Coblyn ar-rived with fifty sand-wiches right around when Earl overheard a telephone conversa-tion about how more

The palace, 1965. Photo Dean Savage.

arrests would be made of people standing outside the jail. Earl pushed her back in the car and drove off. "There went our sandwiches!" Lynn rued.

Did we know that Donna had stayed in the Palace for joining a protest a few years before? She had her own issues with South Carolina. She'd been studying happily at Boston University when, according to her future husband, "Because of all this sociological abnormalcy that goes on in the black community, some damn woman in South Carolina made her go to a black school in the south for a year." He'd met Donnie after she fled back north.

In the footsteps of Jim Sulton and many others who'd been jailed there in 1960 before being shipped by cattle truck to Columbia "Hell Penitentiary," the 53 were led inside, finger-printed, photographed, and locked in collective cells by gender. Those under seventeen were given the option to leave; several did. Butch did not. Downstairs, Lynn and the other women were placed "in a revoltingly dirty cell with three beds. There is a toilet in the room that is disgusting. Also a sink and bathtub. We received no food."

Lynn reported other female prisoners (one black, two white) being "very nice" to the women. "They brought in piles of mattresses (my God—crawling filthy—but something) and blankets." The ladies fared all right that night. "In fact, we were comfortable. I slept well, but everyone was tense and woke up early—6:30. Boy, time goes slowly! I was bored in an hour. The white prisoner made us breakfast. I didn't eat any. Green scrambled eggs don't look appetizing. Neither did the fatback, biscuits and grits. We never got our coffee."

Three dozen boys were in a larger cell upstairs. Three beds. A scared, crying 13-year-old was sent home later that night. Orangeburg SCOPEr Robert Brumbaugh's shoulder had been scraped severely by dragging; another boy was sick; our request for a doctor was ignored.

We had no toilet because, according to one Orangeburg SCOPEr on a KZSU tape, "They got this [square] metal tank which held a prisoner in it where the bathroom was. It was in the middle of the room and we were around it. Apparently it wasn't supposed to be used for prisoners." There was an open shower, so paperless we used the drain. Some lay on narrow benches, more on the dirty floor. The Orangeburg SCOPEr added, "Maybe they had moved out some other prisoners because the other prisoners were stuffed—the colored in one and white in [two other rooms where] there were maybe ten, all in this little room as big as a bathroom. You know, bunks beds and a little bit of—so that not everyone could stand up at the same time. They gave us blankets for that night and talked about [jail, saying] they could sometimes have breaks and come out. The jailer was, I think, one of the trusties, so he was very easy-going."

Mid-late next afternoon we were released on $200 bond times eighteen SCOPErs plus eighteen others, arranged by Earl and covered by SCLC after a scramble to find the cheapest bondsman. Lynn wrote, "Just as they brought us our lunch at 2:00 (beans, rice, cornbread, potatoes, yick!) they announced that we were about to leave. It was exciting as they called each name, and we walked out, signed the bond and were free!"

Of the St. Matthews foursome, only Butch had been inside and arrested. As Lynn was released, Junior "buzzed up in a little VW. He always managed to wangle people's cars. He told us of his evening. He had been to Branchville four times bringing people home who had come to register. Then he stayed in the Orangeburg SCOPE house, taking messages and running errands. I can't believe it of Furman—the one who is always fooling around. He and Harold stayed in Orangeburg until 2:00. John Lee was also there."

Since Butch had declined a *Get-Out-of-Jail-Free* card, the problem was that *now* getting him out required a "parent" to pick him up. Earl was lining up people to stand in as "parents" for him and the other juveniles. Lynn drove Butch's "father" to the jail: "No luck. The man messed up and said he was an uncle—no good. We went to the courthouse to find the man who could authorize Butch to get out. We couldn't find him, so we went back to the Orangeburg SCOPE house. I was quite upset because Butch was the last one. Earl went down himself and was able to get Butch. I was sure glad to see him! He hadn't eaten, so Earl gave me some money, and I walked over with him to a luncheonette. When we got back Furman was there after bombing around in someone's car.

"Butch drove back. Since Furman hadn't eaten we stopped at Quick Charlie's. Furman is such a riot. Not only is every word that comes out of his mouth at 100 mph hysterically funny, but the things he does, too. At Quick Charlie's he was riding a bicycle around. Then he decided to sit on the handlebars and ride it backwards. He went zipping off down the highway."

Back in St. Matthews that evening after supper provided by John Lee's mother, Hope came by to catch up and join some of us at a meeting about the St. Matthews election tomorrow. Terry worked on the registration statistics. Lynn cleaned: "Our house was extraordinarily dirty. We had piles of dirty dishes and garbage, papers strewn all over the living room and chairs everywhere. What a mess."

The Orangeburg trial was set for Friday August 6, then postponed to the 12th. On the 12th the sheriff and chief of police testified about our singing and clapping and added bogus details about our standing on tables. Matthew Perry evoked precedents against arrests for trespass on public property; that charge was withdrawn. We were convicted of disorderly conduct and sentenced to thirty days or $50 fines. (The sentence was nullified later on grounds of unconstitutional vagueness and because no one had told us at the time that we were being disorderly.)

We lay pretty low in St. Matthews most of the election day on Thursday August 5. Three headed out early to Charleston to return the Ramblers we could no longer afford. The one Lynn drove was "on its last rental legs and needed a wheel alignment badly. At super-highway speeds, it was nearly impossible. We were in a hurry, so we had to go fast—problem—at the speed limit (65), the car shook like a dog shaking water out of its coat. I could just barely hold onto the wheel." It ran more smoothly at 68.

We also went to pick up Butch from his summer school final in Orangeburg. In town Lynn saw "an enormous column of thick, black smoke rising into the air. Crowds were hurrying in that direction, including some SCOPE members. Fire engines whizzed down the street. On the news we heard the back buildings of a school were burning—the school used by the tutorial project where some Orangeburg SCOPE people work. The building was totally lost, mainly because the firemen didn't know how to use their new modern equipment. Two fell off ladders, and four were overcome by smoke—all through carelessness—dummies!"

Carol, Citti, Al Szymanski, others, at the hearing. AP wirephoto.

Probably the trial. Where did Citti get the bunny? Photo Dean Savage.

Back in St. Matthews voting was still in progress at the courthouse. Lynn stopped there first and found "all sorts of problems. Outside stood a group of white men, including several police. Police cars were circling. We figured they were expecting us to demonstrate. Fake out on them. I imagine, though, that the presence of these white officials intimidated many of the Negro potential voters."

Some time that day when Terry was outside the courthouse tallying voters, a man drove up with a shotgun, threatening to shoot him. When Carol and Terry reported the matter, Sheriff Rucker reassured her with, "Get back to me after he shoots him."

John Lee was also at the courthouse, taking count of all the voters, and Lynn was hugely impressed by him there. At the same time, "we were all upset by the fact that only one of the three Negro candidates had gotten his poll watcher. When they could have had three people watching, it is sad they had only one."

Late afternoon, Lynn and Mary Ann zoomed back to Orangeburg to Earl, who was being pestered by reporters, to help him compose and type statements documenting the previous day's arrests and jailings. Exhausted, "Earl tried unsuccessfully to stay awake on Jack Daniels, so we took over while he relaxed. Matthew Perry dropped in for a while—what a charming man! Earl ordered sandwiches from a kosher delicatessen—I got a hot pastrami with potato salad—yum. Also good coffee, the first I've had all summer!"

Mary left for a meeting of the CCIL candidates back in St. Matthews; Lynn worked on with Earl. "It was late, and I was tired when I finished, but the evening was just starting. Al [Ziegler or Szymanski] and Earl had been relaxing and working on a letter to the paper from the people of Orangeburg thanking the demonstrators. More of the Orangeburg kids came. They read the letters and statements to see if they agreed."

Phyllis wrote home, "Ish called this evening to say that ballots were being counted—a large white group gathered around the courthouse and two local Negro men were inside watching the ballot count. Ish drove to the courthouse to watch for signs of disturbance, but the sheriff asked that he leave—fearing violence. He assured Ish that he'd protect the men inside. Ish was somewhat uneasy."

At midnight, Lynn and others drove from St. Matthews to a party being held for us and Orangeburg SCOPE at the Equator Club. "They had a whole meal for us, drinks, and I danced with all the boys. Did I have fun!"

What about the town council election results? Although white town voters far outnumbered black, about 120 blacks were registered, and 93 of them braved casting votes. Predictably the CCIL candidates lost, but the turnout ended assumptions that white St. Matthews owned local government.

21. MOMENTUM

Inauspicious Friday the 13th, Thais and Citti came by. So did Liz Hafkin from Richland and Jim Bowers who had dropped in on St. Matthews with Pat in July. Liz and Jim were back from a brief but harrowing trip to DC that Phyllis will describe later on. "Boy, it's good to see them!" thought Lynn.

Lunch turned into "time for a little integration. Because there were so many of us, only some of us could go to the 'hot spot'—Mac's Grill. The others went to The Jacket." To Mac's walked Carol, John Lee, Butch, Terry, and Lynn. "It was crowded. Carol and I sat at the counter. Later, as some people left, Terry,

Butch, and John Lee sat down. We waited. After a while Terry asked to be served. We were told the waitress wouldn't serve us. We asked a second time. When John Lee asked for four hamburgers, the waitress said, 'I'll only serve you. I only have to serve you, I don't have to serve them.' She was very cocky. We explained the reason she wouldn't serve us was that we were with Negroes; and that violated federal law. She didn't care, she wouldn't serve us. We could sit there as long as we liked. I think the other waitress was uncomfortable and wanted to serve us."

They sat a while, then left to confer with Earl.

Thais and Citti stayed over that night for a second integrated Saturday dash to the sea. The rest of the Kershaw crew came, too. Calhoun SCOPE really needed some down time. Our nerves were frayed. Lynn felt "very depressed. I have been for a long time. I kept feeling everyone was picking on me. I couldn't stand anyone except Carol in our group. John Lee bugs me as well as he bugs Harold. I threw a tantrum (after Butch and John Lee tried to strangle me) and went to sleep on the Keitts' porch with their dogs."

Saturday at 3:00 a.m. seventeen were ready to go, but "the Chevy wouldn't start again. Damn! We frantically looked for a second car. Some people looked all over for a fan belt for the second broken car. We found another car, belonging to Rudy Keller. Nine of us were in this car and eight in the Chevy."

The beach was rainy but beautiful. Lynn and Ricky Gurbst sat down near some white boys. "When we got up to leave they sang, 'John Brown had a little n_____.' We took another walk down the beach. It did seem to be clearing. We all got into our suits and went in. We had fun fooling around for a long time. Lunch was spread out on the back of the car since the ground was wet. We were not allowed to use the bathhouse." A hasty note on it now said, "Only for Campers."

After a stop in Charleston late that afternoon, the seventeen mashed themselves back in the cars. Cramped as she was with six in the back seat, Lynn slept all the way home. Next day, she returned the two hours to the beach with most of the Kershaw crew, and got back to St. Matthews in time for a meeting with local leaders about what to do with the rest of August.

Most important was helping CCIL to keep things going in the fall: "They should be the ones devising the plans and contacting people. The biggest chore is organizing precinct leaders who will have section leaders under them. Our duplicate file will go to them." We got suggestions of people to go out and meet individually before the list was set. In a week we hoped to get them all in for a meeting.

Mary Ann, Lynn and Carol devised a second fund-raising letter that Mary Ann took to Orangeburg to run off. Late that night Hope stopped by and went over the county map with us, showing where the precinct lines were. It took some time because he didn't have his glasses with him. Lynn found herself "the only one with patience enough to get each road divided at the right place, and to include all the houses. What a pain! At least Hope knows the roads, so I think we have a fairly accurate map. I wish we had known this all before. Our files would have been better organized."

Whatever the rest of us were up to, Lynn's diary suggests that she did most of the teaming up with John Lee, Harold, Butch, and Junior for August actions in St. Matthews. By August 7, St. Matthews youths were returning from summer jobs. Of that day she wrote, "We discussed direct action. Most of the community was anxious for a boycott of Winn Dixie [a grocery chain]. First we will need to make applications for jobs by qualified people—no problem. If no jobs come, we boycott. The Red & White fortunately hires Negroes, and would receive the additional trade. The small Negro stores would also get a boost."

For black St. Matthews youth, the most attractive target was the "public" white-only pool on Pool Circle, the horseshoe lane that surrounded just the SCOPE house, the Keitts' and the pool—close behind us but fenced and screened off by trees. Since July we'd been scoping it out. The plan we presented to local leaders: 1) Local kids and possibly one or two of us try to get in. 2) Post witnesses. 3) Take pictures. 4) When refused, leave and talk with the mayor. Failing all that, 5) a swim-in. "Actually" Lynn admitted, "I don't feel we are going to accomplish much—this must be reviewed and a more intensive plan put into effect."

Then another St. Matthews youth, Eugene Glover, dropped in to talk, accompanied by several friends. "Is he a sharp kid! We said nothing, and he began talking about what needed to be done and what he wanted to do. Ish kept leading him on to say more. He ended up deciding he wanted to start a youth organization. The first meeting would be Wednesday coming. Eugene said he would get the kids. He sounds good. He thought lots of guys would want to work on this."

Then John Lee came by and wasn't pleased to learn of Eugene's plan. Lynn thought John was feeling jealous. "The old in-group does not want some young agitators to replace them, especially now that John Lee is becoming a leader. John Lee told us not to depend on these 'kids,' as he called them from all of his 21 years. He said their parents would object, and we must talk to the parents first. He said he would talk with Eugene the next day. Fortunately, Eugene did not give in to John Lee."

August 9 or 10, Ham Federick and Ish tried to see a manager at the Beach Party plant. That day or the next, Lynn and Junior walked two hours in the dust and broiling sun to the Hampton-Taylor area to get statements from applicants the factory had turned away. We were probably down to one car then—the Pittsburgh Chevy—out of money for gas and down to generally meager meals. Walking back from Hampton-Taylor, they passed kids swimming in a lake. Lynn was amazed to see a white boy among the Negroes: "The lake must have been more attractive than the pool."

Round about then she also walked "uptown" with Harold and John Lee to Winn-Dixie for job applications. While the lads found the manager, she hid in the aisles, but they had no problem. "The manager was almost pleasant."

On the 10th she set out on foot again with Mary Ann to the laundromat, and quickly got a ride. "It's funny that ordinarily I would never take a ride from white or Negro boys, but here I feel very safe riding with any Negro boys. We went in the colored side. This laundromat is new, and only a partition separates the sides."

The laundry run was needed for Lynn to "make herself decent" before heading off that night with Hope, Butch, and a person named Eliza Brown to an SCLC convention in Birmingham. The car set out after dark.

Beyond Atlanta they stopped for gas, "necessary, but dangerous. Hope doesn't realize that cities are safer to stop in, but also it was late at night, and we couldn't risk running out. As we got to Douglasville we saw a flashing red light on our tail. Butch had been driving about two miles. He stopped. A large policeman pulled open the door. He asked to see license and registration. He began to shine the light in everyone's eyes. When he saw me—! Keeping the light in my face, he asked who I was. I couldn't see him, of course, and I couldn't understand him, so I didn't answer. He went back to his car, talked in his walkie-talkie, and soon two more men drove up. Eliza, who had been sleeping all this time, woke up to find a light in her eyes and cops all around her. She said nothing.

"A policeman yanked the door open next to me. 'Do your parents know you're here?' 'Yes, I just talked to them.' 'Did you run away from home?' 'No.' 'Are you married to him?'—pointing to Butch, although we weren't sitting together. 'No.' 'Are you dating him?' 'No, I've never dated him in my life.' At the same time they had taken Butch out and asked him questions about me, such as what nationality I was—I couldn't be American.

"We were all taken from the car. They clearly wanted to arrest me. If I hadn't been there, there would have been no trouble. One cop began to lecture me, most likely so I would talk back—grounds for arrest. I didn't say a word, just stood there and quaked—I really shook. He gave me the same old shit about how I was a trouble-maker, and should be home minding my own business. The colored folk didn't want me here—they're doing fine themselves. If I were his daughter, he'd shoot me through the face.

"They couldn't create grounds to arrest me, so one of them said, 'Well, you were speeding back there,' to Butch. He had not been speeding—we had been careful to go five miles under the speed limit which is lowered, anyhow, to a ridiculous point. They took Butch and told Hope to follow. They zoomed off, hoping Hope would follow, so he could be caught for speeding, too.

"Our car crept into town. Naturally, we had lost the police cars. We hadn't the faintest idea where to go. We went up and down the main street and finally stopped. Not much later a police car approached. 'You were supposed to follow.' We were led to the station, where Butch was already locked up. The fine was paid, and Butch was released. I thanked the police pleasantly, and we walked out.

"Five minutes later, we were in the next town, crawling cautiously to Birmingham. Hope was driving this time. The first police weren't kidding when they said they had called ahead to warn the towns of our approach. Hope did all the talking—boy, he knows how to talk to these guys! He was charged with speeding—we were not! Hope got us off saying that the policeman had been going over the speed limit because he was catching up to us. All the policeman could do was agree. The charge was dropped, and we went ahead."

At that early hour of morning they were just about to run out of gas when they found a willing station. Around 4:00 a.m. somewhere in Georgia, car noises woke Lynn up. They stopped at a station that couldn't fix it. "I didn't realize, at first, what was going on. As we drove along and sparks and smoke poured out of the side of the car, I learned we had burned out a bearing. It was rather a bad time for an integrated car to be stuck. Hope tried to pack the wheel with grease, but still the sparks came, and the car shook violently. We stopped, let the car cool, went a few feet further and had to stop again. We kept doing this all down the road. Eventually, we saw an open Texaco. O happy sight! We crossed our fingers. Thank God the guy had what we needed and was willing to repair it. What a relief. It took a long time. I sat on a step, had a sandwich and watched the sky grow light, nervous each time a car drove in. But everyone was friendly. A white man even stood around and talked with us about the car."

The three-day conference began August 11. By chance that's the same day, in her grandparents' house on old plantation land about four miles up the road from St. Matthews, Viola Davis was being born. Within two months, her family would leave for good and settle in Rhode Island.

Five days before, SCLC had opposed Calhoun being part of the Orangeburg sit-in and perhaps the sit-in itself. Now, the call was to "march and demonstrate until more registration days were granted...really struggle, and not relent until we have won."

As rebellion ravaged Watts, the SCLC proceedings proceeded and Hope caught up on sleep. Lynn believed it was "the best night of sleep he's had since 1962." She took careful notes of the sessions with her left hand, parrying male advances with her right. After numerous tries she cornered Hosea Williams privately about money to help us out. All-business Hope was itching to get back home where he was needed. When the Calhoun car left the conference early, he carried a check from Hosea for $185.

Ricky Schaffer was also in Birmingham for the convention plus several days that felt like his most rewarding that summer: "While the convention only began today, the past two days have been among the most exciting and enlightening I have ever experienced. About fifteen of us took a trip [to Selma] yesterday to see about organizing a march of unregistered people to the courthouse. (Dallas County received four federal registrars yesterday.) When we got there, 200 people were already waiting—a fantastic, empowering sight—people who a year ago would never have dreamed of getting registered! Their joy was matched only by the rapt expression on the faces of the workers I was with who marched and were beaten there less than half a year ago."

On a fact sheet for VISTA Volunteers, Ricky scrawled, "I am not going to finish out the summer in Columbia—maybe. I have discovered a wonderful project called the Selma Free College that I would like to work on during the next three or seven weeks. It is for people of all ages—about two hundred now attending in art, Negro history, Negro literature, federal laws, French, math, dramatics, and physical ed. But there are really not teachers and students, for the real purpose of the school is to explore the possibility for Negroes and whites to live together in a none-too-friendly social order." But as far as Ricky can recall, he didn't stay and get involved.

Hope's crew got back Friday night. Lynn's parents had just arrived with a station wagon full of books for a library Hope was putting together to be of more use than the small public Negro branch.

Saturday morning Lynn and Ish drove out to pick up the station wagon that had run out of gas while Terry was transporting Head Start kids in Fort Motte. En route, the two refilled at Mr. Smoke's Pure Oil and (finally!) bought and filled a gas can.

That night the Klan assembled, as announced by the *Calhoun Times* and advertised on a poster Ish pulled off a tree by a pond outside town. The Klan did not have far to come, since the leader of St. Matthews Lodge No. 26, United Klans of America, was also St. Matthews' chief of police, as locals knew. The rally took place where it generally met, on his property between Sikes Grocery and the Red & White grocery just outside the western edge of town.

Ben Mack shared some background that Ish boiled down: "There's virtually no Klan here despite the fact that Calhoun was once a stronghold. The Klan hasn't been openly active in South Carolina since the late '40s. Before that they held their rallies in the heart of the Negro communities and commonly dragged men out of their homes."

In the mid-1950s, the civil rights movement had given rise to white Citizens' Councils, a more genteel group than the Klan. Historian Euan Hague has suggested that, when we were there in South Carolina, the Councils were stronger than the Klan, but another writer, Wyn Craig Wade, says that in the '50s and '60s UKA Grand Dragon Robert Scoggin was working diligently to revive the Klan in the state. According to another, Michael Newton, South Carolina authorities held it somewhat in check. For example, the state had passed anti-mask laws,

United Klans Of America, Inc.

KNIGHTS OF THE

KU KLUX KLAN

WILL PRESENT A PROGRAM

Saturday Night, Aug. 14

8:00 P. M.

ST. MATTHEWS, S. C.

Highway No. 6 at Red and White Store

Come Hear The Truth

Several Good Speakers

The White Public Is Invited

Authorized By The Board Of Directors The United Klans Of America, Inc.
National Office: Suite 401, Alston Building, Tuscaloosa, Alabama
S. C. Office: Box 4144, Spartanburg, S. C.
Sponsored by the South Carolina State Office and St. Matthews Lodge No. 26

A pencil correction changes "at" to "near" the grocery.

defied around 1955 by The Association of South Carolina Klans. In 1957, authorities obtained sentences against two Klan members for the beating of Claude Cruell in Greenville. In that instance, six "knights" were arrested; an "Exalted Cyclops" was sentenced to six years; a co-defendant got two. This did not deter the Klan's 1961 assault on Freedom Riders in the state. At that point, Scoggin's UKA was getting trained in marksmanship and demolition.

In 1963-64, says Newton, "As Alabama and Mississippi seethed in violence, the UKA worked more quietly in the Carolinas. Robert Scoggin expanded the Palmetto State realm to twenty klaverns by early 1964, increasing to 55 by 1966. Newton says Scoggin publicly warned against violence, and his followers generally listened, but in 1963 someone set off a bomb near the home of Henri Monteith, Modjeska Simkins' niece who was about to integrate USC.

John Babin thinks the rally in St. Matthews on Saturday featured speakers from Kentucky. As evidence he recalls an incident that summer in which three SCOPE cars convoyed one evening from St. Matthews to Orangeburg. As he tells it, he and Mary Ann were in the front seat of one car with Butch and either Harold or John Lee in the back. En route they noticed they were being tailed by a car with its lights out. Babin flicked his own lights as an SOS to the cars in front. To his surprise, the guys in the back seat pulled out guns. Then the chase car flew by with white teenagers pointing guns, and someone in Babin's took down the number on its Ohio plates. Afterward, says John, ownership was traced back to the head of the Kentucky Klan (Ohio borders northern Kentucky). So, were these teenagers from Kentucky?

This fifty-year-long recollection is suspiciously similar to another tailing incident described by Lynn in which no guns are mentioned. Also, John's is the only mention Ish has found of anyone working with Brandeis SCOPE showing arms in its presence that summer (we'll discuss Mr. Haynes' owl hunt later).

Still, Sherie Labedis' SCOPE account of Berkeley County near Charleston includes much more about arms on the black side, and it's certain that South Carolina farmers—black and white—had been armed since way-back-when, and with the return of black veterans from World War II, blacks had firmed up on defending their homes from whites.

This is how Ish summarized what Ben Mack said about how armed power had begun to shift: "In 1947 an incident set the Negro community into opposition. One night a Negro farmer was called out of bed to the door by two men who said they wanted water for their car. He got a bucket and filled it, and the three of them went a short way to the car. There a number of Klansmen jumped out and grabbed the farmer. He cried out and his wife and 12-year-old son heard. With his father's shotgun, the boy raced out to the road and at gunpoint demanded his father's release. The man in charge told the others to continue binding up the father while he walked toward the boy and asked for the gun in a friendly way. The boy shot him dead. The other men released the farmer and rode away. In the time that followed, several Klansmen were killed nearly every week, and Negroes all over the state simply began to shoot back. Until very recently the Klan was almost non-existent and they haven't returned to the kind of brutality they once practiced. The most we've heard of is that they burned two crosses (one on white property) the night after one of our mass meetings."

Other of Babin's memories of SCOPE have also turned into marvelous yarns. In a recent version of the August rally in St. Matthews, the Klan and onlookers of both races assembled and crosses were lit. Lynn, her father, and Harold were there. A speaker announced that no violence would fall upon anyone there. Meanwhile, John was posted alone at the SCOPE house. At a knock on the door, he found about twenty players from Orangeburg's vaunted SCSC football team "armed to the hilt," inviting him to join them on their way to the rally. But John had to stand by the phone.

Later, he recalls, Lynn and her father swung by and took him. The rally had drawn about a thousand, and the speaker was talking about John, who was always "kind of visible. Here I am standing on the edge of the Klan meeting, lighting a cigar." As he stood there, the athletes mounted the stage from behind, put guns to the heads of the speakers and ordered them out of the county. That ended the meeting, John remembers, and ended the Klan in the county.

Well, it didn't do either. But maybe there were SCSC athletes among the observers that night, since many young Orangeburg blacks took part in SCOPE that summer. The following account, based on diaries and letters, is closer to the truth.

Correctly or not, locals had told us it would be the first public Klan event in the county in ten or twelve years. Since we were known in town, we planned to stay home, but a few guys from Orangeburg SCOPE would attend. Then, since George Goldsmith was in town, he drove Lynn and others past the meeting, where Lynn saw a large crowd listening to speeches. "Up on the stands were people dressed in white robes and the big cheese in red." After the drive-by, "we stayed at home, keeping ourselves occupied." Later, the Orangeburg SCOPE group came by to report what they'd seen, and Mickey Shur mentioned having dropped a SCOPE pin in the pointy white donation hat. In response, according to Mickey, a Klansman on stage announced, "We know you're out there!" Today, Dean Savage, another leader of Orangeburg SCOPE, suspects that Mickey's bit of swagger unwittingly triggered retaliation against our St. Matthews group.

As a member of the Orangeburg convoy, Thais recalls "hiding behind bushes on the outskirts of a field, the speakers' platform with the giant wooden cross lit by the headlights of the trucks." She recalls her shock at the speakers' emphasis on "very graphic descriptions of our supposed miscegenation! Which I assure you were 100% invented. Everybody was focused on the stage. We were behind all that. An awful lot of what they had to say was about the sexual predilections of us northerners. The families, little kids on their shoulders, they're all listening to this, specific sexual descriptions. I was horrified. Sex between blacks and whites was the trigger point for those folks. I was shocked. I didn't think of myself as a prude, but those explicit descriptions, in front of the children, brought home to me the eternal and essential link between racism and sexual insecurity. To this day I believe that is the foundation of the current 'white rights' movement in the US."

What she says she heard is compatible with a letter handed out that summer from Grand Dragon Scoggin, though his focus is not the sexual act but the "diabolical program to wipe out the white race by mongrelization," whites being slaughtered in the Congo and how the white race—a minority that had bestowed civilization and wealth on the rest of the world—now needed "white Christians of all denominations" to protect it from "Communist Conspirators."

Later, Lynn and others drove back from the SCOPE house to see the burning cross, "a most frightening sight. We closed up the house tight and went to bed."

Young Melvin Hart's own preoccupation at Klan rallies at this time was different than ours. Perhaps remembering mainly occasions after 1965, he says the Klan rallied at that spot a lot. On a map he shows Ish, "Folk parked over here. There was no real driveway through, so they kind of made a driveway through here to the road...."

Around the time of our summer, the Hart kids added to family income by cutting and selling oak firewood, though Mel says Furman Sr. was "so cheap he'd buy that big McCullough which was so heavy, you'd be tired by the time you get it off the truck." While crosses burned, Melvin and his buddy Tim Randolph would park the truck on Smoak Street and prowl among the Klan cars, puncturing tires. Then he and Tim would skedaddle. "Thirteen or fourteen years old at the time, I was doing crazy things," he admits with a shake of the head. "My dad would have killed me if he'd known."

Melvin says St. Matthews wasn't the Klan's main patch in the county. Unincorporated Sandy Run (best known today as the site of an ongoing Marine Corps "Mud Run") was worse. In 1959, signs around its gas pump and little store on Route 21 said, among other things, "No Negro or ape allowed in building," and, below a portrait of Jesus, "Send them back to Africa where God almighty put them to begin with." (No suggestion of sending Caucasians home to the Caucasus.) In 1965 the signs were briefer: "No dogs, Jews, or N_____s allowed." (At least that's more inclusive?)

Has Sandy Run improved by now in basic human outlook? One can hope, but it do take a while. Around 1980, before practicing law, Martin Banks' summer job was scouting the cotton harvest. On a motorbike he buzzed many times through Elloree (not a cross-roads but a genuine town) just over the Orangeburg County line, past a restaurant on the main drag. Martin would see the white Coca-Cola delivery driver go into the restaurant and come back out with take-outs for himself and his black assistant who wasn't allowed through that door. After witnessing this "many times," Martin wondered, "What the hell was happening. 'Really? Still? Come on, get over it.'"

The Banks were good people, as good as Ish's. The puzzling thing to Ish, an outsider, is how they and other good leading families in St. Matthews left law enforcement to a head policeman they must have detested at times even more than Ish later detested Frank Rizzo, the thuggish Philadelphia police chief. But who really wanted the nasty job? Probably no one else in St. Matthews. And fear of retaliation would have troubled any white individual who too overtly opposed the uniformed violent white extreme. The more Ish learns of this history, the more he needs to remind himself how much racial injustice there was then back in his own home state. In the 1930s Senator Thurmond's mixed-race daughter Essie Mae was sent to be raised in Coatesville, a Pennsylvania steel town where, back then, lynching also still occurred and interracial marriage was troubling to many. In Ish's own time, as he knew, Pittsburgh blacks were barred from many jobs, and several bright black high school friends were counseled away

Sponsored by the chief of police. Photos Dean Savage.

from the college track or told by career adivsors that there was simply no call for Negro artists. Squarely taking that on would have required far more courage and willpower on his part than coming down here. At the same time, here was a community where folks of both races seemed more locked in old patterns, largely from fear, and here seemed to be better leverage for change that outsider presence could enhance. Anyway, here we were.

Ish's own take on the August Klan rally was that black St. Matthews wasn't impressed, though the night was a prelude to attack. Meanwhile, Lynn's parents were beginning to arrange for Harold to live with them during a fifth year of high school in Princeton. This would replace his plan to take a year off (risking the draft) before entering a school of music. For some time, he and Lynn had been talking about education. One night back in July, the gang had gone to pick up the Chevy at Jim Sulton's place. They ended up staying the rest of the evening, and Jim went out to bring back beers. Lynn was glad that Harold and Butch were there to see her home.

"The Sultons," she wrote, were "loaded (by Negro standards)" with a beautiful modern house. "We talked of college, throwing name schools back and forth, and other intellectual-type things. We read magazines, too...a typical evening of bourgeois entertainment. I wonder how Butch and Harold felt."

Harold felt by now that he needed to augment the education he'd received at John Ford High, where agriculture students learned how to can preserves for winter on equipment that—in a win-win spirit—white and black ladies could use by turn to preserve peaches in summer. Butch, too, was interested in Princeton High, but prudently wanted to wait until he'd got his John Ford diploma.

The Saturday night of the UKA rally, a voice had cut into a call Ish was making. "You n_____-lovin' bastard," it growled. A little later, the phone rang, Carol picked up, and the same male voice asked where was the owner and told us to get out of town. Next day we called the FBI.

22. Swim, Read, Shoot

A few days after the 10th, Eugene Glover still had not backed down from John Lee's scolding about the right way to challenge the segregated pool; nor had he acted. Sunday morning the 15th, stirred by last night's Klan performance, John Lee decided to take back command. He may have had a song in mind.

If you miss me in the Mississippi River
And you can't find me nowhere,
Come on over to the swimmin' pool.
I'll be swimmin' right there.

Lynn asked John Lee when he was going to integrate the pool. "Right away," he answered, and left, returning shortly with several "very huge boys." One was the late Willie Joe Holman, on his way to defensive prowess with the Chicago Bears. John Lee also swung by the Harts', where Furman Sr. gave ninety-pound non-swimmer Junior the keys to the pickup and ordered him to join the gang. Meanwhile, the bigger guys changed into swim suits or shorts and walked around Pool Circle and into the bath house to shower, per regulations, before going into the pool. Junior was with them by now, but Harold hung back to observe. Minutes later, back out Pool Circle shot cars full of whites, some of which, before scattering home, circled several times. From inside the SCOPE house, Lynn and others watched them fly by.

Also part of John Lee's swim team were Leonard Woodis and tall Charles Williams (John Ford High School '63, no blood relation to Hope but married at age nineteen to Hope's cousin's daughter Maggie). See Charles in 2016 holding a painting of the pool and bath house back in the day. Martin Banks has just brought it out to from his office to share with Charles and Maggie. Martin loves the painting, which reminds him that, as a youth, his dad had served there as lifeguard.

Charles and Junior have differing memories of what happened at poolside. Junior says he'd already entered the shallow end before any white bathers knew what was up: "When the people realized what was going on, they started popping out one by one. 'Oh my God, look who's here!' It took a while because there were so many people there."

In Charles' memory, the pool was already vacant by the time he and his friends went in. He remembers the lifeguard saying, "That's okay, we'll leave it to them

Charles admires a portrait of the poolhouse by Rene Pendarvis Scanlon.
Photo Martin Banks, who owns the painting.

'cause they can't swim." In answer, Charles, a terrific swimmer, nailed a beautiful dive from the board. So did Butch. Big Joe made a tsunami splash.

Within minutes Sheriff Rucker arrived and gave orders to drain the pool. The guys continued bathing until all the water was gone, the last folks ever to swim in a public pool in St. Matthews.

By the time Junior got back to the pickup, one of its windows was smashed. Traffic circled Pool Circle long into Sunday afternoon. Cars zoomed by with angry white folk. Who could blame them, with August still heating up in every sense? Junior remembers police cars from neighboring counties pouring in to back up the one or two in St. Matthews. That night Ish answered new threats on the phone.

Big Joe later on.

On Monday as the pool was filled with sand, Harold responded in his own way to the Klan provocation. He and Sallie Shuler (a relation of Jean Keitt) crossed the ravine to the public library for whites. Did they know that, a

There were two libraries in St. Matthews in 1965: one for whites
and a Negro Branch.

few years before, Hope had got involved with that issue as well? Whatever the two knew about the history of their county's libraries, it was surely more than we knew.

Martin Banks and Calhoun County Museum director Debbie Roland shared records with Ish about their far-from-wealthy community's decades of efforts to create and maintain a modest collection. A 1932 survey had reported that three-quarters of rural South Carolinians had no library service, and Calhoun fit that pattern. Around 1935, Lillian Murphy Cain began a personal mission of creating one with help from the WPA. The core collection was about 400 books from an old subscription library that had been mingled into the white St. Matthews High School library. Lillian mobilized the school board and white populace to create a free, expanded library that opened in 1936 in small, rent-free quarters downtown, provided by James A. Banks.

One county teacher already had library training; the WPA trained others. Outworn and useless volumes were tossed. Useful, salvageable ones were re-bound. Over the next few years folks donated more books and magazines. Julia Peterkin gave about 500, many from her late physician father's shelves; she also gave up-to-date fiction. Year by year, some new books were bought.

Since 1917 the county had been part of the federal Home Demonstration Agency program. As the library got under way, the HDA agent began to carry items out to her thirteen farm women's clubs. The clubs were white, though some HDA projects around that time did benefit both races—school hot lunch-es, home-making skills training and mattress-making (no lack of cotton). In 1937, the library acquired a book truck for better outreach to the clubs and other lending points, and to rotate small numbers of books to the county's small, outlying schools. At the time, three white public schools already had countable volumes (St. Matthews 2,000, Cameron 500, Lone Star 300). Among six smaller white schools, some had mainly the twenty-volume *Book of Knowledge*. Outside St. Matthews, most of the 25 smaller black schools had less by way of books *or* textbooks.

In careless wording, *The Calhoun Times* asserted in 1938 that "all persons [sic] in Calhoun County have the privilege of using these books free of charge," but the basic library was only for whites. However, Lillian Cain also arranged for black, WPA-funded individual to mend and oversee a smaller set of books for a black West End Branch, housed at Guinyard School. That collection began with 500 books from W.L.C. Riley, a black preacher from Lone Star.

In lots of ten, the local Jeanes Supervisor rotated books out to the other smaller schools. (Jeanes Supervisors were members of the 1908-68 Jeanes movement, an organization of hundreds of black, lower-grade supervisors and teachers across the South in schoolhouses paid for by Julius Rosenwald and other northern philanthropists. Many Jeanes Supervisors played active roles in ending overt segregation, especially from World War II onward.)

Though blacks in the county far outnumbered whites, in 1940 the county spent about $500 for books for white children, about $200 for black. For blacks the library hoped to get more "from WPA or elsewhere." Used to second-class treatment, blacks expressed support. Of 250 advance tickets to a May "library week" dinner event, about sixty were bought by blacks. Of course, Blacks couldn't literally attend the dinner at the white Legion Hut; they would eat in the Guinyard lunch room and eavesdrop by radio on Senator Gressette and other speakers. Storms prevented the broadcast, so all they got was the reading-aloud of the printed list of speakers. Fortunately they'd prepared some words and entertainment of their own.

In 1941 the WPA withdrew, leaving the school board to keep things going. In 1949 the county bought a building that took five years to prepare—the nice old Clark house on Railroad Avenue, where back-to-the-future Harold and Sallie would try to enroll. While the county was buying the house for the main, a new Jeanes Supervisor, Eliza L. Williams, began gathering more books for the Negro branch.

By 1949 the county's white-only library held about 9,300 books, managed by Lillian Cain plus a committee of prominent women: Laurie M. Wannamaker (Wannamaker Seed Company), Katherine Woodside Banks (Martin's grandmother), Isabelle Strait Fairey (Fairey Chevrolet), and Aurelia Antley Smoke (Pure Oil). Doors were open 22 hours a week; on Wednesdays a book truck ventured out to dropoff points including white schools. In search of more funding, Librarian Clara T. McCabe approached the State Library Board, but the county library budget (based on white *per capita* calculations) was too small to merit state funds. By adding blacks to the overall count, she learned, the budget could be made large enough to qualify for state money. "I hope," the state official advised her, "some way will be found to give the rural Negroes some library service." Lillian Cain, her board and staff all must

A Wannamaker shed still stands near the courthouse.

have been genuinely pleased that everyone would benefit by improving service for blacks.

Joining this effort, Jeanes Supervisor Eliza Williams began to weed out many worthless volumes from the black collection and seek out newer, better ones from donors outside the county. Through 1950, black holdings grew to about 3,000—about 1,000 lent from the white branch, 500 from the State Library Board, others from a college in Georgia, and some purchases (mostly children's books). Still under control of the library's white county board, a Negro board was formed, chaired by Walter C. Jackson. New makeshift quarters were found outside Guinyard School for the West End Negro Branch, and a black woman, Earleane Whitmore, was hired to staff it ten hours a week in 1950-51. For the county as a whole, registered library patrons then totaled about 3,800 whites (mostly adults) making 48,000 checkouts, plus 940 blacks (mostly children) making 2,800 checkouts.

By 1957 if not before, Hope Williams was part of a bi-racial committee to improve the black service and move it out of rented rooms. As everyone knew, the black library and related services in no way equaled those for whites—a more and more sensitive point as years flowed by after *Brown v. Board*. Overall, most of the value of creating the library for the county's blacks had actually accrued to the whites. For example, the 1957-58 county library budget shows most of the money going to the white St. Matthews branch (total salaries $3,326) rather than the black one (still in temporary quarters; total salaries for it and a white Cameron branch $480). Three years later the white collection was about 16,000 items, the black collection 4,500. In 1960, Sen. Gressette dedicated a newly built, one-room Negro branch. What Hope thought about things after that seems obvious from the fact that in 1965 he was asking us to help him gather a separate collection.

As for books and so forth in classrooms that summer, Lynn reported, "The Negro schools are far inferior to the not-too-good white schools. No white teachers may teach in Negro schools. The children have very few books, sometimes only four textbooks (and those quite outdated) for a whole class."

So: On burial day for the pool, Harold and Sallie walked up the steps of the white branch seeking borrower cards. Told the librarian was on vacation, they left with plans to come back later. When they returned the building was closed, the hours sign gone, but the librarian visible inside. Next morning, the AP and *The State* reported the closures of it and the pool. Our telephone tinkled with more racist calls. Ish wrote home, "I don't think they're seriously considering closing the white portion of the public library rather than admit Negroes," but that's what Gressette had ordered.

Not all of the library board members bowed. One member in 1965 was Julia Peterkin's daughter-in-law, Genevieve Chandler Peterkin, who'd taken to heart what she'd been taught in the 1940s at Baptist-rooted Coker College, "that the Jim Crow laws were a disgrace." She was out of the county on the day that Harold and Sallie stepped in, but returned for a meeting in which Gressette issued the order to close. She objected and "Our senator was furious at me. He expected the Justice Department to investigate, and he was telling us what to say. When I refused to go along, he said, 'Mrs. Peterkin, I cannot conceive of a Southern white lady thinking as you do.' Actually he said 'Southern woman' because I'd given up my ladyship status.... [Integration] finally did prevail, and after many, many years that angry senator did become my friend. They couldn't close that library for all eternity. Nothing down here on earth lasts forever."

Back to Harold: Around that same time, on his own, he'd also begun collecting evidence of other discrimination by going around to gas stations asking to use "bathroom #2" —the one reserved for whites. In each case he was flatly refused and told to use the colored.

Tuesday August 17, three days after the cross-burning, Lynn noticed the mercury rising in every respect: "The whites are really scared. We now receive threatening calls every day. We had a meeting this morning to discuss what had to be done." Personally she vowed to expand Hope's library with brochures about government programs that people could use.

Around this time, we switched our grocery patronage to the Red & White out on Highway 6 (next to Klan central), where several blacks were employed, anticipating a community "selective buying" campaign against Winn-Dixie. Ben Mack said not to use the word "boycott." When he came by, Lynn was "annoyed that everyone was scared of his coming and had prepared a big story about how we had nothing to do with the swimming pool integration—Dean Zion had sent orders to participate in absolutely no demonstrations. As it turned out, Mr. Mack hadn't even heard about it, and like dummies, John Babin and Ish began speeches anyway about how we hadn't had anything to do with it. Mr. Mack didn't even care. Those idiots! In spite of everybody's fears, our chat was pleasant and friendly—I told them it would be. After all, Mr. Mack is human, and he knows what's going on.

"Our workers are really getting active! Today they went to Mayor Bob Gressette—another of Marion's seven siblings—and had a talk with him about the pool. John Lee had a very friendly chat [with him] and was told to come back anytime. He also talked to Councilman Fair [Fairey?] about his job application for policeman. Later on, four kids went down to talk to Senator Gressette. They really told him off! He didn't get away with a thing! They put it to his face that the library had been closed because they had tried to integrate it. They said they weren't happy with the way things are. Of course, Gressette blamed everything on the outside agitators from SCOPE. We put ideas into their heads."

Lynn's highlight on the 17th was the night arrival from Orangeburg of Thais, Citti and Gerard Williams who had visited earlier that day as well ("what a boy!"). This was the teenager Lynn had driven to Camden for the registration August 5. "I was glad at least to have the chance to talk to Gerard alone. Both of us feel a decided attraction. Gerard is an extremely beautiful boy. He is very sweet and has good manners. He told me he thought boys should be clean cut. I told him girls liked boys that way."

Also along on the 17th was Dr. Thomas' son Reginald, who'd been first to go to jail in the Orangeburg Movement arrests of 1961, according to Cecil Williams. Melvin Hart says Reggie and his siblings had been arrested as much as anyone else. But Lynn wrote simply that "Dr. Thomas is so loaded [wealthy], and Reggie's car was an enormous new Mercury. What a brat!" Gerard and Reggie "made real pests of themselves." But in the remaining two weeks of the project, Lynn and Gerard continued canvassing together and seeing each other in Orangeburg when they could to talk, party and eventually date.

Tension was still running high that evening. Lynn saw Carol get out the shaving cream and begin "disappearing outside and running around the house. Then they started in for real—she and John Lee got covered. It was smeared all over them. Especially Carol was coated—camera time. Then things got violent. Carol was struggling to get free. Our precinct map nearly got ripped. With all the fighting a glass of water was broken on the porch. The house was soaking and a shambles. Carol emerged like a drowned rat. The Orangeburg kids were quite amused. Finally things calmed down and they left. John Lee drove his shaving-stuff-covered car home, and we got back to work at 1:00. Unfortunately our attempt to get in touch with the FBI was in vain—the operator wouldn't cooperate (I can't imagine why)."

We were all surely randy that late in the summer. Within days, if not already, John Babin and Terry at least were hitting on the girls. If Ish was, too, he's forgotten. As Lynn would scribble a few days later, "These boys are feeling quite desperate. Living with girls must have been harder on the boys than we found living with them." And a handful of locals of various ages were making plays as well. Tuesday August 24, Quick Charlie "was beginning to want more than just talking." Lynn was proud of being able to hold off the advances of undesired men. "Charlie kept insisting that I see him again."

Unfortunately, two white Calhoun brothers were worked up in a violent sense. Their names and penchants were apparently known to the sheriff and just about everyone else. Ish recalls their names being passed on to us. The evening of Wednesday August 18, we were scattered to various places. Late evening, Terry was first to get home. There he saw and learned that, sometime between 8:00 and 9:00, someone had driven by with a shotgun and blasted the living-room picture window that faced onto Church Street, ten steps from the road. The blind was down, so the shooter apparently hadn't really known whether anyone might be inside. Terry called the police, FBI, State Law Enforcement (SLED), and UPI.

Around 10:30 others returned from a meeting. "What a sight! A hole about a foot in diameter. The glass was cracked in all directions. The shade was splat-

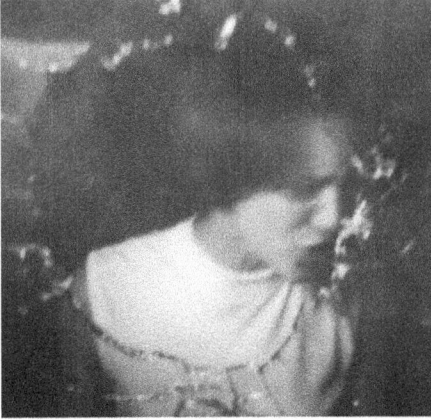

Mr. Johnson's living-room picture window next day. The photo from the street shows the shot was head-high for anyone sitting on the sofa facing the window. Photos Lynn Goldberg.

tered with shot holes. Inside was unbelievable. Shattered glass strewn over every inch of the room. The back wall dotted with holes.

"The police had been by to look things over. They said they would return with the Sheriff in the morning. We called [SLED] Chief [J.P. "Pete"] Strom for protection during the night. Matthew Perry was also informed. It was scary. Earl and the Orangeburg kids left us making precautions for the night. Our beds were moved and windows blocked. Pleasant dreams!"

(In a broader perspective on public order around those years, historian Millicent Brown credits J.P. Strom's "commitment to the maintenance of 'order' and restraint on the part of his officers" with bringing "a degree of confidence throughout the period.... He and a few other public officials professed themselves unwilling to provoke chaos even as official stands were taken in opposition to the demonstrations or desegregation goals.")

Early next morning SLED arrived. Alternately silent and shooting questions, they took pictures and pried some pellets from the wall above the couch. St. Matthews police drove round the block.

That day, Lynn drove briefly up to Fort Motte to tell Hope about an extra day-and-a-half of registration in September. Beyond that, the group stayed home inside, taking death-threats on the phone. But, as Lynn noted, "Someone sent us a huge box of cookies—we ate them nervously all day long—that was all we ate. It was nerve-wracking, sitting in the house. I lay on my bed in our stuffy, blocked-up room trying to occupy myself with my diary, which had gotten very far behind since my Birmingham trip. I also called home."

That evening, three of us watched our house from the Keitts'. Lynn, Mary Ann and probably Terry absconded with Harold, Junior, John Lee, Effie, and Betty Sellars to a barbecue in Orangeburg, followed by drinking and dancing at Earl Ishmael's Rotunda Club in Neeses, Orangeburg County. But "We were silly to think we could just drive out of St. Matthews. Wwe were followed," wrote

Lynn. "We tried slowing down real slow, and even on a four-lane section, we were not passed. Mary Ann flashed her lights at John Lee ahead of us, and he turned off the road. We stopped, and the car following us suddenly sped up and tried to get away. Everyone strained and we caught the license number that will go to the FBI: C27-906—a light blue Valiant."

This may have been the moment when Mary Ann resolved to stay on that fall. At least it was when she decided to see about a new black Mustang she would quickly buy. She'd need it if she stayed.

August 20 we "were able to sleep quite safely with patrol cars circling past our house, and shining flood lights on it. We wonder, though, whose side they're on." Next day or two, by Lynn's account, SLED arrested a suspect in the shooting. This was our next-door neighbor, "dear old Mr. Haynes," who brought us eggs now and then and who, the night before, according to Lynn, had been out and "about to shoot a hawk that was after his chickens. We told him not to. SLED also asked him not to—and he didn't. [But] they searched his house today, and what did they find? Bootleg liquor. They questioned him and let him off."

A hawk? At night? Ish's version home said that Mr. Haynes "woke us up about 12:30 at night a few days after the shooting and asked to borrow a flashlight so he could shoot an owl out of his tree that was about to eat up all his chickens. We argued but gave him the flashlight, and before he got a chance to use his shotgun, the police came by and forbade it. It wasn't a very good idea, under the circumstances," Ish sagely observed.

John Babin's account in 2015 might hold some added truth. According to him, deputies entered Haynes' house and arrested him for the attack on the SCOPE house based on their finding a disassembled shotgun. An hour or so after the old man was taken away, the Sheriff and a deputy came by, entered Haynes' house again, and came out with paper bags concealing bottles of moonshine. John says he asked Harold what was going on. Harold replied that Mr. Haynes was a source for bootleg in St. Matthews. His clientele were uniformed, civilian, black and white. The arrest was a shakedown. "All a big show," says Babin. He says Harold said that Mr. Johnson was involved in this side enterprise with Haynes. Whatever the truth, in a few days the charges were dropped.

The assault on the house scared us plenty but didn't stop the canvassing in sweltering heat. More and more Lynn saw "hundreds of Negroes, from toddlers to tottering old people, half-buried in the fields. They all wear hats to protect themselves from an unbearable sun. The roadways are lined with piles of white cotton, just pulled from the boles. At one house where we stopped, a white man drove up to pick up the woman and all her kids, to bring them to the field.

"A real change can be seen now in canvassing. It is so rewarding to see that we have gotten through. John Babin and I went to Cameron. It has now been done three or four times. The people know who we are and have talked about us. A response and an understanding can be felt. They may not have gone to register, but we keep hitting them with our pitch—they are aware."

Nor did the shotgun episode end our Sunday visits to outlying ramshackle churches, nor driving to Kershaw to help out with its last registrations in August. It didn't stop some of us from frequent travel back and forth the twenty miles to Orangeburg for clubbing, dancing and drinking. Mary Ann's Mustang came in handy.

23. BEHIND BLUE EYES

The shoot-up was a sobering moment for all, including whites who came out of the woodwork here and there. While the Klan had stirred the most hostile, others had been appalled by the rally, and even more by the shotgun assault. Here are a few more notes about our occasional contacts with whites. We generally steered clear, but couldn't always in a place where whites owned pretty much every office or business.

Here in paraphrase is John Babin's possibly embroidered account of a verified incident his first or second day in St. Matthews. "Downtown" near the seed store, Bridge Street crossed the railroad. There Babin, Harold and maybe Junior were hanging out when a white man stopped ten feet way in his pickup and asked John if he was looking for a job. John didn't reply but the two made eye contact. As a Somerville denizen, John knew this was not a good thing, and already threats had come in by phone at the Harts'. John avoided any sudden move, just backed away "real slow." Before leaving, the white man threatened to shoot him. Harold and other kids then informed him he'd just encountered "the most dangerous man in the county," well known for beating up blacks.

The SCOPERs complained to the FBI. Agents came and questioned John and probably Harold and sent a report. In later years John acquired his FBI file, which had tracked his pro-labor doings and such. Among the redacted copy he received was a teletype showing that J. Edgar Hoover recognized there were violations of the law but instructed the agents not to investigate or do anything else unless someone got hurt or killed.

Lynn's entries mention other dealings with whites beginning Sunday July 11: "At about 9:00, Carol, Butch and I went to The Jacket to pick up fried chicken. What a riot! The people were so shocked at seeing us with a colored boy. We brought Butch home and returned to get our order. The lady took an incredibly long time. She stopped in the middle to make some phone calls, and made all kinds of excuses. Meanwhile we bothered her even more by talking to all the colored people who came up. We know almost everyone."

Mid-July: "Caw-Caw township has many white people who often live in poorer houses than the colored folk. That presents many problems. It's quite a shock to knock on a white person's door. 'Where is Route 19? Thank you, good-bye.' Then we scoot."

The Savitz department store is now a café.

Seeking out sympathetic whites in St. Matthews, Lynn and Mary Ann talked long with Mr. Savitz, owner of the largest "department store (if you can call it that)." They guessed he was Jewish. Other stores in town were owned by Jews. The highly regarded Perlstines owned the railroad depot wholesale outlet that supplied small stores like the Floyds'. The shoe store was Goldinger's.

As a child, Martin Banks was not aware that these families and their children, his classmates, were Jewish. In retrospect he remembers a small but "very healthy" Jewish population that was "absolutely part of the community. I never thought twice about it. Nobody did."

Lynn and Mary Ann found Mr. Savitz "very nice, especially after he found out we were Jews." From him they learned how much the Jewish families had blended into the town. He was now Episcopalian, which they suspected wasn't unusual. He still felt strongly Jewish. "He was willing to talk to us, which in itself is hazardous, as everyone is bound to know about it ten minutes later. He admitted frankly that he wasn't brave enough to take any stand supporting us. Well, what could we expect. We spent quite a while with him, and parted friends. This is a first step."

But the step doesn't seem to have been followed up.

July 17: "We found a friendly bank which lets us cash personal checks. The Bank of Orangeburg [in St. Matthews] will be our bank soon. We will open an account there with Mr. Hart. These people may be able to help us. I think they are quietly supporting us. It does seem unusual that they would cash our checks, especially large ones. They always talk with us when we go into their little trailer on Railroad Ave."

A little after noon one day, Lynn took a break to do some shopping. "It's always interesting uptown. Little incidents happen. I was walking up the street and smiled at a colored man, and it dawned on him that I was one of those Civil Rights workers. He was very excited to talk to me. I bothered all the whites by stopping to chat with Mrs. Hart and her baby Euell while they were parked in town. I also managed to bug Sheriff Rucker who was stopping in the five-

and-ten-cent store. In the post office the lady was giving a colored girl a really tough time. She kept scowling at her for losing a slip to pick up a package which couldn't be found. Next I got groceries at Winn-Dixie. I have never seen anybody so anxious to get rid of me. She practically pushed me out the door."

Same day while canvassing, "Carol was asked into a white segregationist's house. Her co-workers sweated for a whole hour before Carol reappeared from behind the closed door. It was quite a shaking experience. Other people had been chased off farms by the whites."

Despite Julia Peterkin's early empathy with the people she'd portrayed around Fort Motte, despite her "adoring young people and their straining against the norms" (according to scholar Elizabeth Robeson), despite her doubts about whites recommending themselves as moral examples to blacks, it seems unlikely Julia understood Hope Williams or would have welcomed us. Around the publication of *Gone With the Wind* (1936) which she admired, she was lapsing back into the myths of a contented antebellum South. Near her passing in 1961, according to Susan Williams' biography, she was "terrified of racial integration. She fretted that 'outside instigators' were coming...posing as Bible salesmen and 'stirring up unpleasantness among the people.' 'Desegregation will cause trouble here,' [Julia] wrote...in a shaky hand in 1956. 'Neither race wants it.' The idea that her grandchildren might go to school with blacks [which happened after her death] was enough to make her cringe. When she dropped her art, she dropped her sympathy for those who were oppressed. Julia lived out her last years indignant at the way the world had changed."

The wonderful irony is that we were apparently welcomed and encouraged by her daughter-in-law, Genevieve Peterkin, mentioned above in connection with libraries. When she arrived in Fort Motte in the late 1950s, she writes in memoir, she "couldn't believe the paternalism, the dependence." She supposed the difference between Fort Motte and her coastal home, Murrells Inlet, was "only one of degree, but on Lang Syne black families were still living in the cabins the slaves had occupied. Nothing had changed."

In 1965, she wrote, she and her husband Bill Peterkin were marked as the most liberally active white pair in the county. "Soon civil rights workers were coming into our county to register black voters. Our own black workers told us they were being visited, so I began to approach these young women and say, 'When you're out on our farm come by and see Bill and me. We'd like to know you, too.' We started having them to lunch in our house. Interesting people."

We don't remember, but according to Genevieve one of the women was from New York state. That could have been Carol. Another's Indiana roots suggest Mary Ann, who was likely at later meetings Genevieve also attended where, according to the latter, "They were organizing something revolutionary called the OEO, and at others they were discussing food stamps—all of which seems awfully innocent today. Still, this was not a popular course of action for a white woman in those days, and fortunately I was blessed with a husband who felt as I did." (Also among county white women who would invite OEO was county museum director Debbie Roland's mother. According to Debbie, as years went by, a lot of people supported Hope's work.) Mary Ann remembers "another woman who befriended me but her husband frequently maligned Hope and only tolerated me for his wife's sake."

Some months after her library tussle with Gressette, Genevieve attended a women's church convention in Charleston at which the Episcopal bishop told the group to join or organize a biracial community where they lived. So Genevieve contacted Hope Williams, whom she knew but not well: "he was the most unlikely of people for me to be friends with. But we started the group and, in truth, weren't very successful, at least with attendance. The only whites who would meet with us were two dear young Methodist ministers who had little country churches. Every black minister in the county attended. We kept that group going for a long time, and some serious confrontations were avoided because we met. I could at least contact the powers that be and tell them what was being thought and said in the black community. We made a difference at that time. But it was scary—very scary.

"On the surface I can't say that my place in the white community ever changed. I never felt any real rejection from them then or even earlier, but if I hadn't been married to Bill, I would have had a different experience. One meeting I even said, 'If I were married to someone else and living in a mobile home, my reception in Fort Motte would be a hell of a lot different.' It helped that Bill was farming, growing soybeans that he could sell to whomever he wanted. I came out of one meeting, and a woman whispered that she wished she could speak up like I did but her husband sold trucks to the county. No doubt I was insulated from the consequences of my actions. But that was just in public. Plenty of anonymous threats were made."

Julia Peterkin biographer Susan Williams writes that Genevieve also "made sure that the few farm laborers who remained had window screens, modern kitchens and bathrooms in their houses, and that their medical bills and burial expenses were paid. And she helped Bill see it as cause for rejoicing when someone would once worked the Lang Syne cotton fields dropped by on his way to march with Jesse Jackson" in the Charleston hospital workers' strike of 1969. By Genevieve's own account, "When the chance came up, my stepson William and I bought fifteen acres near Fort Motte and offered this at a reasonable price for home sites to those who wanted to own their own home, and some of the younger people did accept."

Bill and Genevieve Peterkin weren't the only county whites resisting the anti-integration majority and the violent few. But they do seem nearly the only ones who were able, by courage and social position, to withstand the pressure before the late 1960s.

What about local white *youth*? How did they feel about integration? We weren't there to visit white churches, but southern-born Al Ziegler attended one where he found "only lip service to brotherhood. Among the young people I got the response that integration really is long overdue. I saw no indication that they were ready to make it a going concern there, but they accepted the idea. [They had] many reservations, for they could see why their parents felt the way they felt. [There] didn't seem to be any possibility of people coming from there to lead anything, although a readiness to accept the inevitable was certainly present."

Martin Banks was about age 4½ at the time. He recalls riding in the back of a pickup loaded with siblings past the Klan rally on their way home from an evening harvesting in the family's garden east of town. Although Martin dimly recalls that night, and although he's a county history buff, until Ish contacted him in 2015, he wasn't aware that civil rights workers had come to the county during the '60s. In that respect he'd felt Calhoun a little "left out" and neglected. So he was delighted to know. So was Julian Wiles, another white Calhoun native whose anti-integration father "Pally" Wiles had taken up farming up around Fort Motte late in the '40s, perhaps a beneficiary of Hope Williams' loss. Pally's path must have crossed Hope's. In 1965 Julian Wiles was thirteen and troubled by obvious injustice. Melvin Hart remembers Julian warmly as an eighth grade classmate after that and suggested I get in touch. Today Julian directs the Charleston Stage theater company. It recently mounted "Seat of Justice," his moving play about the central role of Clarendon County blacks in *Brown v. Board of Education*. Melvin recalls civil treatment from Julian's dad on a county committee some years after the '60s.

Martin Banks' older cousin C. Richard Banks was 45 in '65 and Clerk of Calhoun County. (Around that time in kindergarten, Martin was also a county employee: Dick had hired him as "jury boy" after Martin's older brother Jim proved too fidgety for the task. The job was drawing jury names out of a cigar box, which could only be done by "a child of tender years." On certain mornings Martin had to dress up and walk from kindergarten to the courthouse, passing by the "horrible, horrible" two-story county jail where the drunks would yell at him. At least Martin "thought they were drunk—or crazy or just bored, yelling out the un-air-conditioned barred windows.")

For generations the Banks family has been prominent in St. Matthews. Among other enterprises, Dick's grandfather had started a lumber company, and the family sold coal to the town. The lumber connection may been part of how in 1940-41 Dick, a professional photographer, happened to document part of the WPA Santee-Cooper Project, a damming of rivers on the county's eastern edge to create Lakes Moultrie and Marion. Long after, Dick remembered one owner still occupying a corner of an historic home as it was dismantled; and another killing himself. On Dick's death in 2010 one mourner said he had friends "too many to count. Dick loved people and they loved him."

Hope's Kids

Dick came by to talk. Carol says, "He would only meet us at night. Lynn and I went for a ride with him. We drove around for a while. I remember being nervous getting into that car, wondering if he really was on our side."

His contact was informative, friendly. We thought from his manner, status, and talk about travels he might be gay, as people there tended to think about older bachelors living alone. This seems worth mentioning because it might be seen as part of the pattern by which Peter Lee and Bayard Rustin became leaders in the gay rights movement. In Ish's impression it's often the outsider trapped "inside" who questions social constraints. Martin has wondered about Dick, too, though alone as a boy with his adult cousin "many, many times" he never felt ill at ease. Neither has Martin ever heard rumor that Dick ever had sex with anyone. "He was a strong Christian man." According to Martin, he gave his tiny Episcopal church first option to inherit his considerable wealth. "He was opposed to gay clergy in his denomination. If he was gay, I believe he chose to be celibate. You can print that."

Lynn and Ish noted Dick's help. To illustrate the connectedness among whites in the county, he told them how campaigning for the elected office of county clerk required visiting every voting household. He knew everything about everyone. One would never have guessed a sickly childhood had prevented his ever attending school. Taught by his mother at home, says Martin, Dick's penmanship rivaled John Hancock's.

Six evenings after the shotgun blast, Dick invited Carol and Terry for a drive and conveyed what was going on across town. "There is quite a stir," Lynn reported. "Banks would like us to get together with the whites. I'm glad to know the whites are so concerned." From Dick we learned that the whites were "quite affected by our presence" and that wild rumors had spread "that one of us (not specified who) has married Furman Hart. Butch is suspected of having done the same thing—and has run away." It *is* true Butch had gone to New York for some vacation before school started again, based on connections laid down by his mother years before, when she'd worked up north as a housekeeper.

"The shooting is thought to have been done by some Negroes, fighting over us girls. The whites have been expecting us all along to be doing much more than we've done. All summer they've been waiting for us to blow things up, demonstrate, and provoke all sorts of antagonism."

Next day, Wednesday August 25, Junior offered to help Lynn with laundry. She guessed that didn't "help the rumors any for me and Furman to come together with laundry. We carried it to the laundromat in three bags—everything, sheets, towels and clothes. We entered the white side, but the big machines are on the colored side so we used them. While I stayed to watch our things, I was reading a magazine when Isaac Prickett, the owner (white) came over to me. I was nervous, I admit. He told me I was only seeing one side of the picture. I was advised to go knock on some white people's doors, and I would be surprised how nice they would be.

"He told me about all his colored friends—his cook, his attendants, etc.—he has more colored friends than white friends. Mr. Prickett was most proud of his 'separate but equal' laundromat. He tried to please his customers. You didn't see an ugly, water-filled room for the Negroes like in the other laundromat. In fact, the big machines were on the colored side because the colored people liked them. If the whites wanted to use them, they could go to the other side. A loss of some white customers would be balanced by a gain in colored.

"Mr. Prickett showed off for me by being very fatherly toward the attendant's little boy. This Negro child was 'like his own son.' I said little myself and agreed that there were problems in the North, too. I was constantly jabbed by the wrongs of the North. 'There's nothing wrong with the South'—I haven't seen anything bad. 'But look at the North!' I made a feeble attempt to point out that I had seen much wrong with the South, but I was not going to start an argument, since clearly he would never see my view. 'All those colored people do is spend money on cars (a complete myth) and drinking (partly true, but do you blame them?). They shouldn't have more money.'"

So the shotgun had opened channels for talk, though with little time left for SCOPE to take part.

24. HOPE'S KIDS

We were down to the last few days. The girls especially must have felt the sadness of ending the project, the loss of side-by-side connection with John Lee, Harold, Junior, and Butch. Tuesday August 24, Lynn's afternoon canvass was "unbearable" with John Lee who was "very unpleasant lately, especially with me." At the SCOPE house she and Harold "went into a bedroom to talk (as private as might be found in our house)." She wanted to encourage him, also to warn him about what to expect at Princeton High. "Mary Ann and Carol came in to escape a drunken gentleman who had walked in, so that was the end of our conversation—the closest one Harold and I have had this summer. He and I don't talk much in words—Harold is quiet, in general, especially with me—he admitted it. Mary Ann and Carol and I were in a crazy mood. We kidded around and laughed. Mary started drinking. I climbed into bed, and was sleeping while the others were still fiddling around."

We continued to canvass for September registrations, still sorting out maps and precincts. Lynn went to a movie in Orangeburg with Gerard, "The Sons of Katie Elder." The integrated group caused little stir "although Gerard was the only Negro sitting downstairs. Other Negroes sat in the balcony. One couple behind us got up and moved to another part of the theater. It was great to sit eating popcorn and watching a western."

By Friday she and Carol had picked up a virus. Mary Ann made an enormous rib roast, beans and salad. Since Lynn had a date, she ate early and was off to a football game with Gerard in which Wilkinson High School lost to its rival, Brewer.

She couldn't believe it was merely a high school game. The stadium ("and I do mean *stadium*") was as big as any college's, she thought, with concession stands underneath, and ticket booths outside the gates. "The field is fully equipped for night games, since it is always too warm to play during the day. The excitement was high. Everyone was very well dressed (typical of the Negro high school students). The band had fantastic uniforms, and the cheerleaders were already going. They didn't stop until after the game. A constant chant kept up the whole time, and the cheerleaders did fancy steps."

Lynn stayed over that night—her last of the project—in the quarters of Orangeburg SCOPE and found Gerard waiting for her downstairs Saturday morning. "I didn't realize how upset Gerard was, busily puffing cigarettes. I couldn't really talk to him at all. We sat outside with some other kids while I waited for all the last-minute things to be taken care of—phone calls, breakfast, packing. Gerard and I really grossed out a local Uncle Tom who stopped to say hello—we were standing on the steps with our arms around each other. The man left quickly."

After a "very wild" lunch at the Floyds' in St. Matthews, a huge dinner and tortured goodbyes also with the Harts and John Lee's mother, Lynn left for Columbia an emotional mess. In the city came more goodbyes. She "chatted with Mrs. Bowman, and gave my love to the rest of the family. Rev. Bowman we met outside and thanked for all his help. By this time I was a nervous wreck. I just wanted to get out."

She was riding in the Chevy Ish was returning to Pittsburgh. In Ridgewood they replaced a bad spare. To Lynn the area looked poor. Ben Mack's neighbor was suspicious of our taking a tire from the back of the house, but we assured him it was all right. "One last place—a gas station to put the tire on the rim for a spare. At last—to Chapel Hill."

Late that night Ish, Carol, John Babin, Citti, Lynn, and Lesley Straley reached the Straleys' laid-back North Carolina home, en route to Princeton, Teaneck and other points north. Last out of Columbia were Elias and Kathy, returning their car to its grad student owner at Brandeis.

Mary Ann didn't leave with the rest. She stayed on a year, driving on Sundays to "as many black churches as I could to encourage people to register to vote, send their children to white schools and whatever else seemed possible." She traveled the state helping black communities create community action agencies and trying to get school principals informed about federal aid. One goal was to help them get *Title One* funds and not spend them all on dubious products from scores of catalogues. She became involved in a Junior League project to expand career options. In Calhoun and Orangeburg she joined Doc Thomas, Earl and others in the effort to introduce a federal anti-poverty (and Food Stamps) Community Action Program. The holdup was that CAPs had to be implemented through the SC state OEO, which would not act until approached by white-run county delegations that still showed little interest in programs of major use to blacks. As Earl had said, the key was at the county level. The way around this, he felt, was to create a truly bi-racial community committee that would pressure the delegations or gain recognition on its own. In late fall 1965, there were signs of progress in Orangeburg, none in Calhoun.

In Calhoun County Mary Ann worked "in close collaboration with wonderful Hope, and developing friendships with a wide variety of people." Driving in the county she was chased by the sheriff's son and arrested a second time.

Mary Ann's first new living arrangement was with Rosa Schweitzer, "a dear older black woman in Calhoun County who lived alone. I can't remember how I met her, likely seeking to get her to register, which she eventually did. I can still see her in line at the courthouse and remember how pleased she was about it. I stayed in the house we shared until the owner came home at the end of the summer. He was a small, elderly man with blue eyes and could barely lift his feet off the floor. One day he asked me to move out as, he said, people were talking about us. As I didn't have a place to stay, I had to stay in a motel. Rosa told me I could stay with her any night so long as I came after dark. We spent many an evening rocking near her wood stove before I bought a very small, used trailer that Doc Thomas let me put on a piece of his land."

Thanksgiving found Mary Ann and others taking food to ten poor families in St. Matthews. In a Christmas fundraising letter she wrote to friends, "You have never seen such conditions in your life. Those of you who were here this summer know how bad things are, but you never saw these homes in the winter. At one house, which was a fire hazardous wooden shack with no electricity, no water, no toilet, a wood stove (empty), there were three little children and no adults although it was 9:00 at night. The house stank and was extremely cold. Inside on an old wooden bureau, a gas-soaked rag burned in a bottle. The children live there with their father, their mother is dead, the father can't work, and they live on almost nothing. We handed them apples which they grabbed and devoured. The houses we visited were only a few. There are so many more."

In a friendly late autumn note to Harold in Princeton she wrote, "If you decide to give up studying for sewing, you can get a job at Beach Party. It's integrated by three now, but there are plans to set up a training program and hire between 50 and 75 or even more workers, largely Negro." Fifty years later John Babin recalls our being helped at Beach Party by David Dubinsky, president of the International Ladies' Garment Workers Union (ILGWU), who had meaningful ties with Brandeis.

"Also," Mary Ann added to Harold, "your stint at the library caused more stir than you knew. It's open again but one of the trustees resigned over Gressette's order to close it. Problem now is getting other kids to use it."

As Jean Keitt summed up the summer when Ish visited her in Orangeburg in 2016: "It paid off. It was good."

Mary Ann would go on to law school. As for Ish, what he learned about himself that summer was that he wasn't cut out for confrontations. Dr. King, Bayard Rustin, SCOPE, and the Quakers would help him channel passivity into pacifism. Three years later, after restorative time teaching in Africa and discovering Melville, he began work as a conscientious objector for the Medical Committee for Human Rights, itself a product of the civil rights movement. Its outrageous claim at the time was "Heath care is a human right."

In registration numbers, Hope, SCOPE and their friends did well in Calhoun County, where black class distinctions were minimal. At the outset of June, 490 black voters had been on the rolls. The VEP made no entry for June. From July through December, monthly additions were these:

July	115
August	144
September	366
October	139
November	65
December	155
Total	984

Local continuity and Mary Ann's staying on must have boosted the fall registrations. In 1966, a county NAACP would form. Hope may have been its first president; Toot Hart would also serve in that way. Today, in her foundation office in Washington, Mary Ann often looks up at her photo of Hope and feels strength in recalling "an extraordinary man...our beautiful friendship" and how much she gained from working with him.

Integrated schools would take some "getting used to." Token school desegregation in Charleston began in 1963, in Orangeburg the following year. Calhoun County schools began around the end of 1965 with introducing one black child into each formerly all-white grade or classroom. St. Matthews children came from the Hart, Floyd, Keitt, Murphy, Hopkins, Michaels, Wright, Bronson, and Bonaparte families, plus Gideon and Gladys Howell's daughter, two doors down from the Murphys. It was a painful choice for parents, subjecting their children to a stressful, often ugly immersion. At least one Calhoun eighth grader didn't last because of the taunting from white kids each day as he stepped off the bus. In 1969 Junie Keitt and Brenda Hopkins Moseley were the first to graduate from the formerly all-white high school.

Martin Banks' older brother Dave (St. Matthews High '72) had "a great experience" staying on playing sports with black and white teammates after full-scale integration was launched around 1971. Dave says they bonded over football and, in his awareness, never had a racial problem or conflict. In his senior year he remembers about fifteen black males at the school, including a brother of John Lee Anderson.

Martin Banks remembers no commotion when Daryl Murphy ("a super kid, great kid, the whole family is just top-drawer") entered his St. Matthews first-grade class at the start of 1966, but by third grade Martin's family removed him to private, all-white schooling.

Genevieve Peterkin's memoir reflects the challenge for white Calhoun families who dared to embrace school integration. Jim, their son, approached his first day of fourth grade with integration about to begin. They talked with him about the rightness of it. Shortly after school began, they received a note from the principal adivising them that Jim needed to *When in Rome do as the Romans. We do not plan for this to work in our school.*" Visiting Jim's teacher about this, Genevieve learned the problem was that Jim was playing with his black classmates, picking them to be on his kickball team. "We don't plan for that to happen on our playground," the teacher told her.

The Peterkins (Bill a Calhoun *Roman* if there ever was one) didn't know what to do. Genevieve didn't see how they could very well "untrain our son from being a decent human being," but she and Bill did warn Jim that others didn't share the same feelings and could make things difficult. "And it was difficult— so difficult that he was soon calling home, complaining of a stomach ache. By spring I was carrying him straight from the school to the doctor's office. Jim had an ulcer." A pediatrician told them the cause was stress and suggested Jim be hospitalized in a few weeks when school was over. "I was to tell the teacher what was happening and make her understand how important it was for Jim to finish the year with as little fuss as possible. We were going to let him coast with his grades." But the first time Jim left the classroom for a piano lesson, the teacher told his classmates he was very ill with "an ulcer in his stomach.'

"Well, one of our neighbors had cancer at the time, and she too was said to be 'very ill.' Some of those classmates knew this and assumed an ulcer and cancer were the same. That was the end of the stress-free finish to the school year. We took him out, and once he was in the hospital the doctor was wise enough to get the truth out of our son.... We kept him on a strict diet that summer and he healed, but the doctor said he shouldn't go back. So there [we] were, the biggest liberals in the county, and the only alternative we had was to move our son into one of the [new] all-white private schools. We kept him there until the eighth grade and enrolled him in boarding school. Our son had grown up playing with black children at Fort Motte. You work so hard for things to work out, and sometimes they don't. It's like you've been hit below the belt. But then the discrimination that this single white child experienced was being experienced by hundreds of thousands of black children. But this single white child was our Jim."

"After actual integration came," says Martin, "man, they threw up that private school in no time, literally overnight," and all the whites were gone. With that, real county school integration died, and is said to remain dead today. In the late 1990s, 70-year-old Genevieve was still frustrated about how "education hasn't improved in South Carolina since I started school. I mean, it has, of course, and yet the state is still at the bottom in all the national testing...because we've never spent the money." In 2017, *U.S. News & World Report* still ranked Palmetto schools dead last.

At the end of 1965, eighth grader Melvin Hart moved from Guinyard elementary over to the white school. Nine years later he graduated from SC State. In the meantime he sometimes rode with Hope on political work. In late 1967 Hope undertook intensive community development training at an SCLC retreat, the Quaker-founded Penn Center in Frogmore on St. Helena Island. According to NAACP's Felder, as late as 1947 it was "the only place in South Carolina and the South where black and white people could meet, eat together, and sleep in the same buildings." On other occasions, says Melvin, Hope took "a bunch of us down to Frogmore—with Septima Clark and all those folk. I think I went to Atlanta with him. I don't remember meeting Dr. Martin Luther King, but the Rev. C.T. Vivian [another SCLC leader] was doing some of the same kind of work in Atlanta as your dad was doing here," Melvin tells Abraham Williams on a recent Sunday afternoon. Hope "had no fear of white folk whatsoever. He wasn't afraid of nothing."

"He wasn't afraid of anything," Abraham corrects him politely. "Oh, I know that already."

"We'd go places and he would sing," says Melvin. That was the downside of travels with Hope, worse than the overnight drive on a can of beans or sardines. "Now to him, he could sing like Stevie Wonder. He would sing all those civil rights songs. *Keep your eyes on the prize, hold on.* Your daddy loved to sing. He wasn't that good of a singer."

"No, no, he had no singing voice," Abe agrees and laughs.

Genevieve Peterkin passed no judgment on Hope's vocal chops, but her memoir recalls his love of music. In 1969, as part of the state's tri-centennial festivities, she was asked to chair the county's $1,500 week-long celebration. She "assumed the county's money should be spent on a celebration suitable to the whole community. However the rest of the committee hadn't gotten that message at all. I held a public meeting at the courthouse to try and get everyone involved. That evening I was really praying. Except for the committee, no one showed up but the black leaders—political leaders, church leaders, even many of the teachers. It was obvious that they expected and should have expected to be included in the celebration. I was thinking, 'My God, what can we do?'"

One member of the committee suggested a tour of white houses, supposing that "some of our black friends would be willing to open their homes as well. This was meant to be a peace offering, but it sure wasn't going to work in Calhoun County back in the 1960s.

"The notion of spirituals popped into my mind. Our big event was to be on the last night out at the town's park at this beautiful lake. Four months ahead I went every Sunday to different black churches and listened to their choirs. They were so happy to be included and they would be performing music that was beyond the capabilities of most of the white citizens. They'd be contributing what the white community couldn't."

No one thought there would be any problem with what they might sing by way of a Christian hymn, but to avoid duplication each church was asked to report its two selections in advance. But Hope Williams, deacon of his church, wrote down a traditional Gospel song called "We Shall Overcome." Genevieve and her mother drove to his place and found him in the yard chopping wood: "I introduced my mother and told him, 'If you come to the park and sing "We Shall Overcome," it will be just like the whites getting up and singing "Dixie" to you.' He said that hadn't occurred to him.... He said, 'We sing it every Sunday in church, but you're right. I tell you what we'll do. We'll sing "Let Jesus Fix It for You." They both say the same thing, don't they?' Oh, he was a wise man and patient. And a true diplomat. Then he turned to Mama and added, 'Mrs. Chandler, we'll dedicate that one to you.'"

For weeks before the performance, Genevieve was terrified by threatening phone calls: "Mrs. Peterkin, you have opened a can of worms that never should have been opened in this county." "You are going to cause the biggest race riots South Carolina ever saw." She was so frightened she could hardly face using the phone. "All this over singing about God's love and Boy Scouts floating candles on the lake. I didn't know who to turn to, for this was the one time in my life I kept a secret from my husband. If I'd told, he'd pack me up and move me to another continent to get me out of danger. I didn't trust the local sheriff. Maybe I could have but I didn't. Finally I went to the chairman of the [county] Democratic Party and told him I was very frightened but that this program was going to go on. He told me not to worry." He also got in touch with SLED, which stationed plainclothesmen all over the park that night. Next morning the Orangeburg newspaper ran the headline, "Calhoun County's Most Memorable Night in History."

For decades after 1965, often accompanied by his daughter Roberta, Hope continued to travel in-county and out. Sometime after he formed the county NAACP, the graying, ever-wily Fox empowered him to register voters wherever he met them. For many years, Hope also served on the Calhoun County Board of Education and Voter Participation and in other community organizations. A few people looked on these activities as joining the other side, but the greatness of Hope was that, for him, there was no "other side" to a community becoming more whole.

By the mid-1990s things were surely better in the county but far from mended. When Elizabeth Robeson visited Hope then to hear what he might know about Julia Peterkin, she mentioned a trestle bridge across the Congaree River that appears in Julia's stories. Hope offered to ride over to see it. At the river they were accosted by two beefy whites in paramilitary dress who objected to their being there—a dignified 80-something black man together with a much, much younger white female scholar. Elizabeth felt dismayed, humiliated, enraged when Hope affected a shuck-and-jive to placate the louts. As Martin Banks says, "Really? Still? Come on, get over it."

One late afternoon around 1993 when Ish also dropped by from afar to see him, Hope was nearly deaf but otherwise still in reasonable shape, living with family still out in Fort Motte. He sat in a chair in a good-looking suit, perhaps pausing before going out. Ish identified himself. Mr. Hope beamed and turned to his granddaughter saying proudly, "They were my kids!"

We've always felt the same.

A round 1969 when 18-year-old Melvin Hart and his buddy Tim went to the courthouse to register, the registrar recognized him as a former schoolmate of her sons. At first she told him he wasn't old enough to vote. He says, "We were young and radical, I guess, so we said, well, we heard on the news that we're old enough to vote. If you were eighteen you could register and vote. She said, 'No, that's only if you're voting for President. You have to be 21 to vote.' She got out a registration form, gave it to us, typed it up, a greenish card, and then she reached in her desk drawer for a rubber stamp and stamped it 'Presidential Only.'" Martin Banks thinks the stamp was a dodge to continue keeping blacks out of local affairs.

Melvin Hart's career in media took an adventurous turn years later when he managed Cecil Williams' 1984 US Senatorial campaign, hoping they could unseat the un-unseatable Strom Thurmond. According to Wikipedia, in the Democratic primary against white Rev. Melvin Purvis, out of 300,000 votes Cecil lost by less than 1,200. Cecil says the gap was 412, insofar as recounts could be done. Right after the voting, he and Melvin spotted fishy numbers in five counties and began requesting second counts. The first county they notified burned the ballots before re-counters could get there. In the end, Strom pulverized Purvis and hung on to his Senate seat until his death in 2003.

What became of Melvin's older brother, Furman Hart Jr.? For a year or so after high school he'd hung around trying out various jobs, including a short stint with W.M. Keitt at Utica Tool and an even shorter one with LeRoy Guinyard attempting to hang onto the end of a jackhammer. Jobs were scarce. Shortly after our summer, he drove with his high school friend and classmate "Jumpy" Jackson and Eugene Glover up to New York, where family connections helped him settle. By 1969 Junior was happily married and starting three decades of driving a bus.

What about John Lee Anderson? He's dropped the middle name. Junior thinks he may have gone into the air force. Today he lives on edge of the county and his first cousin, Helen Carson-Peterson, is the first black mayor of St. Matthews. (She's related to Eugene Glover, as well.)

After Princeton High, Harold went into the army. In the mid-1990s he held civilian employment at Fort Jackson and lived with his wife Corine in St. Matthews in a comfy mobile home where they raised daughters Gloria and Sonia, the latter named after Sonya Goldsmith. Over the years, friendships expanded between Goldsmiths and McKenzies. Until his death in the early 2000's, Harold and Lynn exchanged notes now and then on life and the state of the county.

In August 2000 he wrote to her about the 82nd annual "Good Hope Picnic" in Lone Star, where he'd been convicted of trespass 35 years before: "Small rides, traditional baseball game and of course lots and lots of food. What made the event unique was the colorful people (Blacks & Whites), mingled as if this event was always for the general public. Lynn, I honestly believe that race relations have changed for the better in Calhoun County, but there are many Blacks who feel they are less than.... Yes, there will always be discrimination. But it is not as noticeable as in past years." But in September he wrote to her bluntly that "hatred has caused [St. Matthews] to die."

Butch Jackson's life was shorter. After graduating from John Ford he returned to New York to settle. In the summer of 1967 he returned to St. Matthews to visit. There one night he was pulled over by police on the corner of Belleville Road where mayor Carson's funeral home is now. There seem to have been no witnesses, but according to Charles Williams Butch was dragged from his car. "They wanted to take him, you know," say Charles, "they said that he was drinking. I couldn't say he was and I couldn't say he wasn't. But he was known to drink. They got into a tussle and _____ shot him." He was shot in the stomach. In 1967 the NAACP reported this incident as the unprovoked shooting of one of its workers. After recovering from the wound, Butch returned to New York where he worked for some time as a bank teller, but Harold said he was never the same. According to Freddie Jackson, Butch died at age 38 of complications of diabetes.

Was the shooting a reprisal for his civil rights work? The several men Ish talked to about it seemed disinclined to fault the shooter. It wasn't the chief of police, by the way, but another man, much better liked and respected by both

Mr. Hope in his prime. Photo Carol Sable.

sides of town. County museum director Debbie Roland remembers the officer as "the kindest man I ever met."

Few of the older generation are still around. William and Jean Keitt live in Orangeburg. Ham Federick has passed, but in 1993 Ish found him still as vocal as ever, employed as a school bus driver. In 2016 Lynn (Goldsmith) Goldberg retired from Vermont to South Carolina and visited with various Harts, McKenzies, Floyds, Murphys, and others at a small reunion in St. Matthews.

In 1968, Orangeburg experienced the most horrendous event in South Carolina racial history from then until the 2016 racist murder of nine in a highly symbolic black Charleston church. Cecil Williams relates the Orangeburg Massacre story in first-hand photos and words. As an extension of desegregation efforts in the winter of 1968, about forty students marched toward a still white-only bowling alley about a mile from the colleges. Blocked by the police, they disbanded. The next evening, a larger group led by local leaders marched again to the bowling alley where a score were clubbed and fifteen arrested. Next day, with classes cancelled, about 600 students broke off another march when authorities demanded a permit. That winter night, about fifty gathered for warmth around small bonfires on the edge of State College. A force of about seventy police opened fire with M-1 rifles, revolvers, and lethal-load shotguns, killing three young men—Samuel Hammond Jr., Delano Middleton and Henry Smith—and wounding 27 others, mainly in the sides and backs. So the movement bled on.

Change Gon' Come

Looking back, Ish can't help but see how so many older people (Drew Pearsons, Hosea and Hope Williamses, Goldsmiths, Simkinses, Stewarts, Dibbles, Harts, Floyds, Peterkins) arranged and abetted the mojo of youth. He'd be humbled if he were still young.

Though Lynn enjoyed some cruising with Gerard and SCOPE did travel at night in integrated cars between St. Matthews and Orangeburg, mixed driving was always risky. Phyllis Greenfield learned that in early August when she and Liz Hafkin talked James Bowers into driving them to the weekend conference in DC. As noted, Jim had been part of the second group of students integratting USC.

Liz's memory of the ride corroborates Phyllis' more detailed remembrance. Phyl begins with how the long, hot days of canvassing and meetings running late into the night wore her down and made her long for brief escape. She got permission to leave the project for a weekend. "Liz wanted to go as well. James was reluctant to take us along, but agreed on the condition that we leave after dark and drive straight through. He had a small rented car. About 2:00 in the morning, very tired and cramped, we noticed an all-night diner in Raleigh. A large truck was parked in front, and a black man—the trucker we supposed—was being served at the counter. We were relieved to find a safe place to stop, took a booth and ordered coffee.

"Suddenly, James put money on the table and told us under his breath to move quickly to the car. We followed him outside, noticing three white men across the room getting up to leave as well. This was the beginning of a harrowing chase, zigzagging up Route 1 at 93 miles an hour to keep from being driven off the road, pursued for miles by a large car, inches from our bumper, blinding us with its bright lights, sometimes bumping up against us, the men hurling things out the windows that struck our car. Liz began to sing freedom songs at the top of her lungs in the back seat, then she seemed to pass out. James and I were sure our lives were over. We hardly knew each other. 'You know what they will do to me,' he said, then asked if I was going to remain nonviolent. We made a pact to fight back when we were caught. Then suddenly our pursuers turned off the road and, miraculously, we had escaped."

In Washington Phyllis sat in on sessions and aided a picket line. Back in Columbia after the weekend she was still in a state of shock and surprised to be alive. She told Elias what had happened. "Elias said, 'Get some sleep. Don't tell anyone about this or everyone will want to go home.' He [had] me taken to a comfortable house outside town where I slept for two days. When I returned, I told no one, not even Lesley, what had happened, and, almost magically, the memories associated with this experience disappeared."

To her parents she wrote breezily, "Hey, folks, got home safely. Lovely trip except for signs of discrimination everywhere. Let me tell you about it when I come home—much to tell that can't be written—must be thought out first."

Within a week she was flown home sick. Early in the summer she recalls, she'd "wanted so to talk about whatever we heard, to sort it out with another person that mattered to me and shared my commitment to understanding." She thinks the sickness grew out of her amnesia and silence. Decades later she wrote that she'd been "dependent on dialogue with others—speaking, writing, even interior dialogue—to process what was happening inside and around me. When that was denied, and the memory was too frightening for me to turn over in my mind alone, I 'shut down' in a way that cut me off from who I was at that moment, and ultimately flattened my memory of the entire summer in the south, especially who I was. That flattening temporarily lessened my sense of loss after [the terror in North Carolina] caused me to disconnect from myself: if I was an un-thinking, naive person, unaware of the dangers of the situation, then not so much was lost."

But years later when she re-encountered her younger self in her letters, she found "a vibrant, active, thoughtful and purposeful young woman, and my response was to grieve the loss of so much of myself for so many years. I discovered, too, that in all my time in the south, I had missed the risk I posed to others—to the families I stayed with and especially to James, who ultimately saved my life by driving the way he had learned to do as a black teenager, pursued by whites on the dirt roads near his home."

Recently Phyllis got back in touch with Jim to talk about those times and these. After USC he'd studied law at Harvard, then returned to become USC's first black law professor before settling into a career in corporate compliance. "I felt like I was going to crack corporate America," he told an interviewer in 2009. "I felt I could do more within the institution than challenging the institution. I've always tried to find situations where I could open up people's thinking."

He must be a man of hard-learned patience. Some folks are tedious-slow to change. It was not until the millennium that South Carolina's black populace managed to pressure legislators into removing the Confederate battle flag from the capitol dome and chambers. It took another fifteen years and the demented massacre in Charleston for it finally to be removed in 2015 from the capitol lawn.

On a rainy, hurricane-scrambled visit in October 2016, driving from Orangeburg to St. Matthews, Ish was startled to pass an enormous "Stars and Bars" on a very tall flagpole close to pleasant-sounding Edisto River Creamery & Kitchen. What was that all about? Six months later he found out in a *New Yorker* piece about Piggie Park. Maurice Bessinger's barbecue empire had expanded since the 1960s, based mainly on white clientele. Shortly before his death in 2014, his heirs removed the Confederate flags from his bottled sauce and outlets. They also stopped offering pamphlets claiming that "African slaves blessed the Lord for allowing them to be enslaved and sent to America." But unfortunate Edisto Creamery had moved into an old Piggie Park building, and the flagpole was on an otherwise useless scrap of ground that Bessinger was said to have donated to the Sons of Confederate Veterans. As of this writing, judges are sorting out whether the SCV does own the land.

In 2017 a small group in Civil War dress was once again ceremoniously re-raising the flag briefly on the statehouse lawn. Like the rest of this country, South Carolina still has rivers to cross.

COMPANIONS, FRIENDS, HELPERS

These were the Brandeis SCOPE volunteers. All were typical of college students at the time in having entered college as teens. As a proxy of age, see their initially intended graduation years. All started in Richland County, and this group remained there:

Kathy Davis '65 Wellesley
Elias Dickerman '66
Phyllis Greenfield '68
William Greenhill '65
Elizabeth Hafkin '67
David Jacobson '66
Alan Kern '67
David Kricker '66
Elizabeth Milgram '68
Frederick Schaffer '68 Harvard
Alan Segal '68
Lesley Straley '68

These moved to Calhoun County:

John Babin '68
Mary Ann Efroymson '65 Wellesley
Lynn Goldsmith '68
Arthur Parsons G1
Carol Sable '66
Alan Venable '66 Harvard

These moved to Kershaw County:

Catherine Allsup '68 Wheaton
Kathleen Courts '67
Richard Gurbst '68
William Kornrich '67
Margot Thornton '68

Jo Freeman, another SCOPE veteran and author of a broader forthcoming history of SCLC-SCOPE, generously goaded Ish into undertaking this book based mainly on the candid chronicles of Lynn Goldsmith Goldberg and Phyllis Greenfield Ross, whose friendships and inspiration he treasures. This book is really theirs. Others also graciously opened their diaries and letters, or did their best to remember.

These additional Brandeis faculty and staff helped launch, train and assist the group: Arnold Abrams, Eugenia Hanfmann, Karen W. Klein, Kermit K. Schooler, Carol Thometz, Roland Warren.

Brandeis librarian Chloe Morse-Harding kindly opened Ish's way to archives containing Lynn's diary and related documents. Thanks to David Kricker for helping Ish retrieve them.

These people and groups were listed on our program of welcome in Columbia. The format was a religious service, including organ prelude, call to worship, choir selection, scripture lesson, and offering. Presenters and speakers were Rev. William McKinley Bowman, Ernest W. Pressley (organist), Rev. J.W. Mungin (scripture and invocation), Mrs. A.W. (Modjeska) Simpkins (purpose of meeting), Bill Roberts (introduction of student visitors), and B.I. Piper (introduction of community leaders).

This was the sponsoring committee:

Adam Stewart, President, Richland County Citizen's Committee
I.D. Newman, Secretary, NAACP
I.S. Leevy, Chairman, Richland County VEP
W.M. Bowman, Financial Chairman, Palmetto Voter's Association;
also Gethsemane Sunday School Convention
James T. McCain, Field Secretary, CORE
Alice Spearman, Executive Secretary, Council of Human Relations
Dr. J. Arthur Holmes, President, Columbia Ministerial Brotherhood
Rev. W.S. Bookhart, President, Baptist Minister Union
William Blakely, President, Lower Richland County Agency
Ben Mack, President, Richland County SCLC
Rev. C.J. Whittaker, President, North Columbia Civic Club

Richland County Library archivist Debbie Bloom made a pleasure of viewing materials there and went on helping Ish remotely. Lifelong activist Brett Bursey, director of the South Carolina Progressive Network, shared insights into his much-missed mentor, Modjeska Simpkins. Columbia welcomer Jill Asouzu put Ish in touch with Columbia historical tour guide Andrena Davis, who braved his driving to show him her city, infusing history and pride with personal memories. Among other things she pointed out how highway construction and "urban renewal" disrupted old black communities, much as happened in Pittsburgh and San Francisco.

In Kershaw County, Camden Archives & Museum staff helped Ish find old newspaper coverage. Since then, research assistant Lon Outen has helped with other details. Kershaw resident Rev. William B. Gaither, an NAACP officer and a veteran of SCLC/SCOPE, helped correct misunderstandings and gaps regarding Miss James Dibble. On an evening in Camden in 2016, the generous owner of Books on Broad put Ish on the trail of more history.

About Calhoun County, activist and historian Elizabeth Robeson helped enormously with perspective, correction, local records, memories of Hope, deep knowledge of Julia Mood Peterkin, and other support. Calhoun County Museum director Debbie Roland and her assistants provided similar extensive help, supplying facts and doing their best to correct Ish's misunderstandings and outsider bias. Debbie and her colleague Jeff Reid also added firsthand details. Orangeburg History Society staffer Wayne Hughes was also helpful.

Abraham Williams answered many questions about his father and family. Corine and Joan McKenzie shared information on Harold. From retirement in West Virginia, still spirited Earl Coblyn shared vivid memories of Orangeburg and his beloved late wife Donnessa. Toward the end of the 1960s they moved to DC, where she helped create a new children's museum. Earl says Strom Thurmond's wife hunted her down there, asking her back with, "I'd like you to be working with me, and I think your husband might be interested in a judge-ship." The Coblyns declined.

Finally, no one gave Ish more personal pleasure and help than Calhoun county natives and friends Martin Banks and Melvin Hart, who tag-teamed back and forth to locate and introduce or re-introduce him to people, places, and lore. Off in San Francisco before he met them, Ish was writing in a fog.

Some Readings

Bass, Jack, & Marilyn W. Thompson. *Strom: The Complicated Personal and Political Life of Strom Thurmond*. New York: Perseus Book Group, 2005.

Bessinger, Maurice. *Defending My Heritage: The Maurice Bessinger Story*. West Columbia, SC: LMBONE-LEHONE, 2001. Life and segregationist perspective of the founder of the Piggie Park barbecue chain.

Brown, Millicent E. "Somebody had to do it." Website hosted by College of Charleston Library. A school desegregation resource created by historian Brown, including video interviews of people who as children began the 1960s desegregation of South Carolina public schools. *ldhi.library.cofc.edu/exhibits/show/somebody_had_to_do_it*

Civil Rights Movement Veterans. Website hosted by Tougaloo College. A large and growing archive of accounts from people in SNCC, CORE, SCLC, SCOPE, and related organizations. *crmvet.org*

Clyburn, James E. "Tribute to Hope Williams, Jr.," April 27, 2006. *capitolwords. org/date/2006/04/27/E649-2_tribute-to-hope-williams-jr/*

Cohen, Robert, & David J. Snyder (eds.). *Rebellion in Black and White: Southern Student Activism in the 1960s*. Baltimore, MD: The Johns Hopkins University Press, 2013. Several contributors discuss South Carolina.

Collins, Lauren. "Secrets in the sauce: The politics of barbecue and the legacy of a white supremacist." *The New Yorker*, April 24, 2017. All you care to know about Maurice Bessinger and Piggie Park.

Crawford, Lindsay, et al. *The Camden African American Heritage Project*. Public History Program, University of South Carolina, June 1, 2006. *scholarcommons.sc.edu/cgi/viewcontent.cgi?article=1001&context=pubhist_books*

Deas-Moore, Vennie. *Columbia South Carolina*. Charleston: Arcadia Publishing, 2000. Black America Series. A repository of 20th-century photos.

Demerath, N.J., Gerald Marwell & Michael T. Aiken. *Dynamics of Idealism: White Activists in a Black Movement*. San Francisco: Jossey-Bass, 1971. Many details and conclusions about the overall conduct and success of SCLC-SCOPE.

Felder, James L. *Civil Rights in South Carolina: From Peaceful Protests to Groundbreaking Rulings*. Charleston, SC: The History Press, 2012. Mainly an NAACP perspective by a leader at the time.

Freeman, Jo. Forthcoming broad history of SCLC-SCOPE.

Gellman, Erik S. "Chapter five: The world's 'firing line: South Carolina's post-war internationalism." in *Death Blow to Jim Crow: The National Negro Congress and the Rise of Militant Civil Rights*. Chapel Hill: University of North Carolina Press, 2012. An analytic account of this aspect of Modjeska Simkins' work in the 1940s.

Gitin, Maria. *This Bright Light of Ours: Stories from the Voting Rights Fight*. Tusca-loosa, AL: University of Alabama Press, 2014. Her difficult SCOPE experience in Wilcox County, Alabama.

Goldberg, Lynn. "Lynn Goldberg File." Brandeis University Robert D. Farber University Archives. Lynn Goldsmith's (Goldberg's) diary plus various items from Brandeis SCOPE.

Grose, Philip G. *South Carolina at the Brink: Robert McNair and the Politics of Civil Rights*. Columbia: University of South Carolina Press, 2006.

Hague, Euan. "The Citizens' Council." *citizenscouncils.com*

Jones-Branch, Cherisse. "Modjeska Monteith Simkins: I cannot be bought and will not be sold." In Marjorie Julian Spruill et al. (eds.) *South Carolina Women: Their Lives and Times Vol. 3*. Athens: University of Georgia Press, 2012.

"KZSU Project South Interviews." Summer 1965 interview recordings and tran-scripts throughout the South with SCOPE and other projects. Most relevant box/folder parts for this book: 4/102, 104; 7/183, 8/184-186. The transcripts are sometimes faulty. *oac.cdlib.org/findaid/ark:/13030/tf7489n969/*

Kita, Miyuki. *Lynn Goldsmith: A Jewish Student Volunteer in the Civil Rights Movement, Summer 1965*. Japan: Sairyusha, 2016). A Japanese language account of SCOPE based mainly on Lynn's experience.

Labedis, Sherie Holbrook. *You Came Here to Die, Didn't You: Registering Black Vot-ers One Soul at a Time*. Roseville, CA: Smokey Hill Books, 2011. Her memoir of SCOPE in Charleston and in Berkeley County, SC.

Leventhal, Willy Siegel. *The SCOPE of Freedom: The leadership of Hosea Williams with Dr. King's Summer '65 Student Volunteers*. Montgomery, AL: Challenge Press, 2005. A thick, somewhat scattered collection of original documents related to SCOPE, with commentary by SCOPE-veteran Siegel.

Lewis, Daniel. "Hosea Williams, 74, rights crusader, dies." *The New York Times*, November 17, 2000.

Livingston, Dean B. *Yesteryears: A Newsman's Look Back at the Events and People Who Have Influenced the Histories of Orangeburg and Calhoun Counties*. Orangeburg: Trippett Press, 2006. Includes Calhoun County economic history and sketches of James Sulton and Cecil J. Williams.

Logan, Sadye L.M. (ed.). *The Spirit of an Activist: The Life and Work of I. De-Quincey Newman*. Columbia: University of South Carolina Press, 2014. A rich description of this remarkable man and SC-NAACP. Especially useful was the chapter by Millicent E. Brown.

Malan, Douglas S. "Cracking Corporate America: Legal career shaped by tumultuous civil rights era." *Connecticut Law Tribune Vol. 35, No. 35*, August 31, 2009. Recent perspectives of James Bowers. *ctlawtribune.com*

Moore, John Hammond. *Columbia and Richland County: A South Carolina Community, 1740-1990*. Columbia: University of South Carolina Press, 1993.

Myers, Andrew H. *Black, White, & Olive Drab: Racial Integration at Fort Jackson, South Carolina, and the Civil Rights Movement*. Charlottesville: University of Virginia Press, 2006. The army base was a factor in Columbia's integration.

Newton, Michael. *White Robes and Burning Crosses*. Jefferson, NC: McFarland, 2014. Includes South Carolina.

"Oral history interview with Modjeska Simkins," July 28, 1976. Interview G-0056-2, Oral Histories of the American South, Southern Oral History Program Collection. (#4007). A meaty interview revealing Modjeska's personality and much about her state. *docsouth.unc.edu/sohp/G-0056-2/*

Peterkin, Genevieve C. *Heaven is a Beautiful Place: A Memoir of the South Carolina Coast*. Columbia, SC: University of South Carolina Press, 2000. By the spirited liberal daughter-in-law of Julia Peterkin, this book includes about twelve pages dealing with Fort Motte in the 1950s and 1960s.

Peterkin, Julia. *Scarlet Sister Mary*. Indianapolis: Bobbs-Merrill, 1928.

Peterkin, Julia, & Doris Ulman. *Roll, Jordan, Roll*. New York: Bobbs-Merrill, 1933.

Reavis, Dick J. *If White Kids Die: Memories Of A Civil Rights Movement Volunteer*. Denton: University of North Texas Press, 2001. SCOPE 1965 and more, including glimpses of Pat Gandy.

Robbins, Becci. *Modjeska Monteith Simkins: A South Carolina Revolutionary*. Columbia, SC: S.C. Progressive Network Education Fund. 2014. A booklet with many good quotes and photos.

Sachar, Abram L. *Brandeis University: A Host at Last*. Brandeis Institutional Repository, 1995. A lengthy account of the school's origins, history, and social involvement by its first president. *hdl.handle.net/10192/26652*

Sears, James Thomas. *Rebels, Rubyfruit, and Rhinestones: Queering Space in the Stonewall South*. New Brunswick: Rutgers University Press, 2001. Contains brief material about Peter Lee.

Sims, Patsy. *The Klan, Second Edition*. Lexington: University Press of Kentucky, 1996. A substantial chapter describes interviewing R.E. Scoggin during Carter's presidency, 1977-1980.

Sproat, John G. "'Firm flexibility': Perspectives on desegregation in South Carolina." In Abzug, Robert H. and Stephen E. Maizlish (eds.) *New Perspectives on Race and Slavery in America*. Lexington: University Press of Kentucky, 1986.

Venable, Alan H. "Generational aspects of liberal activism." Senior honors thesis, Department of Social Relations, Harvard College, 1966.

Wade, Wyn Craig. *The Fiery Cross: The Ku Klux Klan in America*. Oxford University Press, 1998.

Washington-Williams, Essie Mae & William Stadiem. *Dear Senator: A Memoir by the Daughter of Strom Thurmond*. New York: Harper-Collins, 2005.

Williams, Cecil J. *Freedom & Justice: Four Decades of the Civil Rights Struggle as Seen by a Black Photographer of the Deep South*. Macon, GA: Mercer University Press, 1995. Mainly South Carolina. Overlaps a good deal with the next reference, but the two combined are great. Top-notch photos with eye-witnessed and researched narrative.

Williams, Cecil. *Out-of-the-Box in Dixie: Cecil Williams' Photography of the South Carolina Events that Changed America*. Orangeburg: Cecil J. Williams Photography/Publishing, 2010. An extensive narrative with hundreds of great photos. The best single book for getting the context and human feel of the struggle in the 1950s and 1960s in Orangeburg and Columbia, as led by the NAACP.

Williams, Mildred M., et al. *The Jeanes Story: A Chapter in the History of American Education 1908-1968*. Jackson, MS: Jackson State University, 1979.

Williams, Susan Millar. *A Devil and a Good Woman, Too: The Lives of Julia Peterkin*. Athens: University of Georgia Press, 1999.

Woods, Barbara A. "Modjeska Simkins and the South Carolina Conference of the NAACP, 1939-1957." In Crawford, Vicki L., et al. (eds.) *Women in the Civil Rights Movement: Trailblazers & Torchbearers, 1941-1965*. Bloomington: Indiana University Press, 1993.

INDEX

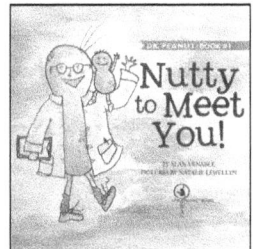

www.ingramcontent.com/pod-product-compliance
Lightning Source LLC
Chambersburg PA
CBHW052037090426
42739CB00010B/1951